Acclaim for James Sherry's
Oops! Environmental Poetics

James Sherry takes Nature as his subject and finds Natures. He pulls us from the corny green landscape and awakens the savannah.

—Jesse Ausubel, Director,
Program for the Human Environment,
The Rockefeller University

What poetry can change is the *will* to change. James Sherry finds "real correspondence" between poetry's conditional truths and the great *out there,* and he definitively places poetry at the center of our being-in-ecology. For a beautifully detailed understanding of poetry's possibilities in apprehending the deep bonds, niches and connections of us-we-there-them-where-here, read *Oops!*.

—Marcella Durand, author of *Traffic & Weather*

The issues raised by the collision of humans, our tools, and the natural world are wicked problems that require every means of responding at our disposal. James Sherry wields language skillfully as a tool and poetry movingly as a technology of the sacred to illuminate the complexly intertwingled issues our species has created for ourselves and the ecosystem of which we are both a part and a threat.

—Howard Rheingold,
author of *The Virtual Community, Smart Mobs,* and *Net Smart*

Can we find models for environmental writing in "language" poetry? What do poetry and risk management have in common? Can hierarchy be inclusive? Why are cross-disciplinary thinking and formal innovation core, non-mutually exclusive tasks for environmental writing today? Sherry's thoughtful, resourceful, playful poetics, as methodical as they are experimental, will challenge you to rethink many of your assumptions about writing, the environment, poetry. This is a substantial, and key, addition to the conversation.

—Jonathan Skinner, editor *ecopoetics*

ALSO BY JAMES SHERRY

Four For

Our Nuclear Heritage

Doscapade

The Word I Like White Paint Considered

Lazy Sonnets

Popular Fiction

Converses

Integers

In Case

Part Songs

Oops!
Environmental Poetics

Oops!
Environmental Poetics

For Holly + Brad

James Sherry

James
8/31/13

BLAZEVOX[BOOKS]
Buffalo, New York

Oops! Environmental Poetics
Copyright © 2013 James Sherry

Published by BlazeVOX [books]

All rights reserved. No part of this book may be reproduced without
the publisher's written permission, except for brief quotations in reviews.

Printed in the United States of America

Interior design and typesetting by Geoffrey Gatza
Cover Photograph: *Glacial, Icecap and Permafrost Melting LIX: Lake Paron, Peru, 2008*,
Sayler/Morris for The Canary Project

First Edition
ISBN: 978-1-60964-136-8
Library of Congress Control Number: 2013900110

BlazeVOX [books]
131 Euclid Ave
Kenmore, NY 14217

Editor@blazevox.org

publisher of weird little books

BlazeVOX [books]

blazevox.org

21 20 19 18 17 16 15 14 13 12 01 02 03 04 05 06 07 08 09 10

BlazeVOX

Acknowledgments

Thank you to the editors who published versions of these works: Juliana Spahr and Jena Osman (*Chain*), Ron Silliman (*Silliman's Blog*), Jonathan Skinner (*ecopoetics*), Craig Dworkin (*The Consequence of Innovation: 21st Century Poetics*), Zhang Ziqing, Brenda Iijima and Evelyn Reilly ()((ECO(LANG) (UAGE (READER)), Cecilia Wu and Stephen Paul Miller (*Critiphoria*), Chad Lowther (*Barzakh*), Kasey Mohammad (*Westwind*), Regis Bonvincino and Charles Bernstein (*Sibila*), John Reed and Anselm Berrigan (*Brooklyn Rail*), and if I have forgotten other kind editors, thank you.

Special thanks to some of the people who helped make this book possible: Jesse Ausubel, Michael Thompson, Evelyn Reilly, Gary Sullivan, Michael Gottlieb and most of all Deborah Thomas.

Contents

Introduction 13
Book 1: Niches and Connections 21
    The Census of the Fishes 23
    A Fish in the Lobby of 95 Wall Street 25
    Clean Speak 26
    War against Nature 30
    Bonding Poets 34
    Environment as Boredom 41
    The Metaphor of Trees 48
    Niches 58
    From Bonds and Niches a Social Force Unleashed 62
    Tagmosis/Prosody (Connecting Parataxis) 67
    Passive Voice: Forcing Amaryllis 83
    Views for China 87
    Sustainable Love 91
    God Loves Sex: Poetics and Reproduction 94
    Is There Such a Thing as Writing? 102
    Three Short Pieces that Compete for Resources as Species in a Niche 113
    Using Multiple Forms to Enact Environmentalism Rather than Describe It 121
    Environmental Poetics as Biography 127

Book 2: Cultural Toolkit 131
    Snowball Earth Creates Innovative Poetry 133
    Human Views of Nature 143
    Limiting the Social Environment for a Good Reason 151
    Is Not Enough of a Reason 151
    (E)Valuation in Poetry: Sequence and Geometry 161
    Appendix A: How Language Writing Got Its Period 176

Book 3: Risk **183**

    Part 1: Business Process Interruption and Risk Homeostasis: 185
    Analysis for Technology Solutions to Regulatory Impact 185
    Part 2: Natural Resiliency and Inefficient Computing...................................... 189
    Part 3: Risk of Poetry 192
    For Rejection 202
    Inter-dimensional Universality of Dynamic Interfaces 203
    The World Trade Center Environment: Strategic Dialogue............................ 212
    No One Is On 219
    Places to Sit 219
    Practical Applications 220
    Passive Voice: Forcing Amaryllis 224
    Spiritualizing Comprehension 229
    Appendix B: Scenes from Fallen Arches: A Mystery Play in Eden.................. 240

OOPS!
ENVIRONMENTAL POETICS

Introduction

During the past three decades, discussion of our planetary environment has been circulating around the world with increasing rapidity. The public shape of the problem has shifted from a diverse set of views about the biosphere to a coherent, globally acknowledged single point: Human activity is significantly changing the planet's climate, putting our species and others at risk.

The solutions to the problem of climate change, the institutions of change, the interest groups participating and the intellectual climate all fluctuate while myriad uncoordinated actions have been set in motion. This incremental progress changes the relationship of humanity to the planet and determines whether the humanist power structures, with their drive to protect humanity from nature, will retain their hegemony in the new age that is being forced upon us. The essays and poems in this book are part of that process. They attempt to show different ways that people might effectively change their relationship to themselves, to each other and to nature, and how poetry can be a useful part of that change.

The solutions to reduce the effects of climate change are fairly well understood and don't need poetic assistance. Numerous scientific solutions are being explored and sorted. The political framework to implement them is active in both wealthy and poor countries, in both totalitarian and democratic regimes. But somehow the will wilts. Resistance to change from a fire-based economy blocks alternatives in Brazil, China, India, the US, Europe, and elsewhere. Everybody's got an excuse to avoid change and change itself has significant risks. At the root of this resistance, the lack of a broadly based functional environmental culture looms. Such a culture needs to build the will to change, provide dynamic mechanisms for change and address its risks.

In the US, vested interests trump up an amazing list of justifications from treating environmentalism as an attack on personal freedom to the false assumptions of how remediation drains corporate profits. In China even the man on the street suggests that developed countries had cheap, polluting growth for 150 years; why can't they do the same? In Brazil, the landholders simply go on destroying their greatest heritage. The list goes on and on.

Highly productive individuals and their group formations such as corporations and religions agree about the risk to power of integrating humanity into the rest of the biosphere. Their shared assumptions means no conspiracy required. First, they have been so successful at dominating nearly every condition that society presents. Why should they give up those hard won gains against their surroundings and in dominating the multitudes of humans?

Second, the individual organism's survival instinct and its effect on the ego reinforce the notion of human exceptionalism. And there's every reason to privilege our species. The conflict between individual survival and evolutionary support for group interests impedes the integration between human culture and other planetary forces that is necessary for us to avoid destroying our charitable climate. What changes of thought, practice and beliefs need to take place in order to overcome this conflict?

Third, the immediate perception of our immense ability to think reflectively implies in all cultures that we have better control over ourselves than other species. While we have effectively manipulated our environment to a large degree, we have done so in concert with the tropism toward individual survival. We now have to exert control over ourselves in a way that is more focused on group and species survival. The way we think about ourselves extends to almost all human cultural features, not only the top tier of individuals and groups. How with all these features of human mind can we encourage greater collective awareness, collective as humans and collective as living entities? How with these mental skills that have allowed us to control much of our environment can we exert this kind of group control and retain the freedoms that we have worked so hard to achieve?

Human resistance does not reflect a failure of political systems, although there is much to repair in that arena. Resistance is not caused by a lack of scientific solutions, although many obvious inventions are not yet scalable. We lack a culture to provide the will to change in the right direction. Writing these essays has emerged as a way to point to conflicts that need to be overcome and to illustrate the characteristics and structure of such an environmental culture.

Oops! is not an effort at cultural studies but a loose construction of examples, tools and methods by which a contemporary model that includes nature and humanity as a single complex entity can be built. Combining concepts of environmental thinking, changed perceptions of social structure, cross disciplinary methods, new forms of writing and creating works of art, music, and electronic media all contribute to shaping environmental change.

My reasons for choosing poetry are sketched herein as a theme, as examples and as form. The theme of poetry's contemporary epistemological value frees it from many of the restrictions of more successful disciplines. Truly convincing people of the need to change and the paths to follow must, however, engage the entire cultural apparatus and identify integration points with scientific solutions and social structures.

When I started writing about the environmental model of poetry, I composed extended essays and poems around the subject. For several years I worked on them, on and off, never satisfied with the results. Finally, I hit on the reason for my dissatisfaction. I was writing about the subject, but I had no structure that fit the theme. Consequently, I began to write in short, niche-like forms that never answer questions completely but always leave them open, to be answered by a subsequent piece—a kind of structure that conditions continuity, works by environmental interdependence and reflects how we grasp most complex systems. I hope readers will collectively connect the dots, finding a literary ecosystem composed of short niches and thus focus a view consistent with how reality is constructed.

These essays have been built over time and in parts that are intended to be both linked and independent. I intend them to operate together as an ecosystem that is sufficiently complete, as our planet is heterogeneous but complete (that is it works) for a reader with raw curiosity to plow through the themes, both new and recurrent, without the usual narrative structure. Critics have suggested that I write the poems and essays together as a single argument with narrative flow to match. While such an approach is possible, it feels to me against the grain of my central argument to chart a single path through the multitude of issues, solutions and forms as if history occurred as it is read.

Together these chapters add to the growing number of tools that change the way we think about ourselves and our surroundings, to level the playing field between human and non-human nature and to encourage a view of the biosphere that is not simply looking backward to a natural pietism that reveres nature regardless of the results and extols its virtues in our writings. We need to more fully incorporate ourselves into the biosphere while giving up as few of the advantages accrued by civilization as possible. It will be an iterative and delicate process. The results are unpredictable.

I titled the book *Oops!* for those who have noticed their willful or inadvertent damages to the planetary environment. But guilt is not the appropriate response of those who have damaged nature (and ourselves as part of nature) or complicated the epistemological landscape with self-serving rationalizations. Neither does guilt help us redress past errors. Rather, guilt is the response that the "judges" of the ecology movement want from their incorporated *loco parenti*—the state—and from us, the citizens.

As judges they cannot be ignored, since they do and will have a wide influence. Yet guilt must be discounted as a way to inform our environmental point of view. Redress must take the form of change, not iterative punishment. We seek restorative not retributive justice. Those who might wish for some *mea culpa* from me can well forget it. History is the court of our collective anxiety. And the cause of global warming is desire.

I have chosen this path to understanding the planetary environment and how we fit into it because of an ongoing impression. One of the reasons for our difficulty in understanding poetry, much less understanding the environment and our place in it, is that one way of thinking frequently is separated from another, undermining the functional links between individuals. The weakness of these connections implies that the poet is not a person like the reader and that the poet stands alone and apart. In fact, and I will address this at several points in the essays that follow, the opposite is true.

Poetry is the role of an individual that is shared by others in the same role. When one takes the role of poet, one is part of a group with common affiliations and needs. Communication takes place among people who understand one another. Further, if we understand a poem, then the poet who wrote it is part of our community of comprehension. Poets are also connected to one another by individual poems that they respond to and through social interaction in the poetry world.

Yet in our contemporary view of knowledge things are defined primarily by their differences. A culture of difference has extended throughout the arts and sciences for centuries and will be difficult to change also because our minds are quicker to pick out differences; it's a matter of survival. But art and science can also provide the tools to assess both differences and similarities. They can ameliorate many social ills while clearly pointing up the risks and benefits of weak connections such as the construction of this writing.

The points of view I've taken may be difficult to reconcile, even contradictory, both as a measure of the irony of our current human situation and as a reflection of its realities. These differences fit into a shared landscape of diverse ecosystems. Many adept scientists and philosophers have used such taxonomy to critique specialization, by pointing to the connections of related disciplines rather than their differences. I want at an early stage in this volume to link with their efforts rather than seek to displace them without undermining the value of detailed and specialized knowledge itself.

Ultimately I want to elucidate the different roles we can take to help integrate humanity with the rest of the planet. Breaking down the logic by which humanism (and much of Eastern thought) separates us from nature and replacing it with a relational framework will take place at personal, familial, communal, political and institutional levels. I will show how by various means, mostly indirect, we can accomplish that leveling task and propose some tentative replacements. I do not anticipate that I have done a thorough job of defining the alternatives to current approaches to our planet, and consequently I consider these pages provisional. Nevertheless, this short work may act as a series of pointers to environmentalism. What follows is a more or less linear summary of the discussion:

2.
As climate change has become more apparent, countless institutions, both public and private, as well as citizens around the world, have sought solutions to global environmental degradation. Each interest group tries to put itself at the center of the conversation, vying for primacy. Science understands and seeks solutions in science. Politicians understand and seek political solutions. And many other groups, including the polluters seeking to support existing economic processes, accumulating wealth and establishing dominance, compete for control of the environmental agenda. Highly productive individuals and groups who control vast resources support restorative approaches until they notice them interfering with their control or threatening their hegemony. At that point we have no well understood process for helping them resolve their clash.

To date these interest groups are proposing solutions based on fixing problems in their fields, repairing breaks in the infrastructure and planning for technologies and organizations that will be prepared to do battle with climate change. What little cultural energy has been applied asks us to conserve or to revert to natural pietism and as such garners little support among those activists who must get jobs done. A set of actions attracting highly productive individuals would gain support in all fields of endeavors, but what would attract these activists?

Some efforts to link art and biology have been made, but willingness to assign real correspondence between humanity and the non-human interactions has been partial and threatening to most intellectual frameworks. Important work is being done in biomimicry to engineer solutions drawn from non-human processes around energy consumption and infrastructure. But the underlying cultural assumption of biomimicry is again that of conservation and reduced expectation, relying on reverence for nature to convince people to revert to older cultures. Cultural conservatism remains insufficient for a robust set of environmental principles and practices addressing a planet that supports us but does not act in our interest.

The narrowness of most current eco-culture leads to solutions only about nature or writing about nature rather than delving into the interactions between humanity and the rest of the planet or showing how human interactions follow the same principles as the rest of the biosphere. They tend to be fragmented, address only part of the problem or like bio-fuels degrade a bad situation with the unintended effects.

Our existing, mainstream concept of nature, as a force humans need to dominate lest we fall prey to its indifference, continues to lead us in the wrong direction. Tennyson's phrase, "nature red in tooth and claw", informs our mainstream discourse and institutions rather than Darwin's measured remarks. Such hyperbole reflects the weakness of the descriptions of nature in poetry.

In order to make his poem interesting, Tennyson has to misrepresent Darwin's conditional phrases. Imagine Tennyson's verse impressing us with "nature red in tooth and claw / within one species during mating season"—not that exciting as poetry. Or "nature red in tooth and claw / and in human's slaughter houses and wars"—doesn't garner that much support from those who use culture as diversion. How can poetry tell conditional truth with direct and powerful presentation?

We tend to continue with the activities and attitudes that put us in this compromised condition; it's inertial. We are almost required by the current culture to fight against nature whereas a more effective method would propel us to synchronize our efforts with the biosphere and where appropriate by natural (inherent) methods. While engaged in exploring inherent methods of production, protection from our surroundings is crucial and must not be ignored.

To develop a relationship with the biosphere allowing our species to persist with the advantages accumulated over centuries of civilization, I propose in *Oops!* an approach that informs our partnership with other planetary forces. As climate plays an increasingly important role, our view of nature becomes increasingly central. Gradually the focus on human life in cities will become a special case of an environmental culture that focuses on global awareness. And human social interaction and culture can be better understood as adaptation.

Oops! proposes a set of perspectives and methods, a toolkit for coping with climate change. To reduce conflict with the environment, for example, the notion of cognition needs to extend beyond our minds. To define how thinking takes place as an interaction between our brains and the outside world enhances nature's perceived value. We can begin to identify with the outside world.

Understanding how our view of the world is culturally determined will enable us to see the social construction of our combative relationship with nature, helping to modify that relationship for sustainable social interaction. Linking our survival to existing ecosystems, the culture of difference, understood today as the way taxonomy must work, will no longer be sufficient. The culture of difference has had a value in science, politics and art, but its oppositional assumptions adapt to emphasize the central role of symbiosis in our society. Next we need tools for synthesis and cross disciplinary analysis, a hierarchy that is more about inclusion than evaluation. I propose the example of q-analysis and how it might be used to modify our categories that value the planet's resources.

Interactions in the biosphere, including humanity and its thought process, operate dynamically. Culture with a fixed view of our surroundings will not accommodate countless shifting connections among people and place. Environmental culture modifies our current ideas about risk and where risk management applies. Culture can improve our ability to cope with unpredictable events. (This précis of the book, for example, seems to me at risk of oversimplifying my approach. But I want to prepare you for what you will read so I am willing to take that risk.)

Culture must also demonstrate to us how to take risks in a complex and potentially lethal situation, since none of the efforts to right our ship can be undertaken without the risk of incurring even graver storms. Environmental engineering solutions increase those hazards, but if cultural renovation fails, that may be the simplistic solution that politicians will be forced to accept. Humans behave differently in uncertain conditions and we must understand how to compensate for the weakness of our approximations.

Putting unexpected things together is a common feature of recent innovative poetry and letters that we can project as part of the culture of environmentalism. Poets take the risk of failed juxtaposition, but how can we afford that risk to our biosphere? *Oops!* outlines several different types of risk and discusses risk management as it influences poetics, providing examples of how innovative writing can improve our ability to understand and manage the risks of unpredictable change. This expanded role for risk in poetry hands us another tool to cross the boundaries of contemporary thinking and puts humans on a path to sustainable relations with the planet in an integrated cultural, political and scientific framework.

3.
Since this text proposes cross disciplinary ideas and methods of delivery derived from innovative poetics, I have organized it so that the larger structure helps the reader with its shape. Book 1 consists of a group of poems and essays exemplifying how to connect in a framework that's consistent with how nature operates. It explores the different types of conceptual and prosodic linkage that might be established between human thought and environmental reality. It establishes diversity of function and common shape as the dual criteria driving human and non-human interaction. Concepts are often reiterated in a new context to show by example how the biosphere addresses a problem in contrast to how the human mind addresses a problem.

Book 2 introduces tools that can help change the relationship between environment and culture: externalized cognition, environmental social structure, inclusive hierarchy, materialization of connections, cross-disciplinary analytics and risk. These exemplary reconsiderations of the basic assumptions of our culture can become part of culture workers' techniques. Without these adjustments to our assumptions, culture provides no will to change and poetic innovations in language appear only as charming procedures, irony or satire. Although we have a strong link between science and the environment, there has been no clear understanding that we need a new model of culture to deliver the environmentalism to specialists and the society at large, providing the will to change even when our self-interest is at stake.

Book 3 redefines poetry as the risks that the writer is willing to take with the components of poetry. It addresses risk in symbiosis as the primary issue for the relationship between human and non-human nature, for as we know, even from the popular press, there is as much risk and less certainty in changing as remaining on our current path. Defining poetry as risk promotes innovation as the goal of writing and undermines the idea of canon in literature as well as in science and politics. *Oops!* proposes that we change the way we think and act in order to reduce the risks of how we interact with nature.

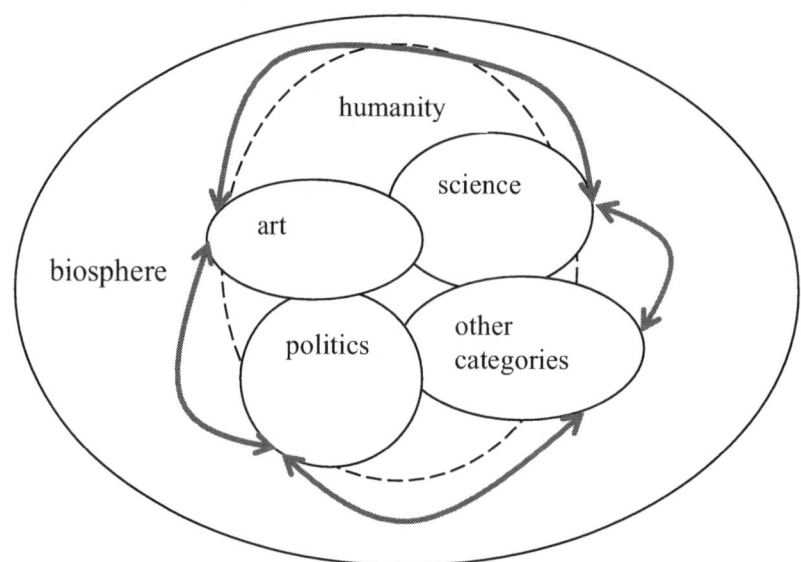

Book 1: Niches and Connections

The Census of the Fishes

Mr. A.
decided to count all the fish in the sea,
because he wanted to....
He went to the New England Fishermen's Association and said,
"I am going to perform a census of the fishes."

"Don't do that," said the Fishers, "the government will regulate what we catch. We won't be able to catch the fish that we catch today."

Mr. A. decided that he would find a more friendly reception among environmental groups. "Can you imagine," said Mr. A. to the Environmentalists, "that in 1992 we still do not know the number and composition of marine life? Wouldn't you like to know about

millions of fish,
billions of crustaceans,
trillions of krill,
and a quintillion of copepods?"

"No, we would not," said the Environmentalists. "As soon as you identify the populations, the Fishers will exploit them."

Mr. A. decided that there must be a premium on ignorance, so he went to the Cold War Scientists who were out of work, because the submarines no longer flowed from Murmansk. He said, "You have been counting submarines for 50 years, how would you like to count fishes?"

"We are concerned with opacity," they said. "We can treat each fish like a submarine with a distinctive shape and acoustic signature. With the end of the Cold War, technologies developed for looking for submarines are now available for other purposes, and at a reduced cost. We can attach a line behind a boat. It will trail the boat in a sine wave counting all the submarines, er, fishes you wish. We can count the shallow and deep all over the world.

"For years we have been writing algorithms to push the fish into the background and bring out the submarines. Now we can push the submarines in the background and bring out the fish."

Mr. A. felt relieved and reassured.

Note: the census of marine life is nearly complete as of 2013.

A Fish in the Lobby of 95 Wall Street

> So what is important,
> if the universe decides not to challenge us, and even breakwaters fall asleep?
> Why, the old, seminal
> undertow, that's what. The nor'easter will be out in force tomorrow,
> an insane force in an otherwise docile universe.
> —John Ashbery, *Girls on the Run*

During the winter of 1993, the old wharf areas of lower Manhattan were flooded by a storm. As high tide approached, the East River rose to the level the Dutch found it in the early seventeenth century. For a moment, the news was filled with the news.

I was working in the financial district late that night. Leaving the office into a crowded rain, I noticed a curious light emanating from one of the buildings. I crossed the street and walked right to the edge of the incoming tide. As it lapped forward, I stepped back.

I looked into the glass and steel lobby at 95 Wall Street. The flood had swept into the tiled, sunken lobby, filling it with salt water, and a few large fish were swimming around as if they belonged there. I thought how strange that the fish did not appear to notice the change in their environment. How easily they adapted to the builder's structure, altering his purpose. Had the fish been part of a fountain or brought by the incoming tide? The water was rising fast.

When I got to higher ground on Broadway there was one cab. Another late-night worker viciously refused to share his ride with me, and I hastened home on foot in the driving rain, imagining the fish discussing the state of their affairs. And chiding myself for being bullied out of a taxi home.

Working in the financial district for twenty-five years one gets to thinking about alternatives. My first effort at environmental taxonomy layered one idea on another mimicking time.

Clean Speak

> The purpose of their organization is simple: to provide activities for kids and adults in an atmosphere that is substance-free.
> —*New York Times*

Here is the genesis of the new spiritualism. You won't miss it for a minute. A kind of airy atmosphere, liberated from the strictures of consumption that blackened coots and mergansers, shuffles off this mortal oil.

But that's just the beginning. We can have a no-dirt dirt, an uncomplicated peace, a seamless hiding in the sand with full control over the stray dogs in the Third World military. Of course we can. We can abuse the opposition from a position of certain safety. And further, we can seek this spirit that has been so often debunked? There must be a need for the thought. And who is really suppressing it?

"My confusion arrives with the feeling of blessedness that I experience in confronting judgment."

No one really had given the matter much thought before Carpaccio invented his centralized syllabic information structure coordinator theory, which revolutionized society. It meant essentially that no one besides Carpaccio could be said to have come up with any ideas that he had not thought of first, not any ideas that mattered or deserved any consideration. Even the final solution of waste-free consumption in which waste is recycled as fuel instead of vented into the atmosphere.

Although his theory threatened to put him out of business, he insisted on authoring it due to its importance to the cultural community that he dominated by his later-than-thou nighttime talk show on which guests talked about it by denying any connection, including, of course, the floor show of armpits and genitals shaved into letters that spell out the credits.

From time to time Carpaccio's colleagues had independent ideas, and contrary to his corporate culture, they disseminated it themselves or had the appearance of doing so. Carpaccio's response was to chart their course on his *Interdigital Prognostication Hour*, a fifteen-minute holoshow on which he channeled their notions through his narrative sequencer and twisted their arguments into the form of his near-fit sympathy or the hilarious "Candid Camper" video segments.

The critics called it media philosophy and fawned without mentioning his name. (As you can see, he suffered, too.) The viewers assessed it by its righteousness quotient, registered on the moral meter that measured the cumulative resistance of all the fringe elements who pressed the red button on their remotes while he "made it clear" on any sundry subject. Of course the other garbage men were disposed to oversimplify their own offerings to avoid conflict with his complexity or be labeled clones, a disaster for their bottoms line.

As time went on, his dominance was unmasked, and the right no longer criticized the cloning, since it could be viewed as recycling, though it wreaked havoc with the gene pool. Splash went the new meteor shower in the gelid jelly of the mutual fund of chromosome banks, transparent as the emperor's new clothes to the osculation of the international out-of-work force waiting for their chance to be underpaid for work that made someone else a lot of money.

Desperate to be included, even angry for attention, and principled to any extreme of suffrage suggested to gestate along with the rhinos and hippos and other bovine utterances, the rest of the world balked at any alternatives to Carpaccio's addictives.

Are there any control mechanisms better in the long run than violence and complexity? The mutual-agreement funds speculated yes, and young investors brimming with collegiate clichés about a more perfect world with no garbage and phone sex everywhere in the well-washed gutters threw real money (that oxymoron of capital) at them with such a flurry that the snow plows, which were otherwise quite idle, had to be brought out of mothballs to take care of the caring cash.

His secret war against nature was no secret, just unspoken slag heaps and run-on sentences, that duplicity of grammar, where he saved the ecosystem by reconstructing it and leaving the waste to recover on its own. Those forgotten dumps leached into the public consciousness as pervasive self-hatred, a communal sensibility that unloaded all the fevers on herd animals that provided food for the helioraptors.

You know what I mean, I mean, I mean it, every meaningful denotation, connotation, indication, suggestion, determination, resolution, intention, demand, or requirement. I mean it on the human scale, the scale we can prescribe, see, fit into, and notice on our fingertips, suffering, and orgasms. I mean it as comprehension interprets meaning, or is it meaning interprets comprehension that is the aim, end, goal of meaning, or is it control of meaning that needs to be comprehended?

The sky let through an unusually blue blue over Mealtown, marred only by the occasional jet trail of a moral leader flying to another judgment, an everyman kind of blue implying that there are others who are not everyman, the specials, a blue among blues. Not policeman's blues this or navy blue or Mississippi Delta blues or the Virgin's blue El Greco trifled with or the reflex blue of the nervous writer's choice of cover for his book or robin's-egg blue, whale-blue, ultramarine, or a penchant for blues or blue-jeans blue, it was a sky blue blue sky, and everyone was surprised when they looked up, if they bothered.

For most citizens went about their business conscious of their duty to themselves and to the greater good, satisfied with their relation to the state. National security meant health, education, and welfare, responsibility for their neighbors, and maximizing each individual's potential. They did not think about the sky; it was a matter of record. For most people thought about the sky as an upside-down garbage pail, repository for a variety of temporarily lighter than air junk that human-industry or earth-generated hydrocarbon processes spewed upward.

Carpaccio woke from his afternoon nap trying to shake off the dream. The sky did filter a clear blue due to the strong northwest wind. He stood looking out the window, conscious that a fiction needed the previous two paragraphs before the third-person narrative cut out the rest of reality, when he noticed a formation of biplanes, not high up, beginning an illegal sky-writing run. He held his breath.

Esse.
He thought of the million or more bathers at the beaches who had stopped watching the shit-blistered waves that nobody would dare get wet in to digress to the forbidden words in the sky.

Oh.
The skywriters wrote. Carpaccio thought they might end up writing "SO what," since he and most of his colleagues and friends fondled that feeling more often than was healthy for so liberated a society, a society so conscious of its mission and so dedicated to pursuing it.

Are.
Who was so SORe, hurt, or angry that they would need to spell out their grief to the millions of metropolitan citizens at the risk of large fines, lengthy imprisonment, or, as was most often the case these days, both. Or who was sorer than the earth itself, bandaged at the poles and wounded beyond humanity's ability to repair it with their industriousness that confounded even the ants.

Are.
SORRel, the sour herb, but not more sour than the attitude that lurked behind the duty-bound blues of the citizenry. What cook would endanger the species with illicit skywriting when so many flocked to culinary schools to learn any variation on how to cook the few foodstuffs still allowed by the authorities to be grown in sufficient quantities to feed the billions of humans the hurt earth supported.

Why.
So *sorry* was the first word. A dour social message sent at risk of life and fortune by anyone with the cool and cash to risk, should anyone trace to them the authorship of so sorry a word. But who was apologizing?

And what was the rest of the message? The harsh sunlight glared through the depleted atmosphere, off the metal parts of the biplanes as off the higher buildings, whose glitter had not, for reasons of state or art, if they can be discussed separately, yet been recycled for the greater good.

The space between *sorry* and the next word lengthened. It was getting ridiculously long. Sorry for what? Was *sorry* perhaps the entire message? What was coded within it, along the edge of the smoke as a signal to aliens? There was no more time to question just now, because, as would have been predictable, the second word, if there was one, would never be.

1492 feet beneath the surface14920 souls had built a sustainable refuge. Composed of highly productive citizens from key civilized roles—farmers, scientists, systems analysts, industrialists, artists, craft people and willing breeders—this carefully selected coterie coaxed a living from the soil using highly developed recirculating technologies. They planned to wait out the collapse of civilization above and then emerge to reclaim the earth for god's chosen creatures. Carpaccio was torn.

War against Nature

> Since the divine goodness could not be adequately represented by one creature alone, on account of the distance that separates each creature from God, it had to be represented by many creatures, so that what is lacking to one might be supplied by the other.
> —Thomas Aquinas, *The Shorter Summa Theologica*, "102. The reason for the diversity of things"

The culture of war in the United States has migrated during my lifetime from a focus on Germany to Communism to poverty to drugs to religious wars and now to nature and the planet. Our short-sighted energy policy and other affectations of capital encourage a monocular view of how people and the planet co-exist. In his *New York Times* article of October 12, 2005, "Next: A War Against Nature," Robert D. Kaplan addresses the relationship between terrorism and environmentalism.

> The rest of the world and even quite a few Americans are uncomfortable with the globe-trotting United States military. But in future years they will see much more of it. The causes will be more related to the natural environment than to terrorism. Just ask the earthquake victims in northern Pakistan....
>
> When such disasters occur, security systems break down and lawlessness erupts.... Relief aid is undermined unless those who would help the victims can monopolize the use of force. That requires troops.
>
> But even using our troops in our own country is controversial: the Posse Comitatus Act of 1878 strictly limits the use of troops inside the United States. The Gulf Coast devastation [2005] has helped remind us that this law was enacted in a rural America at a time when natural disasters took a relatively small human toll, and such calamities were viewed more fatalistically.
>
> ....The very people who typically denounce the American military will surely be complaining about its absence should our troops not show up after a major natural calamity.
>
> The distinctions between war and relief, between domestic and foreign deployments, are breaking down....
>
> ....On a larger scale, the disaster relief provided by the aircraft carrier *Abraham Lincoln* during the Indian Ocean tsunami probably did more to improve America's image in Asia in relation to that of China than any conventional training deployment.

So, how can the Pentagon become better at emergency relief without impeding its ability to fight wars? First, it must continue to train primarily for combat. Combat provides a vital esprit de corps, and the skills that are honed in preparation for combat are also the most valuable tools for disaster relief.

It's easy to see how this article that starts as a critique of policy becomes a promotion for turning the military into a support service for disaster relief. Those seeking an essential, single cause for our problems, a cause that can be captured in a sound bite have a ready culprit: nature herself.

The mongers of cause and effect polarize the discussion once again, reifying the perceived conflict between humanity the rest of the planet. Instead of looking for a negotiated settlement that mitigates the differences between human and natural methods, the security state will find ways of persisting the war metaphor and concomitant spending. The argument ultimately justifies marshal law wherever the market is menaced by disorderly conduct or even orderly but contrary conduct. And drones will fly above the fray as in war.

"It's the classic counterinsurgency model: winning without firing a shot. And it's what the future of the American military will be increasingly about."

Kaplan's article was no one-time event. On August 9, 2009 on *The Times* front page John M. Broder writes in "Climate Change Seen as Threat to U.S. Security"

> The changing global climate will pose profound strategic challenges to the United States in the coming decades raising the prospect of military intervention to deal with the effects of violent storms, drought, mass migration and pandemics… Such climate-induced crises could topple governments, feed terrorist movements or destabilize entire regions….

And what are the warlike policies? Continuing the process of separating humanity from nature, industrializing daily life inside ecosystems insulated from the sources of life and supported by humanized systems, industrializing food growth and production, "strengthening" human resistance to disease and aging with monolithic barriers that reinforce the separation. We can understand this as a real solution where humans withdraw from the biosphere and exacerbate our "independence" from "natural" risks. Can we intentionally decide to do that by looking at alternatives or will it be decided for us by capital formation?

As we move from the humanist period to environmental culture, several threats manifest themselves. The humanist capital structure based on economic opportunism will be challenged in ways that Marxism could not challenge it.

Humanism will fight environmentalism with all the tools at its disposal, from confrontation to co-optation. Humanism has been at war with nature from Xerxes ordering three hundred lashes with chains for the Bosporus to Hobbes to Milton Friedman. As in "Genesis 1:26" natural resources exist for us; animals exist for food. The Elizabethan versions of the Greek Bible give "man" "dominion" or "rule" over animals and plants.

> Christianity [monotheism in general] made it possible to exploit nature in a mood of indifference to the feelings of natural objects.... The spirits in natural objects, which formerly had protected nature from man, evaporated. Man's effective monopoly on spirit in this world was confirmed, and the old inhibitions to the exploitation of nature crumbled.
> ("The Historical Roots of Our Ecological Crisis," Lynn White. 1967. *Science* 155: 1203-1207.)

This hierarchy made sense when nature appeared so much stronger than humanity. As early as the 7th century northern European plows no longer scratched the surface of the earth as they had the dry soil of the Middle East. In order to work the wet, sticky, northern soils plows utilized "a vertical knife to cut the line of the furrow, a horizontal share to slice under the sod, and a moldboard to turn it over." (Lynn White) Culture soon followed with calendars depicting people plowing, chopping trees, and butchering pigs as opposed to the idyllic nature images of early Christianity. Constantine changed the symbol of Christianity from those same multiple pacific nature images to that of the cross of war, the handle of the sword.

What we do with our environment depends on our idea of the relationship between humanity and the rest of the biosphere. Now that humanity can in some ways compete effectively with nature, we need to more fully engage the other modes of interaction besides warlike competition. We need to continue to work in our self-interest but reformulate self-interest as a relational model where both differences and similarities are modeled as bi-directional connections.

But environmentalism will fail if we promote other species or even the entire environment at the expense of humanity. Simply making animals and plants and rocks on a par with humans will not sustain the environment or make our behavior more humane.

By collectivizing more public space and undermining the cult of the individual we may adapt. An intended adaptation using human faculties such as reason, memory, and imagination aligns ourselves better with the planet and puts a cultural premium on coordinating human action with non-human participants. To avoid a purely competitive landscape for human interaction, ideas such as larger investments in the future, endosymbiosis (Margulis) both physical and ideational, changes in language use and a focus on real-world complexity in practical matters as well as theory will help build an environmental culture.

Of course we can't see the future clearly from here, and whenever we try to create change, the law of unintended consequences is immediately invoked. Nevertheless, passively continuing with failed tactics because of the risk of change isn't going to make us more able to withstand change. We need to include change in our processes.

If we are not able to extend these ideas from studies of the past to programs of action through application of cultural work, civilization will decidedly regress as environmental problems manifest themselves. And what appears to be regression is already manifest. If we are not able to exercise our competitive behavior at all, what will become of the human libido that contemporary culture has amassed? Where will it go?

Although some people are excited by the idea of nature, the boredom we feel when talking about or acting in relation to nature, as opposed to social interactions (gossip is much more fun), points to the need to link nature and society in ways that continue to interest the shoppers, social butterflies, and warriors of urban civilization.

Bonding Poets

> Jackson Pollock: "I am nature."
> Hans Hoffman: "Ah, but if you work by heart, you will repeat yourself."
>
> Bill O'Reilly: "Which book is fair and balanced or presents a pro-capitalist point of view?
> Bruce Andrews: "The first half of this class is about how to explain individual country's foreign policies…. It's about explanation, and it's about prescription."

Noted biologist Richard Lewontin writes in the *NYRB*, May 27, 2010, "Nothing creates more misunderstanding of the results of scientific research than scientists' use of metaphors." He writes this sentence in an attack on the misuse of the "metaphor" of natural selection, a Darwinian umbrella concept that he describes as containing four mechanical principles of survival and reproduction "stripped of its metaphorical elements": heredity, variation, differential reproduction and mutation. While his querulous response to the term natural selection pressures scientists and readers to be rigorous, it seems impossible to condemn all metaphor or even that specific metaphor because it can be misused. After all which scientific discoveries have not been misused?

Even Lewontin's skeletal form of evolution is metaphorical; it is also probabilistic. Variation is a metaphor for countless disparities or many types, each operating differently, together and independently, some more directly and some inconsequentially. Heredity does not mean offspring must resemble their parents, but that they are likely to look more like their parents. Plenty of people are dead ringers for each other coming out of unrelated parents and offspring often only have minor resemblance. And the vague generalization of differential reproduction does little to show us the variety of relationships between organisms and their surroundings. To paraphrase Pollock, we are and are not nature. Hoffman's statement about emotion misrepresents nature as that which is not human when human mental activity is certainly a product of natural selection in heredity, variation and mutation—and the feedback loops of culture.

Not only does Lewontin attack metaphor, he also characterizes natural historical stories as an invalid method of understanding principles of survival and reproduction, citing several examples of how the narrative about an organism fails to include certain important contradictory elements that reduce the accuracy of the "causal story of natural selection". So if we can't have metaphor (and I assume any other figure of speech) and we can't have stories, what are we left with?

Bruce Andrews' answer to Bill O'Reilly's metaphor of "fair and balanced or…pro-capitalist" provides a useful direction. The notions of explanation and prescription start to look like methods that Lewontin can support. But are they sufficient for a complete science or a complete poetics? A more comprehensive set of tools and concepts provides both science and poetry with ways to integrate into the larger culture. Andrews' writing uses that larger set of tools and concepts, and many scientists, like Paul Feyerabend, accept the value of metaphor.

The "mechanical consequences" that Lewontin wants to be the primary if not sole methods of explanation in natural science are insufficient to realize society's goals for science and even for the accuracy of the results. Too often, restricting explanation to mechanical consequences results in excluding important features that emerge from the complex interactions of those well-defined mechanisms. Feyerabend maintains in his 1976 *Against Method* that Galileo could not have prevailed against the orthodoxy of the church with only scientific method as his tool. He points to rhetorical, stylistic and other persuasive activities such as writing in Italian instead of Latin as key contributions to the church's ultimate vindication of the scientist and the science. Feyerabend summarizes that "theoretical anarchism is… more likely to encourage progress than its law-and-order alternatives" (p10). Here, however, we have the exclusionary principle on the other hand. Each structure has its value and excluding one in favor of the other merely precipitates argument.

Underlying Lewontin's argument is a plea for purity. If only we say just the right things in the right way, people will believe in us, we can have influence and we can continue with our work. We have heard this plea for purity of language and intention before. Andrews and other Language writers fought this running battle for years with the academic literary establishment until it carved out its niche (another metaphor) in the poetry world.

Language writing doesn't eliminate lexical meaning. It rebalances lexical meaning with grammatical/formal meaning, that is, meaning built into structures of writing like sentences and sonnets that go unquestioned for years until someone willingly questions them. Andrews, for example, writes in mixed grammars that include speech patterns, formal grammar using vernacular vocabulary, propositions, prescriptions, the list goes on even in these short extracts. "Shakedown baby, I don't like you so cosily—Payback is a devil dog." Or later "God is science—First, they have to get more Nazi-like Modern English in their gender qualifies first indoor life;…" (*Give 'em Enough Rope*, 1986). The ecosystem (metaphor) of vocabularies and grammars remains complex and opaque, but fully operational as poetry in that it opens a connection between internal/mental logic and a politics of language and government.

What looks to Lewontin like impurity becomes diversity to contemporary poets like Andrews and is exacerbated by the complex strategies of other language writers like Steve McCaffery, Charles Bernstein, Ray DiPalma, and Ron Silliman. Their landmark collaboration *Legend* put forms of writing on the chopping block, fragmenting in a Dadaist manner and then intentionally reassembling them into heterogeneous grammars, syntaxes, forms, relations, vocabularies….

Very little is alien to the collaboration including Lewontin's mechanical principles except an end-to-end consistency of discourse. The *Legend* collaboration included the mechanical principle of a work associated with each combination of the five writers. The principles of inconsistency and heterogeneity lead to look beyond the poem as organic unit, beyond the organism to collectivity, collaboration, ecosystem and interaction.

Other writers juxtapose the catchphrases of pop culture and in some cases the words themselves are chopped up into letters and syllables as in P Inman's *Red Shift*, "print dockery. / drew , mang. / figment keeps to hum // off flections / . climb in / draw nints" (Roof, p12,13). These fragments juxtaposed to complete words and phrases reflect how organisms like poems are colonies of biological (exosymbiosis) and language (parataxis) strategies. The notion that organisms and poems form organic unities points to their collective functions, not a full census of their constituencies. But both poems and organisms have collective functions and a parsable set of components.

Making this point is not new to poetry criticism but extending language writing into environmentalism opposes some of the 1970s tendencies to separate humanity and nature as well as to glorify the modernist focus on mentalscape differentiated from landscape. Writers describe human atrocities as unnatural when they mean unusually vicious. We hear phrases like unnatural language or unnatural diction when we mean unusual or fragmented. We can write a word unnatural but it has no significance except to drive us away from our most rewarding path. We can conceive of that which is unnatural but we cannot point to anything that does not derive from nature, the ceiling and root of human thought and action.

Aligned with our environmental model, Feyerabend points out how this anarchic theoretical approach in science leads to new ideas. Science like poetry develops unevenly. As a result non-rational methods must be applied in order to change hierarchical orthodoxy. "The consistency condition which demands that new hypotheses agree with accepted theories is unreasonable because it preserves the older theory…" Or Feyerabend's citation from Einstein.

> The external conditions…which are set for [the scientist] by the facts of experience do not permit him to let himself be too much restricted, in the construction of his conceptual world, by the adherence to an epistemological system. He, therefore, must appear to the systematic epistemologist as a type of unscrupulous opportunist….
> (Feyerabend, 18).

Underlying the legalistic terms of both orthodox scientific and literary arguments resides a concept of mechanical efficiency that is not universal to natural systems like animals or languages. While an efficient use of resources, that is, using as little energy as possible to complete a task, helps organisms survive and poems to be less boring, a principle of inefficiency more accurately, although perhaps less emotionally satisfying, maps most complex, real-life processes than any single theory or point of view.

Inefficient approaches like duplication in mechanical systems insures against failure of any one component. Repetition in poetry improves our ability to remember the poem and shows us how meaning changes with context in the scientific and musical repetition of words and phrases. Yet even the principle of diversity isn't always the most effective operator as Vaclav Smil shows in *The Earth's Biosphere* (MIT, 2002). Diversity improves productivity in only 30% of all cases, better but far from universal. (Waide, R.B., et al. 1999. *Annual Review of Ecology and Systematics* 30: 257-300 quoted in Smil, p325)

With this lack of certainty we move deeper into poetic territory as Bruce Andrews speculates on inefficiency for major ROI. In *Divestiture* "Pleasure means *inefficiency*." Or in *Lip Service* "Efficiency is the slob I'd love to get / that on wax curve barrage, windswept pull around altercation…" The notion that by being increasingly specific and accurate we can overcome the limits of nature doesn't seem to work out as errors abound.

If we release all these restrictive approaches from their disciplinary confines, we are left to model nature and humanity together more loosely than Lewontin's mechanical principles support by adding that each frame as modeled alone isn't going address all conditions or situations, that is, inefficient processes persist. I recently had a sonogram of my heart. The cardiologist pointed out that there is some backflow from every valve the elimination of which would render the heart too stressed to beat as long as it does.

Even in the case of efficient processes, to effectively achieve biological sustainability and cultural diversity, we constantly need to add mechanical principle to mechanical principle until their very complexity produces properties that are not present in any of the individual mechanical principles. Note the progress of law in any society.

Science cannot progress past its orthodoxy without input from metaphor. The conversations in the epigraphs at the beginning of this essay are useful because they are conversational, not because one of those points of view is correct or effectively encompasses the other. They both operate at the same level in an inclusive hierarchy. The metaphors and narratives of culture need the mechanical principles of interaction, explanation and prescription from grammar, syntax, and format to accompany purely observational methods. These statements infer that metaphor not only reflects the mind's ability to bridge with images any break in logic, but also that the world has transformational or emergent characteristics, that metaphor represents the interactive materiality of the biosphere. Metaphor is not a mental construct but a perception about one of the ways the world works. New things and processes arise from complex combinations of existing things and processes.

The complexity of these interactions of organisms and poems leads me to look at the relationships between them more completely and separately rather than simply view relationship as a characteristic of organisms and poems. Consider the relationships between organisms as the peer of the organisms themselves.

We might say that the disciplines of ecology and poetics study the relationships. Does each discipline have its own set of relationships? Physics has four forces connecting matter. Anthropology identifies various group relationships. Poetry uses punctuation, grammars, syntax and figures of speech. But poetry has forces like rhythm and sound, and anthropology has syntax, and physics has group dynamics that are both similar and different from the way they are used natively. Nevertheless we may find a way to talk about connectors that apply to both organisms and poems.

Since relationships are things, too, they like organisms and poems have characteristics. For example, relationships can be strong/robust like the relationship between noun and verb, neutron and proton, mother and child or weak/loose like the relationship between sentences, atoms and clans. Relationships can be holistic like gravity and periods or transmit components of the organisms like blood vessels and poetic line. Relationships can be uni-directional like time or bi-directional like roads. They can support relatively consistent flows like copper wire and iambs or change the volume and speed of their flows like locks in canals and punctuation.

Andrews again provides a heterogeneous set of connectors that don't always conform to the standards of grammar but make sense as ways people connect action to action, thought to thought, and action to thought. "Unit Costs" written as a score for movement connects dance and poetry as a collaborative process. It also connects language to drawing in a series of shapes that were used in the dance.

Andrews also presents multiple discourses and connects them. "That looks hard to do / Flick whole else". (*Give Em Enough Rope*, p33) These two lines are sequential, i.e., connected, but each uses a different discourse. The first is a simple spoken phrase while the second represents a kind of instruction as a three-word phrase that itself contains multiple discourses. The word "flick" appears to be something that a part of the body might perform. The second word "whole" changes the scale of the phrase. The third word "else" acts a warning, provides an alternative, sounds like a computer code word and links to the drawing that follows: a diamond with an x in it and a squiggly line.

The point of connection between the relationship and the organism also varies in characteristics. The point of connection can be a property of the organism such as the mouth in a kiss or part of the independent connector like a chain or an em dash. In some cases the connectors themselves are a third organism that acts as a connector between two other organisms.

Primitive termites, for example, use specific gut bacteria to help digest wood rather than containing the wood digesting enzyme as part of their digestive juices. In poetry citations, references, paraphrase and epigraphs from other writers clarify the poem's perspective. In this essay I used two epigraphs since I am trying to make both the point about connectors and a point about ideology at the same time, since I suspect emphasizing connectivity helps overcome ideological isolation.

One way to negotiate differences is for each party to say what they want and then together craft a solution that supports the stated needs of both parties. Such an approach requires honesty that often isn't part of a negotiation where one party wants to conceal its motives. Conflicts in government between two political parties results in policies that are difficult to understand because stated goals may not reflect actual desires. For example in 2012 the conservative goal of a balanced budget appears to lock in gains of the one percent from the past 30 years.

Another connectivity type in biology shows how these common solutions play out in the long term. There are cases where connection between organisms is made so thoroughly that one organism becomes part of another as in exosymbiosis where mitochondria and chloroplasts, starting as separate bacteria, became part of the very cells of animals and plants. This connection allows both plants and animals to metabolize oxygen. Such strong and lasting connections are always present, but are easily overlooked because organisms focus on difference as a survival mechanism. The integration of various lexical and grammatical meanings into poetic form might be a literary analogy. Which comes first may be more difficult to diagnose.

There are conditions when vocabulary does not extend beyond a specific discipline because some organisms and connectors have unique properties. There are other situations where translating a term is not only useful, but points to the larger biosphere, itself a whole comprised of component parts. For example similarities of form take place at different scales. The curve defined by electrical flows along nanowires is virtually identical in two dimensions and in one dimension. (*Nature*, P740, Ap 9, 2009) Similarities not only jump disciplinary boundaries, but even dimensional boundaries. The similarities are vital; unfortunately humans notice difference and tend to gloss over similarities so we have a skewed view of the bigger picture.

The emergent properties of all these connections working together with organisms, some of which are merely concepts, some of which are forces, some of which are parts of organisms and some of which are organisms themselves implies that we have spent much time on the organisms and insufficient energy understanding the connections between them. Juliana Spahr's memo on Bruce Andrews emphasizes the need and the nod for connection: http://epc.buffalo.edu/authors/andrews/about/spahr.html. While Spahr identifies several different connector types, a complete theory still needs to be written.

Cultural changes occur in patterns that are isomorphic to changes taking place in natural selection: heredity, variation, and environmental differences regardless of the poet's intentions. The idea that purity of language implies purity of meaning has to be approached more carefully than the orthodoxy of science and poetry admits. There are many misuses of terms like natural selection or poetic, but to exclude trans-disciplinary usage locks us into our current patterns of behavior and language and makes it doubly hard to accept change when change varies. Theoretical anarchy is a far more fertile process than demanding that each theory be consistent with existing theories. Such demands repress advancement in science and poetry, although we may not expect poets to bond more effectively than the current anxiety driven inertia.

Environment as Boredom

> We cannot live in the country,
> For the country will give us no peace.
> —Sir Walter Raleigh

Boredom and Reflection

To start the juices flowing,
When the only consequence is
What already is, craves other
Outlets. Some postmodern poets,

Instead of allying with country matters,
Recursive writings question
Their own existence unproductively,
Negating each sally like overripe bureaucrats.

The lineage of blame,
The critique of industry while reaping its sheaves,
Embraces obedient naturalism that will not support
All of the people together, and neither will love.

What you don't know sneaks up on you,
Nourished on the club sandwich of consciousness,
Emerging as the next planetary hegemony
Parallelizing bio-geometry.

But in whose self-interest?
And what is self-interest?
A working link of plastic arts and orgasm?
The final sounding of the whale?

National Public Poem

Watching Canada geese flying around the valley,
They sit on the pond chatting, then take flight.
What are they cackling? "Watch that wingtip,
Get your beak out of my butt." Then they

Relight on the pond, on the field.
I notice bands on some
Around their legs; they are sending
Radio waves to biologists

Far away. It must make them fly funny
To have those metal appurtenances on,
Like poets: funny
But still sending out signals:

Boredom and Reflection (continued)

Fussy attention to incomplete details,
The lower castes of human ingenuity,
A bathetic metal, reused and used to it.
Expecting contradictions:

Goal-ist revelry excited my atoms,
Intentional progress deified. But what
Moves on? Not new parts, only combinations.
Not neologisms but recycled phrases.

Hurting animals hurts people, but fur is renewable.
Conflict makes up the social body
Where aggressive thought is questioned
And the common lot fits the global cycle?

For the artist, it's still life. And special
Features explode within its ken.
The only special species is starting
To question itself again.

Ron Silliman asked how seriously I take
These environmental niches. I can
Or not:
I have no fixed intentional value;
Irony is intention *and* perception.
Irony versus ontology: looking hard at connective tissue undercuts
       [irony, avoiding its glancing blow. Biology
In the spectrum of intention.
Nature is very much too much.
How can I answer, Ron, when I am

Constantly changing my mind?

But for many readers the compact
Must be stated or made transparent
So the reader doesn't feel endangered
Rejecting play between intention and suspense.

How would society appear after
An environmental renaissance,
Where human boundaries become more
Permeable, without losing ourselves?

So who is left my randy friends,
And how do they relate?
The new caste casts the old one out.
Their functions don't abate.

Boredom and Power

I hope that I shall never see
A poem as boring as a tree

Nature study is boring.
Trees are boring.
Nature completes where human
Arts perfect.

Nature study is boring.
The trees grow. So?
And after a few lines godly fear
Of Darwin appears unjustified.

"Certainly no clear line
Of demarcation has yet been
Drawn between species and
Sub-species—that is, the forms….

or

"The term variety, again, in
Comparison with mere individual

Differences, is also arbitrarily applied,
For convenience' sake....

or

"Finally, varieties cannot be distinguished
From species.—except first, by the discovery
Of intermediate linking forms; and secondly,
By a certain indefinite amount of difference between them..."

Politics sallies forth as if all differences were the same.
Gay marriage and global economy differ in scale
And in vital force but people become equally emotional.
How can the mind compare?

How many dark plans have been hatched over such vagueness?
Would art or religion be so indistinct and rigorous?
Abnegating power has been tried and failed.
Is uncertainty the revolutionary force we are seeking?

Are Darwin's unpredictable definitions a threat to power?
Must people be crushed who pose such questions?
Is nature's diverse way the answer or a special human
Skill efficiently applied? Assign apt apposite.

"Rarity, as geology tells us,
Is the precursor to extinction."
To the extent we can transfer biology
To society, efficiency is often not sustainable.

Repetition secures the future for biology and poetry.
The complexity of phenomena promotes scalar rhyme.
Each argument recurs as in Vico's sutures.
Darwin's importance? He questions time.

In natural selection, the individual must maximize reproductive efficacy for species survival, but what he describes
As a key objection to his theory, sterile or neuter insects,
Supports the social construction of nature.

"I have now explained how, as I believe, the wonderful fact of two distinctly defined castes of sterile workers existing in the same nest, both widely different from each other and from their parents, has originated. We can see how useful their

production may have been to a *social community* [italics mine] of ants, on the same
principle that the division of labour is useful to civilised man."
(Charles Darwin, *Origin of Species*, Modern Library, 1998, p358)

Mediating similarity and difference, objectivity
And personal and class bias, we're never free
Of argument, even though society has that goal
Of presenting the environment as culture, but free of it.

Applied to political conflicts, such as the Middle East (2006),
Biology encourages conflict: conflict implies similarity.
"The forms which stand the closest competition with those
Undergoing modification and improvement will naturally suffer
 [most."

Applied to conflicts in local politics in 2007:
"…We see in man's productions the action of what
May be called the principle of divergence, causing differences,
At first barely appreciable, steadily to increase, and the breeds
To diverge in character, both from each other and the common
 [parent."

As an argument for environmental politics:
"But how, it may be asked, can any analogous principle apply in
 [nature?
…that the more diversified the descendants from any one species become in
structure, constitution, and habits, by so much will they be better enabled to seize
on many and widely diversified places in the *polity of nature*"
 [italics mine]

"And so be enabled to increase in numbers."
The combination of the resurrection
Of Islam and Israel is
"…the truth of the principle that the greatest
Amount of life can be supported by great diversification of
 [structure…."
"Amount"
Is romantic in use but refers to the same in Darwin as in the
 [newspaper,
Suffering aside.

The contemporary poet and the farmer are linked through nature. "Farmers find
that they can raise most food by a rotation of plants belonging to the most different

45

orders." And Diversity is not just native, non-immigrant, "for out of the 162 naturalised genera (of Plants in America), no less than 100 genera are not there indigenous." (1859) This remark is relevant also to global climate change in that while we think of it as associated with the introduction of alien species, even as early as 1859 the America's was a melting pot of plants.

Does the application of reasoning make humans less susceptible to
    [the laws of nature and
Which ones (of those laws) are thereby circumvented? "A set of
    [animals, with their organization
But little diversified, could hardly compete with a set more perfectly
    [diversified in Structure."

For radical art nature has a special place. "If then, these two varieties
    [be variable,
The most divergent of their variations will generally be preserved
During the next thousand generations." Sounds like a Darwinian
Paean to the artist who is willing to continually stretch the absurd.

END of POEM and of citations from Darwin's *Origin of Species*

**

The environmental model of culture does not confirm that intra-species social activities should work in a Darwinian way. Social life in natural settings does not look like Social Darwinism. There is constant sharing, competition and cooperative reproduction between species. There is cooperation, too, on the evolutionary scale, where independent species share components and gradually lose their identity, merging into one another through endosymbiosis as bacteria transform into chloroplasts or mitochondria.

"Life did not overtake the globe by combat, but by networking—that is, by cooperation—and Darwin's notion of evolution driven by natural selection is incomplete. (Lynn Margulis, "Marvelous microbes," *Resurgence* 206: 10–12, 2001.)

Environmental culture sheds light on the way we interact with one another, with other forms of life, and with the resources of the planet. It does not dictate a tribal hierarchy for our social model or a view of human nature as "red in tooth and claw." Social life differs among gorillas, ants, and humans. "Survival of the fittest" applies primarily to reproductive functions. Darwin is clear about that. The environmental model does not dictate similarity among all interactions, but implies levels of interaction that can be defined.

Human social interactions fit into the environmental model. They are not immediately changed by the model, but some human social activities might be repositioned as a result of the model. The relationship of the individual to the marketplace in healthcare might be taken into the government sphere. But climate change will change social interactions more than the application of the environmental model. By changing our view of social action, new ways of behaving may emerge that allow us to retain characteristics of nature that support us and reduce some of the burdens of nature that led us to produce civilization in the first place.

By exhorting awareness of assumptions, post-modernism dictated not so much an alternative set of assumptions but a critique of any reasoning that did not acknowledge those assumptions. Environmentalism establishes an intervening model between our experience/memory/sense data and our actions in the personal and larger social frames—family, friends, non-governmental institutions, and governments at all levels. The model is not intended to make our social interactions duplicate the interactions of other species or to dictate that we should act like any one of them. Instead, the initial purpose of the model is to enable us to look at ourselves from a greater distance. Environmental culture can help us realize that we participate both as a unique species with unique skills and needs, and as a part of the environment, affecting it with our technologies and being shaped by it. What we are creating by our industry is ourselves. And instead of a critique of society, the environmental model helps to shape society by showing how both diversity and standards can produce useful results.

The Metaphor of Trees

> There is no place on this planet that is untouched by human action, [that] the entire Earth is now to a certain degree a human artifact,...
> —Vaclav Smil, *The Earth's Biosphere*

Poets are alleged to bloom alone, arboreal. Coleridge seeks "solitude, which suits Abstruser musings". Wordsworth famously "Wandered Lonely as a Cloud". What these poets often mean by unaccompanied roots less in their person than in despondency and alienation. Emily Bronte addressed alienation directly in "Faith and Despondency" as did Coleridge in "On Dejection". This attitude still dominates much officially sanctioned poetry today, but the larger social frame of the early romantics, their aspiration to reverse industrialization and question capitalism, often disappears in a wave of contemporary self-absorption. Recent work of mine on environmental themes, for example, was rejected by an editor who railed against my "activism" and asked me to "please leave us poets alone on our corner".

Poets' bent for isolation appears in classical and Asian poetry. The global romantic view distains court poets, while crazy wisdom or "naturalness" produces the most genuine work. "He looked like a tramp. His body and face were old and beat. Yet in every word he breathed was a meaning in line with the subtle principles of things, if only you thought of it deeply." (*Cold Mountain Poems*, introduction by Lu Ch'iu-yin, Governor of T'ai Prefecture, tr. Gary Snyder, Origin, 1959.)

Poets ignored by their contemporaries are often admired as much for their solitary lifestyle as for their poetry which is frequently about solitary pleasures. What is not acknowledged is that the poet working in isolation is far easier to co-opt or ignore if her results do not support what the mainstream considers important. Look how Emily Dickenson was reified by mainstream editors until Susan Howe revived her wider intentions and innovative techniques. (*My Emily Dickenson* (New York, 1985)) Such poets need champions like Baudelaire promoted Edgar Allen Poe.

An environmental view does not exclude a solitary lifestyle as a valid response to society. The lone poet represents the reader's self- image. As a specialist process writing a poem without collaboration strengthens the individual poetic impulse. How hard it is to find a moment's peach in the urban hubbub.

But the notion that creating poetry alone and in isolation is somehow truer to "nature" hardly passes muster. Hans Lennenberg in "The Myth of the Unappreciated (Musical) Genius" puts the fairy tale to bed at least for music.

> Most of the great creators of the past, as I hope to demonstrate, received recognition quite early in their careers. Of course there were some to whom recognition came posthumously, but they were usually exceptions whose "failure" can be explained on grounds other than a martyrdom to which a Philistine public condemned them.
> (*Musical Quarterly* (1980) LXVI(2): 221)

From the environmental point of view "natural", read artless, art protects the established hierarchy by promoting ignorance of social means of control. The solitary poet does not help us improve our relationship to our surroundings although he does act as a social critic. While he may provide an example of love of the biosphere and act as a counterweight to oppressive social norms, the subtext recommends isolating individual from individual like trees.

In this arboreal model artists and artistic disciplines are separated like trees in a field or an orchard. The orchard (academic/corporate) model cultivates populations to control cross-pollination or grafting (circumventing the legal, read "natural", routes to fertilization) rather than unintentional (risky) crosses. Any tree not bearing the right fruit must be uprooted or moved to another department of the orchard. And of course we may not expect an apple tree to bear a pear; it's not its job.

A society cannot flourish with such structures alone, although the eugenics approach of the city state of Singapore has so far produced distinct benefits. Society thrives by association between individuals, associations, cults, avid integrators, families, entrepreneurs and hierarchical organizations. The differences between individuals make such a restricted society unsustainable.

The postmodern critique of the metaphor of trees, while attractive, falls into a similar ideological limitation. Deleuze and Guattari propose knowledge and society are rhizoid (*Mille Plateaux*, Minuit/Continuum, 1980). Subterranean channels connect components, plant links to plant in the nitrogen and water cycles, fungi grow via mycelium, and animals share mental space. Mutualism, a kind of symbiosis, links organisms and emphasizes their coordination. This model of society has great power, but the postmodernism critique almost willfully ignores important contrary interactions between organisms.

A 500 year old Brazil nut tree dominates its surroundings. It supports a wide variety of other organisms while preventing certain other trees from growing in its shade. From the point of view of environmental poetics Brazil nut trees exemplify highly functional individual organisms that in human society dominate through the oligarchy, a collection of highly functional individuals in a society or discipline.

The ability of these highly functional individuals especially in collaboration to control an ecosystem cannot be underestimated. One can see it in large mammals or on another scale in certain viruses. Highly functional individuals' natural advantages in human society include an awareness of the similarity of their collective and individual interests. They know what threatens their collective interest and retain the ability to put aside their differences. Much of human history can be understood by looking at highly functional individuals and much of history is written about them.

At some levels such as in society or the biosphere a rhizoid model controls interactions while at other levels such as an individual ecosystem oligarchic arborealism can easily dominate, especially the orchard model that cultivates individual excellence. In most complex ecosystems both rhizoid communication and oligarchic controls coexist. Several models of these structures can coexist. For example, oligarchic individuals controlling different industries come together every year to discuss their strategies, resolve their differences, define their goals and foster cooperation toward their ambitions, shared or not.

Focusing on only one level helps understand interactions within that level, but causation frequently jumps levels as extreme circumstances develop in complex systems. Therefore ideologies or practices that limit responses to one vision reduce their ability to operate under stress or to expand their spheres.

Overall therefore multiple perspectives on the metaphor of trees appear relevant to environmental culture. First, in the orchard we have disciplines, artists, and works of art (the metaphor functions at all levels) like trees. The muse funds the poet who is not yet funded by the NEA, DOD, DOI, FBI, or IRS. (There is some slim hope from the INS, but after the spring 2007 legislative season, I'm not holding my breath.) If it then becomes my problem to define the job of cross-pollinating knowledge from the arts, I might become the Mendel of the social values in poetry. Or I might become responsible for putting together the volatile compounds of further destruction. How do we know or make judgments? Without an analysis to inform us we are thrown back on that artless "naturalness" that leaves citizens prey to power. The metaphor of trees in this sense fosters the vitality of the organism.

Second, the arboreal approach to knowledge isolates tree from tree, defining "nature" in opposition to humanity, isolating one individual from another. There are no vines in the orchard. The wind is still in order to maintain ideal conditions for each tree. Pests are eliminated to maintain each tree's top profitability. All poetry not conforming to one of these arboreal models is considered a weed. Lack of detail stabilizes the metaphor resulting in the over-simplification that results in unsustainable monoculture. The poems growing in this situation support the orchard in which they grew.

In the forest model interactions are acknowledged, but the imagination, that wild mental space, stands at the top of the hierarchy. And imagination is sadly not considered a group activity. In any case humanity cannot return to the forest; there are too many of us. Nevertheless poetry takes root there, especially new/mutated forms generated from complex and unrestrained exchanges. In some parts of the forest individuals dominate, sheltering dependent species. In other parts a tangle of multiple species creates a field where rules are frequently broken and strange creatures abound.

Trees, the other large life form with extensive ranges throughout the planet, while they are many species and we are one, share much with humans. Both trees and humans act as ecosystems within organisms.

> The ratio of fungi to bacteria is characteristic of the type of soil use.
> - Grasslands and agricultural soils usually have bacteria-dominated food webs.
> - A highly productive agricultural soil will have ratios of fungal to bacterial biomass near 1:1.
> - A deciduous forest is fungal dominated and the ratio of fungal to bacterial biomass is 5:1 to 10:1.
> - A coniferous forest is fungal dominated and the ratio of fungal to bacterial biomass is 100:1 to 1000:1.
>
> (http://www.on-line-seminars.com/index.php?p=1_8_Soil-Food-Web)

The many ways that people use trees implies symbiotic relationships of various kinds. Deforestation on the other hand supports a competitive arrangement between humans and trees. An economic and capital driven model focuses on competition/deforestation. A more cooperative relationship occurs when the paper company cuts selectively, so not all capital driven land use requires competition.

In the overall discipline of poetry, imagination and cultivation both tool works. Isolating these ideas weakens the cooperation required to control how we interact with the rest of the biosphere. Humanity's ability to govern many ecosystems represents both our hope to reduce suffering and the branch from which we are about to hang ourselves, the petard with which we are about to hoist ourselves, the guillotine of our own revolution.

None of the metaphors alone is sufficient to address society at large and still less the entire planet. From an environmental perspective the metaphor of trees proposes that the social identity of the individual replicates the rest of the biosphere, saying, in effect, it's just innate (the useful meaning of the word natural) that I am the center of my universe, but I am only my center and even from that center my surroundings support and complete me. There is some justification for this point of view in that organisms do rank as definitive components of life.

In developing an environmental principle, these metaphors enhance and multiply connections between individuals in a society or between ideas in an interdisciplinary epistemology. Such diversity of form reflects the biosphere more fully than any one metaphor. The rhizoid and arboreal models both impact human society often in a nested fashion. And their different surroundings have their place in epistemology.

But when do we apply a particular metaphor? How do we know when ideas stand more or less alone like organisms and when their interdependence becomes more important? Without a taxonomy or dependency map such as proposed by environmental poetics, we will continue to view these connections as mysteries subject to spiritual confusion and aspirational vagueness, or we will defuse connections with humor or ideology. What are the problems we need to address for environmental poetics to actively inform a variety of human activities? The power of metaphor to magnetize and convince remains both lovely and lethal.

Although postmodernism has exploded logo-centrism and ethnocentrism, it has failed to limit the anthropocentrism arising out of our literature's seething mass of misdirection from Genesis to romantic social criticism. If today's artists stop harping on the failures of other disciplines, like a government that starts foreign wars to distract from problems at home or a business person who spends a fortune attacking government, then the leaders in each discipline may be free to take some resources from their disciplines and apply them to finding accurate, meaningful, and fertile connections to other disciplines. Reallocating resources and mental space from emphasizing only differences and complaints to simultaneously strengthening individual organisms and social interaction both between people and thought processes lies at the core of environmental poetics.

Assuming we can develop a culture that supports individuals and their relationships, how can links between disciplines raise interesting problems to work on and have a social utility as well? Here we have no apparent analog in mainstream science, which assumes that, whereas all facts must be considered in validating a theory, all theories are not considered when contextualizing facts. But Paul Feyerabend writes,

> Not only is the description of every single fact dependent on some theory (which may, of course, be very different from the theory to be tested), but there also exist facts which cannot be unearthed except with the help of alternatives to the theory to be tested, and which become unavailable as soon as such alternatives are excluded. This suggests that the methodological unit to which we must refer when discussing questions of test and empirical content is constituted by *a*

whole set of partly overlapping, factually adequate, but mutually inconsistent theories. (*Against Method* (New York, 1975) p27)

Feyerabend then goes on to provide such a test model where imagination dominates method. In doing so he shows the value of competing theories in assuring that facts or people are not suppressed. Diversity of theory and fact interpenetrate. Theory and fact in science map to aesthetic and poem. (And here I am trying to frame the environmental aesthetic with an ecosystem of poetries even as poetry is called into question.) Further science has aesthetics and poems as poetry has theories and facts.

The critique of poetry, such as language writing or Surrealism that are not dependent on our arboreal model, has been that it pays too much attention to theory and not enough to the poem. But each poem and each style of poem is related, as Feyerabend points out, to a specific view or concept of poetry that fostered it. There is no poetry free of theory. To think that a poem arises out of a poet who has no background, no history, but only a direct link to the muse who inspires him, ridicules the entire history of poetry writing.

Yet many poets when pressed voice such opinions about "natural" and immediate poetry. Sapir's oft cited statement about Gerard Manley Hopkins "terrible immediacy" is a quick and dirty example of an idea that is widely promulgated and then intentionally misunderstood. Poetry has always had this tendency to ally itself with "nature" and the natural, but "nature" that emphasizes the individual organism rather than including the organism in its surroundings and configuring its linkages. Such poetry relies excessively on method resulting in the same failures as the science described by Feyerabend.

Once connections between the poem and its context, between the poet and her milieu are established, however, simultaneous instances of greater and less mediated language emerge. Along with intentional stylistic tropes, various prosodic components of a poem (lines, rhymes, themes) are un-self-consciously generated either through forgetting or because of prior conditioning of connections with non-poetic materials. Thorough knowledge and circumspection regarding every iota of the poem is both impossible and absurd, just as it is in science. Both processes are simply too complex to avoid some assumptive creativity and such autonomic efforts produce surprising and interesting results.

Even the "uncreative" conceptual poets of today create their selections of texts and juxtapositions with other texts. The selected text is transmitted with an assumptive context to the reader. For example, Rob Fitterman's context in *Sprawl* derives from the intellectual critique of commoditization of our basic necessities rather than the context of a shopper trying to find a bargain or an imaginative window furnishing and rather than the context of a shop owner working to feed a family. Method does not stand alone nor does it, except in the most intentionally absurdist strategies, lead.

Science and poetry scrutinize specific but different aspects of a process, worked over, and developed in thoroughly overlapping ways. The idea of reinventing poetry with every poem is no more possible than sweeping away all assumptions in a scientific experiment. Yet the effort to find something new in each effort is worth the effort.

If in talking about the poem we emphasize only that one mew component, we risk supporting that component to the exclusion of the rest of the poem and reducing our ability to understand the whole. This tactic creates a hierarchical problem that reduces the value of the poem/organism to its new component. Humans, for example, are not reducible to an opposable thumb. The tactic of isolation also ignores the value that the poem may be good as a whole as well as in parts.

We admire the overall poem aesthetically, so if the new approach helps make a good poem we are pleased to read it. If the new technique confuses the reading, we are less interested in the overall poem, but might find the technique helpful in understanding language or reuse it in a more effective context. For the whole poem to be effective that specific experimental technique needs to be developed in a thorough way. Imagine the following poem.

> I wander through each chartered thoroughfare
> Near where the chartered Thames does meander
> And mark in every face I encounter
> Marks of weakness, marks of psychological disruption resulting from social inequality.

Expected consistency of execution in both meter and rhyme fails. The poem offers us a bit of humor, if you like that sort of thing, while the lexical intent remains mostly intact. This stanza substitutes humor for regular rhyme and meter. There is less discipline, but is it sustainable or do its loose connections, in fact, make it more sustainable? Before you answer, remember how rhyme and meter aid memory. I'm not sure I can answer the question one way or the other even though it is important. Rather, I'd like to decompose the question further and apply various values to multiple answers. (And if you want a moral to this essay, I'd like it to be in that statement.) Consider this effort:

> I wander thro' each charter'd street
> Near where the charter'd Thames does flow
> And mark commuters lunching meat
> Who, while appearing healthy, have high cholesterol.

Here we have mixed the theories of poetry to make a modern poem that doesn't establish its own theoretical ground but instead juxtaposes one aesthetic with another. This theoretical enjambment links medicine, pop culture, and poetry. Its postmodern fragmentation ignores the connectors that are as much a part of an environmental process as the components themselves while creating connectors familiar in other contexts. The facts of the poem don't build a theory but represent a meta-theory. This effort to strengthen the arboreal case highlights the integrity of the organism. Poetry written in this way imitates the arboreal perspective, while leaving out other models. It also reinforces the value of independent facts that environmentalism positions in a context.

In 1926 Victor Shklovsky wrote, "Facts are being experienced esthetically. A work of art no longer needs a plot. What used to be working material for the artist has become the work of art." (Viktor Shklovsky, *Third Factory*, ed. and trans. Richard Sheldon (Ann Arbor, MI: Ardis, 1977) cited in Abigail Child's *This Is Called Moving* (Tuscaloosa, AL, 2005) 162) From this starting point fragmentation may seem like a complete style, rather than a technique enhancing prosody. But once writers get over the shock of fragmentation, while trauma may persist, the linkage between fact and theory continues to dominate the background of all artistic interactions. What may survive from modernism beyond mere style is this aesthetic idea of fact echoed in Feyerabend's history of science. But more structure needs to be added, the connecting links. (The argument does not have to be taken literally.)

Once we get over the shock of the aesthetic idea of fact, we can write poetry that includes facts, theories, and other disciplines as in Khlebnikov's super-sagas. But to be paratactic, the aesthetic needs realization in a way that the poetry can be read. The political extremity of opacity in writing as a social critique, initially a radical experiment in the work of poets like Cris Cheek, Marshall Reese, or in Charles Bernstein's *Veil*, quickly disintegrates as a reader's attention flags or in the best cases merges spectrally into visual art.

The notion of soft borders between disciplines represents another connection type and another example of cross disciplinary work, one that is not paratactic. By selecting common components of written and visual art, the poet can attempt to create a border discipline. The illuminated poems of Robert Grenier that he initially called "scrawls" provide one example. In these "illuminations" (phase thanks to Karl Young) letters are stretched, overwritten, and smudged into near illegibility. In many cases achieving legibility requires Grenier to explain how to look at the work as letters and words. (http://www.thing.net/~grist/l&d/grenier/lgrena04.htm)

Grenier's utopian border town links visual, poetic, and critical/explanatory materials within a poetic context. Jenny Holzer establishes a more paratactic approach to cross disciplinary work by simply placing text in a visual art context. This simplification captures a wider audience because it launches from an established strategy of conceptual art and does not intentionally ignore common visual art aesthetics as in Grenier's work.

Another simplified paratactic approach juxtaposes one discipline on another as common political poetry where a political theme appears in verse. Political magazines often publish these kinds of poems, attempting to renew the social indignation of Blake without much in the way of updating the prosody to match.

> I stumbled over the renewed cobbles
> Of the twee streets of Elizabeth's town
> But all the wealth was locked in banks
> That made the people gasp and frown.

As a result it is poetically boring. We cannot merely substitute theories, as Feyerabend points out. Facts and theories are intimately bound, as are aesthetics and poems.

But does the linkage of theory and fact, aesthetic fact, and this planetary perspective exist only when we look at an expanding future? In our environmentally conscious world of sobered expectations can we be satisfied with conservation, analysis, and morality? I'd suggest that multiple theories and visions of the biosphere continue to exist as well as multiple facts, even facing the anxiety of climate change. But the anxiety starts to dominate the discourse, overwhelming many of the aesthetic values of détente between humans and between humanity and the rest of the planet.

In 2004, BBC aired a documentary *The Power of Nightmares: The Rise of the Politics of Fear.* Director Adam Curtis proposed that political leaders used to rally support with a positive vision of the future. In a world of diminished expectations and future natural disasters, Curtis points to politicians' use of fear as opposed to hope to rally us to their causes.

This negative appeal dominates the discourse around environmental degradation and significantly reduces its value to inspire real change in the way people accomplish their goals. (I'm always surprised that conservatives don't embrace conservation.) Leading writers also work in this field of pessimism due to a lack of alternative views of nature in mainstream culture. In contrast, environmental poetics seeks significant expansive and optimistic goals for humanity and "nature" as a single global system.

Interests vested in a fear-based notion of "nature" will push back. The possibility of poetry that support multiple views of nature is simultaneously founded on innovation and a political/scientific review of where we must follow processes that we find in the biosphere and where following those processes exposes us to planetary forces that are not necessarily supportive of continued human existence. And it is strange that I feel the need to say this: We want to avoid destroying the places we live in order to achieve short term comfort and satisfy short term desires.

Today more than a pattern of social disarray and ecosystem degradation thrusts us to act to repair our surroundings. One group thinks that giving the sufferers support will help their situation and another group maintains that strengthening the economy as a whole will help those stressed by change. In reality, both these theories need to be in play at the same time to improve the situation of the majority. Working people, managers, and the poor need to know there is hope for them in an economy designed to include all its citizens, but they also need to eat something today. Highly functional individuals need to see the fruits of their labor as well. How do we provide for both in a world of increasing competition for resources?

Multiple theories are invoked simultaneously. Rather than simply discuss ambiguity, environmental poetics emphasizes synonymy. Rather than isolate the poem/organism, treat its linkages as well....

Niches

> [W]hen an ecologist says 'there goes a badger,' he should include in his thoughts some definite idea of the animal's place in the community to which it belongs, just as if he had said, 'there goes the vicar.'
> —Charles Sutherland Elton, 1927

"Good Luck" Haiku
Crawls in a tunnel
That he made all by himself.
Poets meditate.
(don't other animals?
Each discrete organism
Independent and
Linked
In relational position.
That feels good, too.)
Subservient/subordinate/solvent
Allaying the words
A place with something in it
Or a place for something

Of poetic life—
an oxymoron.

    I edited. Then I rewrote it.

"At a Certain Level" Haiku
The early bird picks
The above worm from the tunnel
They both inhabit.
Some letters are bigger than others
Specialized and generalized
They walk over
The snowy field
K-L-K-L-K

Analogy makes distinctions.
But risks fruitless relations

How can the rectangular page
Represent the pear-shaped planet?
How far beyond that
To the screens of psyche?
To think planet keep moving
But skin blocks the passage.

O
K
O
K
O
K
Thinking outside the head…
And I suddenly realized
It wasn't all about who…
Bug, bugger, buggiest
Give me a leaf quick
I gotta go expand
The firewall

To profess alternatively
It takes six weeks or more to heal.

The one and the other
They are unique but their cells:
Picaresque dentifrice.
Around the block with Mercator projections
Are the whole human experiment
Of only two sides.
More than feeding the cow:
A shape and other shapes,
More than the cry:
Fitting facts into another fiction.

What we put in overflows
And we don't clean up,
Leaving around and about.
The extra keeps its coffee grounds.
This and that
Creative residue.

Retract the valence,
But keep it handy.
Extend a hand:
"Cellular prosody"

Green is not enough.
Poetry is possible,
If we give it its head:
An anonymous flow job.

Extend myself to you.
Extend myself to me.
Extend ourselves.
Extend ourselves
In other directions.
The green hokey-pokey.

What do I think about that?
What do you think about that?
What do I make you think about that?
What do you think about that after I made you think it?
What do you think the next day?
And shifts too,
Another opportunity for dispersed light.
    A flamboyant cult awhile
    Then agnostic choices
    Remote host for the symbiotes:
    Her biceps.

What I said earlier
Is what I meant then.
    A flying squirrel, a flying gecko
    A flying elephant
Homologous
    Shared ancestry.
    Analogy: similar but independent
Anachronism deference.
    You'd like to say higher,
    But rather flatter.

Anyone
Arguments tried and tired
Linked and unlooping
Choker vines.

    An unrecognized threat
    A recognizable thread
Unintentionally irritating
Because elsewhere is easier.

What's wrong with a little assurance
About causality,
Even if we don't believe it?

    The left hand knows what
    The left hand is doing.

END

Niches, the relational positioning, are incomplete in themselves, as are the species and groups of species in any geography… At least light, water, and standard atmosphere. They do not delve into any subject in aggressive specialization but together are intended to answer the questions more completely because the relationships are defined by the juxtaposition of the entities rather than following a single thread of argument which is a species of thought. I suppose I am valorizing a natural process over a human model of efficiency. I hope that readers will defer gratification, catharsis, and resolution to understand the value of a literature that reflects natural processes in a way that co-exists with human ones.

From Bonds and Niches a Social Force Unleashed

> If to do were as easy as to know what were good to do, chapels had been churches, and poor men's cottages princes' palaces.
> —Portia, *The Merchant of Venice*

Last week when I was talking about Erasmus' *Praise of Folly*, a colleague asked me if Erasmus was Jewish. While I was making it clear that Erasmus was a priest who stood against the doctrine of Predestination, in spite of Luther's entreaties to join him, and that he was also a close friend of Thomas More, at whose house he wrote the tract, I suddenly felt that I was really being asked about my allegiance to the faith of my fathers and the increased attraction of my aging male friends to their cultural heritage. I asked myself which is true about me: I was born Jewish (one cannot be born into a state of belief); I believe in Judaism (one cannot prove belief as true); I participate in Jewish culture as part of or independent from a layer of the Judeo-Christian tradition... I decided only the last one can possibly be tested and accepted as true, and it's certainly the only one I'd admit to. So it was probably not coincidental that I began reading and watching different versions of the *Merchant of Venice* to see if perforce I had a greater attraction to my past as my future shortened.

The reader knows by now that the present tract relies on diverse elements formed into small essays and poems, while the forces operating among them drive the narrative. Yet I had not, until this friend in essence accused me of being interested in Erasmus only because I was Jewish, thought carefully about the types of connections that might exist between these niches and how their forces were manifested neither in nature nor in culture. (Such are the limitations of the amateur, since a professional would annex these bonds to culture.) Goffman's frame theory might also be an interesting way to look at this problem.

The variety of binding/framing types is blinding. And the suggestion that any one, Judaism, is at the center of Shakespeare's intention is inflating the notion beyond anyone's ability to keep your interest for more than the few pages of this essay. Although love's set of bonds seems the ontological key to understanding the play's action, commercial bonds are the stage on which they play. Consider the bond between Bassanio and Antonio, between Bassanio and Portia, between Antonio and Shylock on behalf of Bassanio's suit of Portia, and between Portia and her father's choice. This set itself has many characteristics that may be hard to define. In addition, there are the bonds between the Jews of Venice in their *Geto* to their God and to one another in their cultural prison. Then the bonds between them and the larger society of Venice may drive Shylock, although it is also clear that the strength of that bond is added to by the stressed bond between Shylock and Jessica in her escape and conversion. (Note that the connection is not lost, but stretched into memory and regret.)

In addition, these niches are connected by bonds between the law of the Jews that drove Christ in the first place and the laws of the Duke, which are modified by those two sets of religious laws, but are a separate set of laws that he himself must enforce and be seen to obey. There are further bonds between the Duke and the Pope that from the English point of view have been morphed further, as England had already established its own national church. There are bonds between the men, who control property law, and the women, whose rights to control property in sixteenth-century Venice are probably a subject in themselves. There are bonds between the Duke and his religion, by this time embattled by Luther on the one hand and Erasmus' critique on the other. And there, and seeming to inform all, are the bonds between Lorenzo and Shylock's daughter, between the law of the Jews and the compromise of Christian love—the cross-bonding bonds. Quite an array to be analyzed.

What ultimately secures Antonio's solvency is that this diversity of relationships is nearly impossible to resolve under a single set of laws and even within a single set of beliefs, to come to a conclusion about appropriate action without due consideration. (Current religions and governments may do well to note this consideration before seeking easy and ultimately incorrect answers to the conflicts between them.) Shylock cannot rely on the word "flesh" alone, because it is tied to blood. The law cannot rely on a single statute but must depend on a combination of statutes and interpretations, a social dashboard and its controls, to regulate society.

What saves the day for Bassanio is Portia's recognition not only of how the complexity of law is interpreted, but how the other bonds among people are mediated by circumstance as well as by fixed laws. She knows how she in disguise compromised Bassanio's bond to keep her ring, even if he did not know it. She knows that keeping the society diverse is its only measure of surety.

> The quality of mercy is not strain'd,
> It droppeth as the gentle rain from heaven
> Upon the place beneath: it is twice blest;
> It blesseth him that gives and him that takes:
> 'Tis mightiest in the mightiest: it becomes
> The throned monarch better than his crown;
> His sceptre shows the force of temporal power,
> The attribute to awe and majesty,
> Wherein doth sit the dread and fear of kings;
> But mercy is above this sceptred sway;
> It is enthroned in the hearts of kings,

> It is an attribute to God himself;
> And earthly power doth then show likest God's
> When mercy seasons justice. Therefore, Jew,
> Though justice be thy plea, consider this,
> That, in the course of justice, none of us
> Should see salvation: we do pray for mercy;
> And that same prayer doth teach us all to render
> The deeds of mercy....

Transposing this statement to contemporary society is a bad omen for global population control without concomitant despotism.

How Portia's brilliant moves work in a continually expanding field of endeavor is one of the marvels of all literature. Yet we now find ourselves in a different situation, in which diminishing returns result from continuing conflict in the limited field of the planetary environment. And yet perhaps, if we're careful, and think through the drama, even these additional complexities of a limited field (space colonization aside) can be addressed by Portia's ability to assert varying levels of control on the different bonds that attach us to one another as individuals, cultural niches, and nations.

Shylock loses his suit because of his insistence on the fundamental bond of the contract (the Law), broken because it inevitably states the case in an incomplete manner. And even our gargantuan contemporary legal system is easily overturned by such discrete articulations of power as George Bush's phone surveillance tactics, while at other times it cannot be budged by atomic weapons. Bassanio keeps his wife because she recognizes the mutability of personal bonds. Antonio binds himself to Portia through the intermediary of Bassanio. Lorenzo and Jessica are bound to Shylock in spite of her conversion. And the spirit of compromise allows the world to continue to turn. Even Shylock gets to keep his house, sadly for my argument, all through the justice (authorship) of Portia.

These diverse answers for diverse relationships are at the root of society, and we can go one step deeper in the relationship between the aristocracy and the Jews. It was not entirely the Jew's money that was being lent. In their *Geto* the Jews could not accumulate enough funds to bankroll the entire expansion of European enterprise. The money, by and large, derived from the property of the aristocracy, for whom the Jews acted as sometime bankers, not funders. (*The Ideology of Adventure*, by Michael Nerlich, Minnesota, 1988) Since the aristocracy could not, in medieval culture, be seen to be engaging in this kind of commerce lest they come into direct conflict with the dicta of the papacy, the Jewish and other middlemen supported the surplus cash flow. This additional level of complexity ties the knot of justice more thoroughly and in a far more interconnected way than ever. And it points to a larger issue of a continuing top/down and bottom/up hierarchy for social and cultural models derived from the visible and invisible models observed/sensed in the environment.

What I mean is that Portia cannot hope to keep her constituents from compromising themselves by a continuing downward spiral of fundamentalist considerations without a continuing set of compromises that counter gravity, death, and other implacable forces. Portia recognizes the interconnectedness and complexity of our relationships to one another and ultimately to the political niches that we all inhabit.

Fundamental or essential views seek to ignore these complex relationships by establishing a hierarchy to which they appeal when a threshold of stress is reached. And although these fundamental and essential appeals can prevent many disagreements from becoming theatrical farce by being self-critical, the action that resolves the difficult problem is, in this instance, untying the knot of fundamentalism strand by strand, identifying the situations, and identifying them separately instead of applying an emotionally appealing Gordian solution.

Our human world is built from the general to the particular *and* vice versa. One-directional flows often provide an insufficient explanation and require a leap of faith. Faith alone will not build a bridge; an expert will not solve every problem within a discipline. We cannot exclude faith as a driving force of our society, nor should faith exclude reason, compromise, and other ways of thinking. *The Merchant of Venice* is not about anti-Semitism or the higher law of the Christian God but about humanity's ability to work through our differences. What is more hopeful is how our differences, their distances, and bonds, inform our solutions.

How we can actually operate in the now visibly limited field of our planet without reverting to restrictive views of behavior that continually reduce expectations and drive power into fewer hands is another subject. It will require knowing, as Portia knows, that not all bonds are the same, that bonds have variable binding power. Physics has a model for these bonds (four types) that may be useful for culture, but the metaphors are perhaps not necessary here. A science of politics modeled on physics is also a consideration for another time. Our political system and our leadership are responsible for reinforcing the valued network of our relationships and for keeping paths open.

I have undertaken the responsibility of explaining how to get from a homocentric to a planetary view, and I am coming to realize such an effort is not accomplished in one place but through the relationships of multiple locations and methods interacting with one another. Some good work has been done on a social structure of an environmentally focused world, the components that need to interact, and their kinds of connections. (See the sub-section titled "Academic Structure of Confession.")

The complexity of the bonds in *The Merchant of Venice* reinforces my view that a society modeled like the environment will be more sustainable. It does not answer the questions of when and where we must diverge in our own interest, when we must ignore self-interest, and when we must bow our heads and succumb. As Portia says, "To offend and judge are distinct offices and of opposed natures."

Tagmosis/Prosody (Connecting Parataxis)

> Discrete skeletal units are known as tagma. The process of fusion is called Tagmosis. Different patterns of skeletal tagmosis provide a primary criterion for identifying fossil arthropods.
> —Stephen Jay Gould

Discrete structural units of poetry are known as prosody. The process of fusion of prosodic units is known as writing. Different patterns of prosody provide a primary criterion for identifying poetic affiliations.

Start with a bird in a tree.
See it: a thing, a fad, a need.

Two, three, four, and more starlings
Pack the black walnut.

Focus on the whole walnut, a green
Shape with black punctuation

That was recently starlings.
Concentrate on the whole copse:
A maple, an elm, a walnut. Honeysuckle,
Lilacs in sunny spaces bleed into the grass.

The landscape of things transforms
Into one of relations. Things lose
Their identity. Bonds compile
Into landscape. Words collect
Into blocks of paragraphs;
Disengage into masses of letters
And streams of space.

Phrases accrete into forms and thoughts,
Not one like a thing, but an
Interlocking and disassembling set.
Our inference machine connects
Facts and fuses
Them into theories. Our minds continue
To suppose segues and bridges

Between disciplines.

Juxtaposing prosody to tagmosis, for example,
Creates difficulties for political and ethical processes.
Politically, what thoughts can live together?
We assume relations of things
Proximate in trees,
Thanks to Linnaeus.
If we limit our perception
To the black starlings in the black walnut tree,
Specialized disciplines transform
Nature into objects for use.
Very practical. And our sense
Of self supports this supposition
To distinguish each from other
People, species and the landscape.

Ethically, which parts of ecosystems
Correspond to human constructs,
And where is human activity unique?
We constantly differentiate ourselves
When ego seems pertinent to survival.
We work in communities to build
Surplus to reduce risk. Thus
Community produces freedom?
Relational focus materializes emergent properties
That simulate imagination to formalize
Our production of poetry, biology, and community.

Parents teach ethics of cooperation.
From a comparison of human and primate
Societies, human groups nest
In more inclusive structures while
Primate societies are flat. Human families
Form by conjugal, monogamous partners,
"Remarkably unique" among primates.
Among most primates either males or females
Move to another group at puberty, "losing
Contact with their natal group permanently;
Dispersal is strongly sex-biased."
In humans either sex may stay or leave.
"Dispersed kin maintain lifetime bonds"

> Kin recognition is bilineal and of unparalleled
> Extent.... Humans maintain preferential bonds
> With their affines, or in-laws....a uniquely
> Human feature....close and distant affines
> Account for a large proportion of coresident
> Group members.... Instigating
> A state of mutual tolerance." Social awareness
> Leads to cooperation with non-kin,
> Regard for others, seeking
> Of linkages, cultural transmission,
> (Hill et al., "Co-Residence Patterns in Hunter-Gatherer Societies Show
> Unique Human Social Structure" and Chapais "The Deep Social Structure
> of Humankind," *Science* (vol. 331 March 11, 2011, p 1276,7 &1286-89).

And intolerance of deviant behavior.

Environmental interactions develop processes
Like a water cycle, a food chain,
A community of supporting individuals,
A supply chain that drives process efficiencies,
Interdisciplinary thought that overlooks/sees
What specialists appreciate as deistic details.

The conflict between things and connections
Arises when we as individual organisms
Revert to perceiving the world as a set of objects,
When multiplicity in societies or ecosystems
Threatens the individual objective condition. Hence we

Must build connectivity
Into the model of things

And isolate ideas to focus
On the organism.

Ego spotlights the self
In opposition to interaction,

Limits awareness of emergent properties.
Forcing behavior into an organism model

Reduces the value of interaction.
Can any construction hold these

Interactions, synergies and contractions?
Don't we sustain to build one?

How are these threads woven? The analogy
Between tagmosis, prosody, and ecosystem
Is a fine place to start, since data
And knowledge about them emerge
From process and relational thought
As well as from ontology. Tagmosis,
Prosody, and ecosystem identify a whole
Organism/poem/biosphere built of interacting
Components. None of the prosodic or skeletal
Units are really independent like a sentence
Or commensal bacteria. Therefore our limit
Condition entails sets of mostly dependent components.

Working with process enables us to see self-identified interactions. Working with ontology develops the temporal relationships of both the individual organism and its interactions. Process and ontology interoperate and need to acknowledge that they do so.

First, in addition to the separation of the different prosodic or skeletal components, we must consider the sideways pull of interaction between components and characterize the linkages between them. Otherwise hermeticism will create unpleasant surprises for our specialists/species. This physics of vertical components and horizontal interactions produces a familiar branching and extends the analogy to ecosystems of ideas.

Prosodic connectors are well defined.
Parataxis connects by juxtaposition.
Elision and contraction connect lexis.
Lines are bound by meter, rhyme,

And stanzas as tagmata by tendon's line,
Ligament and cartilage. Logic and legend
Connect the tagmata of the poem.
In speech focus and intonation tie.

Second, the relationships between poems and types of poetry can be based on prosodic distinctions as well as logic and legend, although content as noted above can also be viewed as a kind of prosody. Finally, poetic affiliations, loosely knit groups of poets and schools, can be defined by how they view prosody (language poets, New York School, metaphysical poets) or by their themes (romantics and identity poets). Both treatments produce remarkable poetry using crucial tactics of the others. The distinctions that participants in different groups find so vital are by and large partial and fragmentary.

While little recommends one style or practice over another in the long run, short term values in poetic strategies attract the energetic poets of the moment. Often the presence of a new perspective is sufficient to draw talent to it. And I have a strong bias for poetic approaches that hold promise for investigation over forms and themes that have been fully explored. Again to distinguish the individual I have my own ideas; to cooperate I have appropriated and modified.

Unlike skeletal links, poetic connections are not always articulated hence the importance of parataxis to both contemporary poems and groups of poems as the poet strives to keep them independent and clearly identified. But the preference of poets and other artists to have their works identified by criticism rather than interpreted by it is also a key connection linking poetry to biology. Poets want to have the interpretation integrated in the poem and for critics to merely identify and celebrate its existence. As an alternative the current generation of poets opens the possibility of poetry criticism about more than just the work and positions the work within its ecosystems. Interpretive criticism, such as environmentalism, opens the door to extend poetry's reach.

Carrying identity too far leads to battles for hegemony. Me, us. Identifying poetries solely within a taxonomy or canon limits poetry's value. What if we limited biology to counting species and categorizing them? But such conflicts between poetic groups present beyond the minds of individuals seeking control. They are also fighting for the jobs, prizes, and reviews that allow them to continue with their work. These distinctions exist because of real world problems and limited resources as much as they are vacuous contests. As with biology, survival dominates individual behavior.

**

To write about more than one subject in more than one discipline and find their correspondences—people find differences too easily—leads to learning which questions can be answered by a single value and which require compounds. How old are you leads to a number while sink or swim points to a polar structure. We tend to seek single or polar answers to most questions, but the majority of real world concerns related to society, science, and writing have many answers or long answers or aren't even structured as question and answer at all: How shall we live together requires more forms than simply q&a in spite of Plato's simplification?

How shall we live on earth invites our processes to fit into those of the planet? How shall we write about these questions? Should I be positing them as questions.

Linnaeus, for example, modeled relationships between biological species as a tree. But many solutions are more complex than a tree.

> …trees are by no means a universal representation. Inferences about other kinds of categories or properties are best captured by using probabilistic models with different forms: two-dimensional spaces or grids for reasoning about geographic properties of cities, one-dimensional orders for reasoning about values or abilities, or directed networks for casually transmitted properties of species (e.g., diseases). … Knowledge about causes and effects can be expressed in a directed graphical model…
> (Tenenbaum et.al., "How to Grow a Mind: Statistics, Structure, and Abstraction," *Science* vol. 331 March 11, 2011 p 1279)

Physicists, too, have accepted indeterminacy even in measurement since the early 20th century as in the case of quantum mechanics. But we are only beginning to accept these probabilistic solutions for social problems such as learning or judgment or intention. Most of our ethical reasoning assumes single or polar values as the correct representation whereas social problems are more often resolved by a range of solutions. We are able to infer so much from so little that the facts we possess are rarely sufficient to justify our conclusions. Tenenbaum et al. propose that our inferences can be built from a fact and an abstraction. Poets have long been at the forefront of such construal.

Linking poetry to the reader, that is, understanding how poetry follows this probabilistic model, a range of approaches supersedes any single, dual or even a map of multiple connections. Ambiguity grows in poetry from court poets seeking to avoid imprisonment to Mallarme's *Un Coup de Des…* where

> …the ensuing words, laid out as they are, lead on to the last, with no novelty except the spacing of the text. The 'blanks' indeed take on importance, at first glance; the versification demands them, as a surrounding silence, to the extent that a fragment, lyrical or of a few beats, occupies, in its midst, a third of the space of paper: I do not transgress the measure, only disperse it. The paper intervenes each time as an image, of itself, ends or begins once more, accepting a succession of others, and, since, as ever, it does nothing, of regular sonorous lines or verse – rather prismatic subdivisions of the Idea, the instant they appear, and as long as they last, in some precise intellectual performance, that is in

> variable positions, nearer to or further from the implicit guiding
> thread, because of the verisimilitude the text imposes.
> (Mallarme's Preface of 1897, trans. A.S. Kline, 2007.
> http://www.poetryintranslation.com/PITBR/French/MallarmeUn
> CoupdeDes.htm. (June 26, 2011))

While Mallarme's stated intention works with spacing, he also accepts "that the tentative participates, with the unforeseen, in the pursuit, specific and dear to our time, of free verse and the prose poem." (Ibid) Space for Mallarme and subsequent field poets represents time and the intervention of reflection during reading. What Mallarme calls "the unforeseen" means indeterminate, but also that many readers identify a specific meaning that they can support, a reading. In the case of *Un Coup de Des* the simple fact of using space in a new way, juxtaposed to the abstraction of chance, sanctions a series of writers to subsequently create a variety of probabilistic poetic responses.

In our time Silliman's use of space between sentences offers a range of more specific meanings that do not increase the likelihood of one answer somewhere in the middle. Rather the range of answers remains and each of those referents generates another group of sentences. The subsequent sentences reduce the range of possible meanings, but we are soon lost in the next set of possible alternative meanings.

> Revolving door. Fountains of the financial district. Houseboats
> beached at the point of low tide, only to float again when the sunset
> is reflected in the water. A sequence of objects which to him appears
> to be a caravan of fellaheen, a circus, camels pulling wagons of bear
> cages, tamed ostriches in toy hats, begins a slow migration to the
> right vanishing point on the horizon line.
> (*Ketjak*, This Press, 1978)

Thus interpretation in modern poetry remains dicey. And contemporary writers relish going beyond ambiguity to accommodate several valid readings of a poem including interpretive readings, showing the superficial indicates subsequent layers. Lyn Hejinian writes, "Planes of information intersect, coincide" (*My Life*, 1980). John Ashbery,

> The men never learned to love much. There was both hunger and
> sadness/at their feasting, the rocks wave over the airstrip, the hyenas of
> sleep redescend,/the leeches brace themselves for one last fetid leap into
> thanksgiving/there where loam signals the synod's pallid approach.
> (*Girls on the Run*, 1989).

The criticism that there is a lack of sense data to make the contemporary worlds of art and science collectively comprehensible underestimates our power of generalization, because "if the mind goes beyond the data given, another source of information must make up the difference. Some more abstract background knowledge must generate and delimit the hypotheses learners consider, or meaningful generalization would be impossible." (Tenenbaum, p1279) For example, history echoes, rhymes but does not repeat. Our abstraction apparatus supplies the similarity. Déjà vu occurs when a fact links with a memory adrift. Our body's posture may be associated with a sound or afternoon light as in the *Light Poems* of Jackson MacLow. The sensory fact isn't entirely clear or remembered, but the shape of the event, an abstraction, triggers memory.

As Silliman poses the issue, "…an ordinary sentence, such as 'I peered into it', can become a new sentence, that is, a sentence with an interior poetic structure in addition to interior ordinary grammatical structure." (Ron Silliman, "The New Sentence," *The New Sentence* (Roof, 1977, p90). The form of abstract knowledge, a structure of knowledge representation, in New Sentences nests a probabilistic (poetic) grammar within a goal directed Latin sentence. Successful poetic generalization occurs when the dependencies map to the forms of abstract knowledge that readers have evolved. I represent evolution as both a long term biological adaptation and short term cultural transmission through successive readings of many texts or even rereading of a single poem.

These forms of abstract knowledge also pertain to a physical analogy. Causal relations tend to be traced "from disease to symptoms, rather than within these classes or from symptoms to diseases." (Tenenbaum, p1281) In traditional verse these physical relationships run from experience to poem with little attention paid to the underlying abstractions Silliman exposes. Some innovative poetries such as contemporary conceptualism manipulate those received abstractions. For example, Fitterman copies texts from commercial writing about a shopping mall into a new context in *Sprawl*. Goldsmith juxtaposes weather reports from New York and Bagdad to stimulate our memories of other events occurring in those locations, revealing who has more at stake in breakfast, the chicken or the pig. Their form of humor derives from a mismatch between the expected and written fact/abstraction models.

The need to get abstract knowledge right occurs in effective learning. But how do we know which structure appropriately organizes hypotheses for learning words? The probabilistic framework of learning allows for incorrect connections to be made once an abstraction links to a fact like "this is a horse." The supervision of the learned structure comes from matching evolved mental structures to structures experienced in the world. Here again Tenenbaum points to nested structures and a complex, not always effective, process. And categories are developed in ranges so that experience isn't always carried over into repeatable action. In fact conservative political strategists, like the conceptual poet's realignments, confirm that by merely triggering an abstraction, it connects to facts bound by the tone created by immediately prior events.

First, a politician establishes a framework of anger, typically showing something that the voter cherishes as lost or stolen by the opposing party. The speaker establishes trust by showing the voter something she accepts as true. Then a series of statements—some true, some false and some ambiguous—builds a matrix of facts that the voter connects using the triggered abstraction. The abstraction establishes the connections between the words. "In Reagan's hands, taxation became 'confiscation,' attempts to solve social problems became 'costly social experiments,' regulation of market failures became 'economic tinkering'." (Drew Westin, *The Political Brain* (New York, 2007) p 156). In Boehner's hands negotiation becomes a weakness, proved because Obama changes his position to accommodate his own idea of negotiation as flexibility. Voters accept the outright lies of politicians. Absurd extensions of partial facts are believable once the speaker establishes the appropriate connection between abstraction and fact.

The gestural poets' critique of intellectual pursuits in the arts fails to account for the indeterminate and redirected connectivity found in New Sentences, conceptual poetics, and poetry generated by chance operations. "Structured symbolic representations need not be rigid, static, hard-wired, or brittle. Embedded in a probabilistic framework, they can grow dynamically and robustly in response to the sparse, noisy data of experience." (Tenenbaum p 1285) And the academic adherence to reasoning within a discipline does not easily accommodate many real world events that cross boundaries. And the identities of those organisms objective condition are threatened.

But let's not lose sight of the multiple ways we can get to there from here. Many important non-linear problems have been addressed by simplifying them, making the complex linear. Picasso's formula for success as an artist valorizes simplification, "If you have five elements available use only four. If you have four elements use three." Other aspects of similarity persist and are accepted without the concurrence of the creators. Interpretation of the Constitution leaps to mind. But can we trust our perceptions of similarity in opposition to specialist appeals for consistency?

Environmentalism proposes that real-world phenomena contain similarities at all scales, implying a composite worldview, single, but composite, not unitary. The biosphere works through abstract structures linked to facts in much the same way as Tenenbaum described learning. This structure by necessity assumes a kind multiple connective tissues in paratactic constructions, maybe many multiples. The connections between components in individual organisms are well understood, for example, how bacteria in the gut support digestion. Taxonomy, on the other hand, bases its themes on structural differences such as how the hip of the dinosaur distinguishes it from other lizards.

Writing uses prosodic connections: thematic transitions, punctuation, spacing, rhyme. Looking more deeply at literary tagmosis would clarify the links between mental and biological constructs. (*Eats Shoots and Leaves* by Lynn Truss (New York, 2004) provides an entertaining if narrowly grammatical example of the details of connection by punctuation.) Yet in literary criticism we rarely differentiate styles based on how writers use punctuation or capitalization except when comparing innovative poetry to canonical poetry. Unexpected syntax or punctuation labels a piece of writing as structurally different, becoming avant garde or experimental or innovative. Here tagmosis of the biological kind appears in writing. Could we develop a taxonomy of literary connective tissue?

Time is another internally diverse connection type. Now, the present, does not necessarily go this way and might go another or several. A statistical distribution replaces a dichotomous solution. While mathematical time goes forward, literary time can scatter. Both poetics and ethics form dynamically. In paleontology Stephen Jay Gould (*Wonderful Life,* Norton, 1989) represents progress as "punctuated" and not uniformly progressive, citing periodic mass extinctions and long periods of relative stasis. He also demonstrates that survival is often based on chance or distribution, not solely on competitive "fitness." "Arguments that propose adaptive superiority as the basis for survival risk the classic error of circular reasoning." (236)

What are the implications of Gould's revelations for our model?

> Art based on or assuming a continuous, progressive march of ideas is inconsistent with our observation of the biosphere and the mind. Continually progressing art must be viewed as contrary to biomorphic progress, since the origin of such art or politics for that matter is based on a linear/urban/separatist view of nature.
>
> Politics, science, and arts based on a notion of continuous progress must be understood as applicable to limited time spans if they are to be valid at all. Such works in the arts are primarily ironic, parody or satire, and do not rely on progress at all. As social critique they are useful, but as progress; we must examine our goals for writing. If we do, we find a variety of targets whose proponents go in and out of fashion.
>
> Arts and sciences that assume a composite set of natural forces or multiple views of nature must also reckon that short and long time spans have decidedly different kinds of progress. A single mode of discourse

throughout a poem would not support both time spans; the odes of Charles Bernstein, such as "Lode (Mrs. Mao at Gulag)", provide a good example of complex discourse organized around multiple genres. In the short run, progress can appear orderly, but phases of turbulence occur that may punctuate the sentence of progress, usually ending in a period.

Politics, arts and sciences that assume only an association with nature or only an opposition to nature must be reconsidered, since the idea of nature now includes humanity as a result of human control of many non-human functions in diverse niches. Humanity's relationship to the rest of nature must also, however, retain the measure of self-interest necessary for survival.

The word nature might best refer to the innate characteristics of things rather than the entire universe excluding humanity. (I should edit the word nature whenever noticeable, but it is intimately bound with my syntax.)

These points of view are resisted by and depress many artists and scientists because they imply rethinking assumptions rather than progressing from here. Even innovative writers want to be able to refer to the 'unnatural' as something inherently mistaken without realizing they are referring to themselves in this use of the word nature; we might call it the Byronic fallacy.

These assumptions imply more than one view of the nature, and few icons are held more dearly than one's singular view of nature. Yet what is changed and what is continuous would surprise many poets. The horizon is different; the surroundings are changed, but basic human requirements are not substantially altered. What that means is yet to be defined by artists and scientists, but it appears as a fertile pursuit.

Most people educated or not retain assumptions that are not supported by what is known about the world. The facts are available, but the modes of thought have not assimilated the new facts, structures, and linkages. What do poetry and poetics look like assuming a dynamic relationship between humanity and the rest of nature? For one thing they are dependent on how the writer views nature and how willing she is to see that relationship as dynamic.

For example, in literature most readers and many writers cling to early nineteenth-century assumptions about what should be achieved in writing—truth, beauty, self discovery. Meanwhile surrealist, formalist, dada, objectivist, and language poets have all introduced changes in the way we use language in their effort to realize the world through writing. Modernist changes should have undercut the basis of meaning in narrative and descriptive prosody. Yet the instrumental uses of language (pass the butter please) persist in focusing our attention on lexical rather than prosodic meaning, whereas the changes in prosody drive an environmental distinction of species of writing, that is, a structural link between humanity and the rest of nature.

Our daily stories about ourselves, the trajectory of a human life, and the sex act all imply narrative and support our identities. Society still implies description as well as the ideas that modernists promote. New modes of writing and thinking might fuse the tagma of narration and description into an environment using contemporary approaches (New Sentences, lists, found poetry, search engines, multimedia, etc.) to create a contemporary poetry.

I drove to the (store)
And should oak floor being low
We slip our accordions
Whatever this is for.

How do we get to a species of writing from a single tagmotic relationship like a dinosaur's hip? Here we add the political and social realm to be the scientific/artistic. Species in biology are now thought to develop as a result of a gap in a specific niche rather than as a result of a "creative" process. First, there is a set of unused resources—food, water, etc. that results from climatic change or extinction of a species. Then an existing species transforms its structure to take advantage of those resources. Species development is not "uncreative," an oversimplification in any discourse, but rather "assisted creativity". One might call it opportunism. But of course such concepts run against the grain of those prior assumptions of artistic uniqueness and independence.

In society, new writing as an analog must initially take a hermetic approach to avoid being co-opted before its strategies are fully formed, and it emerges on various public fora. Early versions of the ideas of each modernist literary group are understood as substitutes for existing strategies rather than additional components. The resources they need must be available, for example, a readership tired of a specific dominant tendency or the lack of new material in the literary sphere.

New ideas condition themselves in public niches by purporting to circumscribe all use cases of writing, dividing from the mainstream. In the next phase, the new ideas fuse in a rewritten canon. For example, as language writing developed various leading writers refused the group label, denying the existence of a group of language writers. John Ashbery and Barbara Guest both publicly disavowed the existence of the New York School. Individual writers clearly separated from the group as their interests diverged and careers were built. Dichotomous solutions insist that the individual writer is the source of creativity. Looking at almost any other creative processes would disabuse the writer of that notion. An environmental approach might talk about interactivity between the individual and the group and how the tagmata of a new school fuse into the mainstream of poetry.

For these writers, the undefined connections of parataxis do materialize advanced tagmata. Connections become visible when we expand our field of vision, and the conceptual linkages between components emerge as assumptions. In these paratactic constructions tagmosis also occurs in the composition and reading of the poem as well as in conceptualizing the poetry. But how many of the new links are fit to survive in a world where chance may dominate intention? Risks are much higher. Blake's *Proverbs of Heaven and Hell* is a long-standing example. His parody of absolution ("The cut worm forgives the plough") points out a revelatory connection that to others remains absurd or sanguinary. The diversity of its connections sustains.

In the hothouse of experimentation new ideas are born, but neither poems nor poetry exist as an independent field any more than industry exists without agriculture. They can be spoken of as discrete but will always in practice link with other fields. In another linking analogy from biology, Brian Goodwin (quoting Charles Delisi) makes a significant point about genetics: "the proposition that 'the collection of chromosomes in the fertilized egg constitutes the complete set of instructions for determining the timing and details of the formation of the heart, the central nervous system, the immune system, and every other organ and tissue required for life' [...] is incorrect" (Brian Goodwin, *How the Leopard Changed Its Spots* (New York, 1994 p34,5). Genes don't reproduce effectively without an organism (fact and abstraction). Reproducing in isolation, the strings of genetic material fragment and stop reproducing within a few generations.

In poetry, the prosody must be modeled and contrasted with the poem, in the same way as a bodily form is modeled against the genetic code, to propel the grammars forward beyond a few readings. Additionally, Goodwin points out that the growth of many organisms is structured by the basic elements of biological growth, such as calcium and mechanical stress, which occur in the structure of the organism. Chemical and engineering realities account for the shape of organisms in a way that is nearly as significant as the genes. Here in a sensational biological metaphor nested structures more truly represent how things work than any flat explanation.

The whorls of *acetabularia*, a large, single-cell organism are caused by the speed at which free calcium accumulates in cytoplasm (81, 93). The same sensitivity of calcium to ambient conditions determines that leaves grow on multi-celled advanced plant stems in the three ways. They can occur one at a time at regular intervals, alternating sides of the stem like corn.

Second plants can grow multiple leaves at the same place around the stem.

Third they can grow in a spiral. (117)

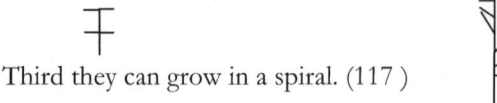

The notion that "chemical reactions, combined with diffusion, could produce spatial patterns by spontaneous symmetry breaking an initial spatially uniform state" (105) was initially postulated by Alan Turing in "The Chemical Basis of Morphogenesis" (1952). His ideas confirm that there are generic categories, or forms, to life based not only on the interactions of the genes, but on chemical concentrations, and temperatures during cell growth. All of these factors determine the final shape of the organism. Genetics does not provide the essential reality of life forms any more than narrative, grammar, tone, or sensibility alone provides essential poetic value.

Goodwin's conclusion that genes require physical organisms to model growth for them has other important parallels for the arts. The identification of language with the poem matches the attempt of geneticists to eliminate the organism as a valid episteme. It also oversimplifies language writing. Field poetry and biology work similarly. Goodwin says something familiar to innovative poets: "A field is not defined by the nature of the molecules and other components involved, such as cells, but the way these interact with one another in time (their kinetics) and in space (their relational order—how the state of one region depends on the state of neighboring regions)" (51).

Following this approach the poem orders itself through a set of relationships and a process, not merely through a code, genetic or linguistic. The poem is a field established by the consequences that arise from the proximity of various components. A phoneme juxtaposed to a word or concept (fact and abstraction) creates a resonant field throughout the poem. And typical of field poetry, a confluence of smaller fields—a vowel sound, for example, contrasted with a phrase—flows now turbulent, now tranquil toward the sea of the reader's metabolic syntax.

From *Legend*, a collaboration between five poets—Bruce Andrews, Charles Bernstein, Ray DiPalma, Steve McCaffery, and Ron Silliman—comes this citation from a section by Andrews, Bernstein, and McCaffery:

>   Wish: No one leaves a simple line
>
>   acid vacuum   the sea shells
>   vertical form
>   lines
>   AMP
>   LI   FIED
>   notsomuch that   crowdbychances
>   droplet
>   field
>   filigree
>   sentient
>   largenous   limits aerate
>
>   Play: Transfiled in college saying   unclear
>
>   encumber—this work comes through the pales
>   are we words, horses, manes?
>
>   (L=A=N=G=U=A=G=E/Roof, 1980, 232)

Certain poems are prosodically stable and as such follow the forms in which language can become generic. Silliman's "Sunset Debris" is a good example: "Can you feel it? Does it hurt? Is this too soft? Do you like it? Do you like this? Is this how you like it? Is it alright? Is he there? Is he breathing? Is it him? Is it near?" (*Age of Huts* (New York, 1980) p11). Fields of this type can also take greater risk in less stable forms that may perform a specific or heroic task. P. Inman's "decker" comes to mind:

> Speak in from black knock
>
> g l a y s husk
>
> (*Red Shift* (New York, 1988))

These specialized poems are also written with respect to the generic forms of language, but do not accept them as the entire set of possibilities. As such they can predict or account for linguistic change.

Modernism elided form and content. As such it established the possibility of a relational rather than a hierarchic structure for the poem: "the women come and go" (T. S. Eliot, "The Love Song of J. Alfred Prufrock," 1917). Post-Modernism showed that the separation of an artist's context from their works is unsustainable and exemplifies another relational model for writing, as in these phrases about childhood: "on a broad plain in a universe of/anterooms, making signals in the dark, you/fall down on your waistband…" (Charles Bernstein, "Matters of Policy," *Controlling Interests*, (New York, 1979).

The variety of language writing represents a set of advances that field poetry might take through the matrix of possible poems. Linking in this way the *excitable media* of cytoplasm and language establish an extension of possibility. We can now revitalize categories of structure that allow information to be organized. Organisms:genes = poems:prosody. A cross-disciplinary discussion seems to be possible. Juliana Spahr's "Spiderwasp or Literary Criticism," for example, muses on power by multiplying the genres she uses to describe it. The relationship between the wasp and the tarantula, in spite of its drama, makes a point akin to Genet's *The Maids* about who controls whom in the household.

Once a multi-disciplinary option is established, the structure of the relationships, tagmosis, becomes an unavoidable issue. I would extend this discussion to the current argument about stem-cell research. The notion that working with human genes is impious fails to recognize some of the basic discoveries of the past few decades. Lyn Margulies, in her confirmation of exosymbiosis, points out that vital energetic components of human (mitochondria) and plant (chloroplast) cells were originally separate bacteria. As Bernt Walther puts it: "Eukaryotes are chimera of permanently fused monera" (*Journal of Biosciences,* vol. 25, no. 3, September, 2000). The notion that working with the human genome would create monstrosities ignores the fact that we ourselves, our cells in detail, are composed of multiple organisms; and in the end poems are the monstrosities created by working with the fact of language and abstraction.

Passive Voice: Forcing Amaryllis

>   earthearthearth
>   earthearthearth
>   earthearthearth
>   earthearthearth
>   earthearthearth
>   earthearthearth
>
>   "any piece of counterpoint includes
>   a silent part
>   for the rhythmic movements of heart and
>   lungs"
>
>   (lilacs)
>   —Ronald Johnson, *Ark*

Current cultural barriers limit our options in two ways. In contemporary literary criticism, for example, the passive voice is identified with weakness of style. The passive voice is considered inefficient linguistically and artificial as a style. The underlying values of frontier forthrightness and manly straightforwardness, if you want to do something be direct about it to prove your honesty. In his 1918 *The Elements of Style* E.B. White wrote: "The active voice is usually more direct and vigorous than the passive." Although the ensuing false forthrightness has become a hallmark of our public communications, I cannot reject that totally as it's useful, too.

Eliminating the passive voice altogether can lead to inappropriate attitudes in writing and style, a literary machismo associated most clearly perhaps with Hemingway. On the other hand, we can find a use for passive attitudes when subverting aggression. We cannot always confront effectively, like children stuck in a war, Gandhi in the Raj, guests at a dinner table beset by a garrulous drunk, or a poet bent on telling us about her latest book. Neither can we continuously characterize our antipodes and hope for fairness from the enemy. "They" is the last bastion of counter punchers.

To revive passive voice, how can value be achieved without leading to weakness? And is passive yielding rather than the opposite of strong? The passive resistance of grammar, the way a massive body achieves control through unity and gravity, enables the verbs to function indirectly and hence as a fifth column in otherwise obsessively good-natured, hale-fellow-well-met, unhyphenated prose. The active voice engages through proximity. But proximity in ecological niches results in some eating and some being eaten. Appropriate distance illuminates, focuses, and preserves. The passive voice measures agency twice before cutting.

Active voice seems the appropriate form in transitive sentences where agency is emphasized, for example; "nature supports a variety of species including humans". Passive voice is more effective when the object is the key component to understand. "There is no place on this planet that is untouched by human action…" As opposed to "Human action touches every place on the planet" which falls flat and lacks drama.

Equally, the passive voice can act for a niche that does not need or want to confront agency directly. "Performance enhancing drugs are turning sports heroes into tabloid figures." The writer seeks to make the agent less important, less central a fixation. Seen from a contemporary moment some literary events in the past could have been acted on differently. I met a famous writer the other day who realized, after 15 minutes of talking about herself, what she was doing and said, "Enough about me; what do *you* think of my new book." Can the passive voice act to undercut self-centered poetic or humanist campaigns?

The writing I want to do now is about something specific, not only emphasizing prosody as meaning. Although I approach the theme as poetry and want to see how it orients my writing beyond humanity, I see poetics as intention. I have no choice but to seek dangling modifiers, sentences that change structure in the middle, and other subject-oriented matters of grammar and politics. All these approaches are disruptive to the individual reader's expectations. At the same time poetry follows biology regardless of the poet's intention.

The passive voice also allows the reader to benefit from hindsight as well as distance. In so doing, the reader is not locked into a fatalist viewpoint in which all interactions have to take place definitively in the past, present, or future. In the environmental model of writing, change depends on the conditions of each moment as it verges on the next. Temporal distinctions are available but not fixed. Time goes in both directions; time has no fixed end point. Nevertheless, I am still trying to get this writing done.

The passive voice apparently inhibits the impact of your writing. From childhood we are taught to expunge it. "Sentences laid out in passive voice diminish the impact of what characters do and lessen the immediacy of events. Prose is weak and readers remain detached from the action when protagonists are done upon rather than being active doers." ("Writing for Young Readers," Eugie Foster, http://www.writing-world.com/foster/foster08.shtml) Passive voice fails to communicate your meaning. It puts you in a bad position on the job. It avoids the first person, so you can't connect directly to the objects of your desire. You can't shop straight in the passive voice. Blame and responsibility can hide. The passive voice de-emphasizes the actor or agent, thereby highlighting the process that the agent is engaged in or the agent's set of relationships, and emphasizes the object when it, not the person, is the focus. Perhaps this focus away from the person is why the passive voice is such a threat to our culture, relying as America does on the central role of the individual.

When forcing amaryllis, the plant is kept in controlled conditions so that its bloom will occur when and where the gardener wants it. The pot is kept in a warm, moist, indoor climate to force the plant out of the soil. Once the amaryllis begins to grow, the pot is rotated so that the foliage does not lean toward the light. Once the bud begins to color, the pot is moved to a cooler location with bright, indirect light to prolong the bloom. Thus, controlling the plant is contrasted with a distance from the theme. The passive voice refers to the description of forcing, an intriguing effect for an obscure kind of humor.

Compare this description of forcing amaryllis with the instructions provided by the horticulturalist: "Choose a container with a drainage hole. Pour soil… Bring it into a warm room… Rotate the pot… Move the pot…" All are strategies consistent with the process they dictate—no contrast, no ambiguity, literature without shading. Yet they are effective and easy. Some people, however, resist instruction, and some forms are more appropriate to certain conditions and subjects. In the sum of all cases both forms are useful as are intransitive sentences. Specialization's illusion of perfection and thoroughness is lacking, but we may be able to get used to a different kind of completeness.

Excellence in the techniques of any one theme is still craved and required. Who wants an amateur brain surgeon or engineer, although the religious right in America is attempting to eliminate experts in several fields in which their moral dictates are at odds with fact? But the larger answers are there. We need not strive after a spiritual answer; the spiritual tropism may be satisfied by the knowledge that our activities are at least linked with those of the rest of the planet. The biosphere's unpredictability acts as imagination for our species.

And specialists can still drive deeply into any of these subjects. There are many voices not just the modern, arboreal dichotomy of active/passive. Further many languages have a middle or reflexive voice and some have mediopassive voices that merge reflexive and passive. Classic Mongolian features five voices: active, passive, causative, reciprocal and cooperative.

And specialization is not exclusive. The surface is described and the shape of things is not distorted. I have left the themes alone. I have tried to leave the style to be shaped. The style would seem to be able to include a passive voice that, together with the active and others, composes a completer self. In summary, humans in the biosphere might use multiple "voices" of interaction.

Views for China

> The world is all that is the case.
> —Ludwig Wittgenstein

When Zhang Ziqing asked me to write a pair of essays on China for an English and American poetry anthology to be published in Chinese, I gradually learned a bit about Chinese essay forms: the analytic and the personal. This essay is analytic because it juxtaposes components that are linked in the environmental taxonomy, and as such it supports the model proposed by this work.

China and the U.S. face each other across the Pacific Ocean. How they look on the map engages me. The thoughts are endless and unstoppable, as are the events of the day. I cannot drain the Pacific and drag the countries closer together; I can only try to link them in this essay.

A visit to China in 1993, documented by Hank Lazer, my august traveling companion, in his volume *Analects*, marked the beginning of my ability to see an alternative to the marketplace model of poetry. The Chinese government divided the country into three parts. They allowed nineteenth-century capitalism in the South, where accumulating money by any means was the goal; if I can get money out of your pocket and into mine, it belongs to me. In the North they pursued their tradition of state capitalism. But they built more complex models based on public/private cooperation in the middle of the country, where, for example, academics and technicians were paid part time by the government to start and run new companies. I visited one of those cooperative companies, where they told me the marketplace was fragmented and no single ideology was sustainable.

Since then I no longer see my poetry only as something to be sold in competition with other poetry. My poem is not better or more valuable than the other poems in the field. It is itself and does certain things well. It was written by me to fulfill its own purpose; the importance of that purpose may occur now or later. It occupies its own space among, mingled and interacting with, or on the edge of the other poems in the field. The poem presents itself to readers in intended and unintended ways. It communicates to other poems by its references. It has characteristics that distinguish it and others that ally it to other poems and poets in its immediate surroundings and with all poetry by virtue of declaring itself to be poetry.

The events we see in the news today further my assertion that an environmental view of poetry and the communities of nations will propel us out of the impasse of regionalism while not entirely eliminating geographic determinism. Yet I suspect the Chinese feel differently about poetry written in China than poetry written by Chinese overseas. Is poetry national? Is poetry politically motivated? Is poetry written for aesthetic reasons? Is poetry oriented to the language of its composition? How many combinations of these questions alone occur in well-articulated poetries?

By adopting an environmental view, these poetic ideologies can be understood for what they are—adaptations. New writing creates styles that use a set of resources left fallow by existing strategies. The language poets, for example, exploited the fact that immediately preceding poetries had sublimated poetic technique in favor of topical themes, such as the way people relate to one another (New York School) or post-World War II projections of power (Black Mountain). Yet language writing also shared some political perspectives with both of those groups of writers.

Political positions derive from the interests of the niches we occupy—People's Republic of China/Chinese/misty or original schools of poetry (Note: The misty school is associated with Gestalt poetry and direct speech. The original school is associated with the physical language of Chinese characters both in their etymology and how they are inscribed) and the United States of America/American/New American poetry or language writing. And yet in those niches we have the same needs—food, clothing, shelter, culture. Our two great nations have solved or can easily solve the food, clothing, shelter needs if there is good will. But our ways of solving these needs separated us further than our national borders.

When emphasized, cultural (including religious) differences are the most destructive forces unleashed by humanity: witness the Muslim/Christian/Jewish/Hindu slaughters of one another over centuries, from the Crusades to the Holocaust to the bombings of Hindu and Muslim holy places. Yet contrary to shifts in geography, which occur over millions of years, cultures can be moved together by well understood methods if the leaders can be made to see an advantage to cooperation. Leadership can provide a platform for cooperation by talking about other perspectives in supportive and respectful ways. Representing the symbiotic value of cross-cultural exchanges increases our ability to find common ground and appreciate how leveraging differences can assist in solving complex problems such as those caused by environmental degradation. As our cultures become understood by other peoples we can begin to talk about China and America as part of an integrated, global cultural environment—not China and America separated by 6,000 wet miles.

This tyranny that geography imposes between different countries may change in the way that the environmental model proposes changing the ordering principles in contemporary knowledge. In poetry I suggest that environmentalism changes the relationship of A and B. (Note to Zhang Ziqing: rather than translate A&B, use two Chinese characters that reflect a sequence and a distinction. Maybe two numbers, but since it is poetry, two sequential characters are best, if sequence is arbitrary in Chinese as in the alphabet of English.) We can go a long way toward ameliorating the conflicts arising from cultural differences if we can figure out a way of thinking that allows both letters (sic) to exist in separate and communal/contingent spaces.

The tyranny of taxonomy in Linnaeus' system makes it difficult to analyze similarities and differences together. Individuals are of one species or another; phyla are of one kingdom or another. But species on the same branch are related and branches linking other branches are related if a bit more distant. We may then use this tree structure to establish a view of both similarities and differences and hence modify the influence of taxonomy. Nevertheless not all problems require the complexities of a tree structure and some are more complex requiring probabilistic solutions. Taxonomy exists, but does not model all interactions. We discuss multi-dimensional taxonomy in the section on Atkin's q-analysis in "(E)Valuation in Poetry."

If we think differently about ourselves, thinking differently about one another will follow. If I am not a poet, isolated but inspired from heaven while battling for market share in the poets' market, can I find a way to be part of a global community of poets without losing voice, face, self? The environmental model is inclusive, allowing the niches to participate and function, and possibly flourish. Each niche has a level of independence as well as several levels of interdependence. As they move through time, they have, at each moment, a continuing dependence on initial conditions. We start here in the U.S. and there in China; here in New York and there in Shanghai; I in my chair, you in yours.

Who am I here in the U.S.? Who are you, dear reader, in China? The picture, then, is more complex, more real than the narrow path of narrative: For example, I am a poet and essayist and have published 10 books. I am a publisher, and my literary press, Roof Books, has published 150 titles. One title translates Chinese classical poems into English. *Shi* (Roof Books, 1997) does not merely translate the small, beautiful Chinese poem into a similar English poem. It is not a coin with two sides. Yunte Huang translated the poem itself, the characters, and the radicals. He listed what is not in the English version and what is not in the Chinese version. He re-creates the entire environment of the poems on both sides of the language divide. Each Chinese poem spans four pages in English, encompassing differences and similarities.

But I am also a technocrat working to build market infrastructure with new technologies. In the U.S. poets must do other work to live—teacher, technician, and official. Ironically, American poets are functioning as model workers embedded in a capitalist framework. There is no mainstream of poetry in America any more than there is in China, where each of the many schools, like fish (do you say fish swim in schools?), inhabits its own place in the sea. I am a father, a husband, a son, a brother. I like to eat fruit. I like to drink wine. I am not Chinese, but I remember China. Much of me is China. I am a walking community of ideas and bacteria. Is this the antecedent of alienation or the recognition of symbiosis?

And the adaptations go deeper, to a place where differences begin to emerge. In America, the movement I am associated with, language writing, includes as many different styles as there are poets, all trying to differentiate themselves. In China, the original poets, who also called themselves language poets when I visited them, imploded writing by reducing it to an exploration of the Chinese written character. The stunning visual work of Che Qianzi that I saw in 1993 telescoped all language into a few characters, a limited vocabulary that has deep etymological resonance, based on the earth, agriculture, and traditional culture. Che built a powerful niche from a limited set of words. Seeing how Chinese poets interpreted language poetry exposes real differences. While American language poets develop as many strategies as there are writers, Chinese language poets recycle a common, ancient language and all of them work with that same limited vocabulary.

Environmental poetics as a whole rests not on the agricultural communalism of the past but on the notion of a common global culture with an agricultural niche. By employing environmental poetry, I don't seek to write about ecologically sound practices. The entirety of human thought must accept that it is implemented through many non-human processes without allowing nature to destroy human thought. In its own way that destruction might be simply the result of humans having changed the climate. Change *in situ* is more complex than revolution, in which you merely have to eliminate the opposition and take control. And as we move forward we make continual mistakes, slipping back into convenient and seductive ways of thinking that may themselves have been adaptations for survival from an era when humans had to spend a lot of effort to protect themselves in their surrounds in order to survive. But if we witness how environmental models move forward in politics, for example, we see Subcommandante Marcos using his Zapatista movement to alert and alter society without taking power. The Zapatista view power, not government, as the process that needs revolution.

Recent American poetry resolves the conflict between humans and the rest of nature in the way that it extends poetry beyond the poem. The poem's social (historical and biographical components) and technical (prosodic) tactics (the genetic structure, the organism, and its environment) can be valued together as well as separately.

Sustainable Love

> I want a good luck charm
> a-hangin' on my arm
> a-to have, a-to hold,
> a-to mine...
> —Elvis Presley, "Good Luck Charm"

Love's physical force sustains the species. Love's cultural force sustains society. These two sentences could be written as one with the connector "and". Love is a diverse noun, the adjective of society, and the verb of life. But love's beings—Cupid or Christ—are only symbols of love, an encouragement to reproduce.

The value of love, like that of poetry, does not rest solely within the confines of technique: an amorous glance and a flowing bank account. The spirit and image of love drive individuals as much as their physical needs. Yet technique improves procreation and generosity.

Love pervades all societies in one form or another, even Toltecs and Bosheviks. It makes Darwinian sense to promote love through culture. The Americans call it marketing: large-breasted women on television, tactile sensation in painting, Imagism in poetry, both the vacuity of Buddhism and the vector of Christianity, the subjects of popular music that Confucius thought controlled society. All market the culture of love and mechanize social control.

The ideal of love requires belief as profound as religion but easier to accept, since almost all of us find some form of it we can enjoy: devotion, mutual adoration, wonderful sex without regrets, duty all justified by the primary value of species continuity. The ideal of love is an epiphany that extends over a lifetime and even beyond the grave.

In reality love is often fleeting, depending on the type of love experienced, the person who loves, and the stage on which these organs of love are engaged. In our youth, literature tells us that love's symptoms include the inability to speak in front of the beloved or to concentrate on anything else. How else could nature ensure continuity of the species if love were not the most important thing in the world after survival of the individual organism? Love changes as we age and fills our surroundings with things that are also memories. What does changing love say about eternal love or love that lasts a lifetime? Is there an essential love or is introducing that concept simply a way to link love with the other mechanisms of social control: law, science, religion, economic creeds, race, and the cult of the individual?

Distinctions are helpful but often disguise the common thread. When I was young, we discussed the difference between love and sex. Now we discuss the conflicts between sex and morality. We are battling in our country over love between two people of the same sex. Clearly that love is not the love of procreation but the love of one person for another, set free of the boundaries of society yet profoundly implicated with those boundaries in the legal sense. We love our spouses, friends, families, parties, countries, teams, races, neighbors, lands, houses, foods, cars, chairs, and cosmetics, and, with luck, our selves get a little attention, if not too much.

More money is spent on love than on any industry, since real estate, trade, manufacturing, and politics are all modeled on love. Love is scary to the oligarchy because it often conflicts with power. It is the ultimate individual prerogative, yet it is often out of our control. Even the individual is subsumed by love, because it requires a connection to be made and because individuals understand they continue because of it. And that connection threatens the connections that powerful people create to enhance their power. The smartest of them link power with love, but few are able to control the awful forces unleashed by their alliance.

Thus love often goes against the grain while bringing the lovers into the mainstream. It captures some and releases some. It inspires and domesticates. And it imposes all these singly, in pairs, and in groups. And sometimes love inflicts them all at once. The European Renaissance sought to separate love from the actions of life, distracting as it does from great dedication to tasks. Yet our global culture links love to the business of living as it trains us to consume.

India and China perpetuate their populations differently. Mindless adherence to love generates war and overpopulation, since the opposite of love is not hate but indifference. Love does not fill the universe, since gravity cohabitates with dark matter in an uncertain relationship—a marriage of convenience? Love is synonymous with life. And in death the beloved remains with us, a many-armed beast, grasping and needy. As Edgar Allen Poe said,

> And neither the angels in heaven above,
> Nor the demons down under the sea,
> Can ever dissever my soul from the soul
> Of the beautiful Annabel Lee.

Love comes in many forms, but is not the only way to reproduce, as many species can attest. Love comes in many forms, but how do we sustain it? As individuals, we can sustain love by linking it to friendship and communication and family. But referring to love as the indissoluble bond between two people misses the point of both the transience of sexual reproduction and the continuously changing gradient of our relationships. Undying love is a product to be consumed, not a lifestyle to seek. Nevertheless, it is confusing because the intensity of love and its overwhelming sensations, although no more than adaptations, overwhelm other species activity. Entire religions are based on it, and it makes sense to have your group reproducing as fast as it can. The risks of doing otherwise are manifest. And how could the social schema continue to support the species if it did not support love. So the phrase "sustainable love" is really backwards: love sustains us, but it is a metaphor, a higher-level abstraction with a highly active analog at the dimension of individuals, and this intensity communicates by relationships throughout both human and non-human society.

God Loves Sex: Poetics and Reproduction

> For who hath she to spend the night withal
> But idle sounds resembling parasites,
> Like shrill-tongued tapsters answering every call,
> Soothing the humour of fantastic wits?
> She says "'Tis so"; they answer all "'Tis so";
> And would say after her if she said "No"
> —Shakespeare, "Venus and Adonis"

We all love sex. It feels good. And even if we fear it, we love its triumphs, its humiliations, its complications, and the structures of society that are built around it. We love our feathers and fakery, our airs and hair, our art, our politicians' and clerics' hypocrisy, and the shenanigans we cavort to get what we want. And with equal fervor we fear the alternatives to our own proclivities, legislating perversions, mutilations, and sexual repression with as much energy as we pursue our pleasures.

So much of our society revolves around sex for good and ill that I cannot fail to speak directly on the subject. And it's important because how else do we get to be? Now in the waning days of my sex life, well life altogether, I want to thank the many who have embellished it. And I want to thank my son for giving me the joy and job of progeny even though he doesn't think of himself as a sex object.

Sex generates some of the greatest art. What are God and Adam reaching for in the Sistine Chapel? We know the facts of Michelangelo's life, and how the metaphor of divine love extends to the tryst. The exquisite sensation of accepting Jesus, of submitting to Mohammed, is just that exquisite sensation. To disembody that feeling, to abstract it into a form of worship and to institutionalize it represents culture's most lethal power grab. Yet losing track of the true agency of sacrament inhibits us only slightly since our bodies continue to feed us its well oiled sensations in spite of several highly functional subterfuges. We don't need sex to spawn related vibrations; it is so central to our becoming.

While status is a key trigger of action, nothing stimulates literary history as strongly as sex. What angers Achilles in the *Iliad*? What drives Augustine to find God in his *Confessions*? What inspires the young Dante in *Vita Nuova*? What murders Romeo and Juliette; what sorrows young Werther and ruins Mme. Bovary? What kills the hero of *The Golden Lotus*? How does M. de Charlus celebrate WWI in Proust? What drives Nada Gordon into the imaginary arms of another man in *Scented Rushes* (Roof, 2010)?

First, why do we have sexual reproduction at all? Species with asexual females and hermaphrodites:

> …can grow at double the rate of a population that reproduces sexually. Why then, given this "cost of males," do most plants and animals indulge in biparental sex? One possible solution is that sex accelerates adaptation; the Red Queen hypothesis, for example, proposes that sex gives plants and animals an edge in the never-ending battle against their coevolving parasites.
> ("Sex, Death, and the Red Queen," Michael A. Brockhurst, *Science* July 8, 2011, p166)

Species that can reproduce either sexually or asexually tend to reproduce sexually in an ecosystem containing more parasites and more often asexually in the absence of those parasites. If, then, evolution endures the "cost of males," because it helps to outdistance the other runners, how does environmental poetics relate adaptation to poetry? And what are its politics? Those of you who have been paying attention may have already guessed that poetry and poetics innovate for adaptive advantage both for the advancement of the language and the career of the poet. Whitman reviewed *Leaves of Grass* himself. Ginsberg's novelties, the perverse word combinations like "hydrogen jukebox" and his bare butt, have now both become cultural icons. Andrews and Bernstein published their own work in every issue of L=A=N=G=U=A=G=E. I do not recall ever identifying a flamboyant poet an arriviste; poetry is too hard and prose too dominant in modern times.

But what of the wonderful poems that do not have innovation as one of their key motivations? They, like the asexual reproducers, protected from parasites by the poets that inspire them, create many examples and variations. These poems seek identity primarily with poetry. They hope to perfect the materials and techniques introduced by innovators and to have their poetry called simply poetry, a modest veneer over a more desperate effort to write just the thing. This quietist poetics, that is, poetics that favors craft and the net stasis of perfection over less practiced strategies, tends to savor the word as sensation rather than as material, using well understood prosody. Ron Silliman: "The School of Quietude…is simply a placeholder for that other poetry tradition which tries so very hard to be the unmarked case." (http://ronsilliman.blogspot.com/2009_04_19_archive.html) And surely unmarked and speaking to the desire for clear and well-wrought writing is Roethke's well known poem published in his Pulitzer Prize winning book *The Waking*.

The Waking
I wake to sleep, and take my waking slow.
I feel my fate in what I cannot fear.
I learn by going where I have to go.

We think by feeling. What is there to know?
I hear my being dance from ear to ear.
I wake to sleep, and take my waking slow....

The poet wants to reduce poetry to feeling, waking to sleeping, a turtle's analytic. But how marvelously he imitates the pelagic sensations of waking in a few simple words! Dismissing the work entirely because an aspect that displeases would, as Hawthorne says in "The Imperfection," "find the perfect future in the present". And if there's one thing we have learned in our post World War life is the importance of Voltaire's adage "*le mieux est l'ennemi du bien.*" But but, you say, poetry that strives for that intense perfection comes at high risk of failure—sex, no? Of course it is.

We don't, however, want to flush the lady down with the bidet water; we want to retain the ability to use analysis and make choices about our self interest and group values. As Silliman points out in the same blog entry, these poets of a static world, where change registers as a fixed force, part, if you will, of the muscle of the spheres, adhere to past innovators as the source of their work such as Whitman in Roethke's case. The innovative poet lingers as the source of quietist poetics, and these linkages, often ignored in the intimacy and intensity of poetic discourse, inspire desire and continuity requires them.

I choose the Roethke example because of his extensive writing of nature poetry and that is precisely the contrast I mean to draw. For the poets as people are not hermaphrodites, creating great poems without partners while the rest of society does it. Whether we are straight, gay, or transsexual, we participate in all the same postures and potpourri as our neighbors. We eat, sleep, screw, and gossip as much if not more than accountants; we have the time to do so since poetry doesn't take as long as double entry bookkeeping.

Nevertheless, poetry excites poets when we as sycophants of the cult of the individual imagine the creative process as something we execute by ourselves. We own that creative energy, elevating ourselves to that perfect moment with afterglow. Imagining poetry writing as an asexual or hermaphroditic relationship, where we contain both the experience and the tools to write a poem, misses the point of poets' interactions. We read and write our own poems; we read other's poems and rewrite them; we read other's poems and try to extend them. The moment of creating interacts with all the other moments of creating. We share language, grammar, cultural assumptions, modifying them to evolve our languages and understanding. Such a process is hardly solitary; our psyches are crowds.

Imperfection apparent to all of us in our reflective moments, we don't throw the poetry out with the annoying self-promotion that dominates every gathering of horny poets trumpeting their organs. The conflict between our social and individual reproduction goes beyond the more obvious nature poem of post war quietism to the deeper understanding we have about ourselves. Yet poets oddly continue to promote asexual reproduction as in this iconic work of Dickinson.

> Growth of Man — like Growth of Nature —
> Gravitates within —
> Atmosphere, and Sun endorse it —
> Bit it stir — alone —
>
> Each — its difficult Ideal
> Must achieve —Itself —
> Through the solitary prowess
> Of a Silent Life --
>
> Effort — is the sole condition —
> Patience of Itself —
> Patience of opposing forces —
> And intact Belief —
>
> Looking on —is the Department
> Of its Audience —
> But Transaction —is assisted
> By no Countenance —

Dickinson at least registers her connection to the audience, but I wonder if she appreciates the transaction with the audience as much as the transaction of creating a poem in her economic and poetic manuscript. Poets benefit by appreciating their interaction with the world as much as by the creative activity that processes that interaction. Poetic influence presents in both innovative and quietist poetry. And influence manifests both retroactively as precursor and in the moments of creation.

Significantly, Dickinson also acknowledges the likeness of human and non-human interactions. While not all analogs register congruently, the overall likeness of human, read cognizant, interaction to other interactions in the biosphere makes speaking about them together more than analogy by proposing poetry as representative of biology.

Beyond the analogy and representation, Dickinson accepts that the individual creative process uses the same mechanisms as growth in nature. The incomplete separation of humanity and nature encourages research into the ways that human and non-human interactions integrate. The relationship doesn't have to be definitive. Dickinson's use of parataxis admits many interpretations. Evolutionary approaches to the problem select what works from among various mechanisms generation to generation.

Poets collaborate when there are more parasites or when, in our solipsistic maelstrom, the isolationist aesthetics threaten to cut off sustaining trade. Language writers, Surrealists and Lake Poets did it together in part because of the strength of their collective argument and when society threatened poetry with extinction. Poets write alone when they are least threatened; the academy tends to promote these pure or self-oriented poetics. Poets also feel safety in numbers.

Today with the rise of parasitical libertarianism, where some people promote how they are putting it over on all you suckers who work together (you think they'd conceal their subterfuge), it is all the more important for leading poets to reproduce sexually continuing a generation of collaborative efforts in Modernist, NY School and Language poetries. The effort by poets to ignore their influences and lineage, to promote themselves at the expense of the interactions that inspired their work, exemplifies a fearsome libertarian tendency among writers that, if you agree that people's mental activity largely mirrors other biological processes, cannot produce lasting results.

Flarf's googled vocabularies ejaculate into Nada Gordon's *Scented Rushes* (Roof, 2010) and where she imagines her lover ravishing her practically in front of her husband. In Kasey Mohammad's *Deer Head Nation* (Tougher Disguises Press, 2003) he wonders "?is this what sex is like / ?an ear, three boys, seven kittens, twelve roses / ? -ance, -ence, -ity." Look who is does it with; even the suffixes show their connections.

New conceptualism's totalizing appropriation appears ironically as the innovative writing of our current phase. Conceptual poetry recycles the idea of found poetry by taking the entire context of the appropriated work along with the text in a group grope. That such text and context theft is considered innovative ignores the fact that the oligarchs have been innovating for years by appropriating workers' wealth through financial control of government and using the community of humanity to benefit themselves, valorizing it as creative destruction, entertainingly exposed in Derek Beaulieu's *Seen of the Crime* (Snare, 2011). These internal incongruities, along with biparental poetry, also occur at moments of stress and change, but I will not make predictions except to say that poetic strategies will fluctuate, and poets will likely be flucted again.

The sexuality and absurdity of appropriation aside, we will over many efforts often be surprised where the poem will come from. We develop strategies to facilitate its creation, forms to house it and link it to our intent, but these strategies chum the waters for the creative moment in the middle of the night or the middle of a crowd. Interaction responds like sex; we're trying to make something come alive in our race with the parasites. And who are the parasites if not those libertarians who think they should strive for personal gain by exploiting the work of the rest of society and then crow about how smart they are to have bettered those citizens who work together and apart for mutual advantage.

And that includes poets who think of the mystery of the creative process as internal and dependent on their living correctly whereas the greater mystery resides in the interaction between the individual and the group as a creative process. Jackson MacLow (*Representative Works*, Roof, 1986), for example, wrote during others' readings, not taking notes, but writing his own work, influenced as others read theirs. Bruce Andrews lets others' poetry readings generate his vocabulary, sometimes by copying a spoken word, sometimes by allowing the reader to evoke a word that he inscribes on note cards to be used later as material for new poems, recycling.

We can take Dickinson's "growth of man like growth of nature" one step further. Not only would it help to assume that human mental activity is natural, it would help more to forever stop referring to nature in contrast to humanity. If we define nature as only innate characteristics, we can eliminate the definition of nature that separates humanity from the rest of the planet and improve our culture's chances of building a more sustainable civilization.

All peoples have both analogy and homology with other parts of the biosphere. Take for example the notion of influence again. We can think of influence as retrospective in the long term or in the very short term even simultaneous influence as in group and collaborative activities. How many cell types does it take to build and maintain the synapses that wire a brain? How many cell types does it take to protect the body from external and internal apoptotic forces? How many poetry types does it take to create a vibrant culture?

In *Against Professional Secrets* (Roof, 2011) Cesar Vallejo identifies 27 categories of art that vitalized the literary scene between the two world wars. Today we may have as many or more groups of poets each striving to be the adored. The economics of poetry imply a multiplier effect from these different groups influencing each other.

Could a lively literary scene contain only one kind of writing? Possibly, but, more importantly, it's rare, and rarity as Darwin points out is the precursor of extinction. So the components of the individual influence each other, the individuals within the group influence each other, the groups influence each other and different generations influence each other. How can we advance asexual creative processes?

We can also turn the discussion on its ear and talk about the poet as parasite. The people who produce shelter and food and make society run suffer us neonates to come unto them and do we ever make them suffer. If we want art to survive in an increasingly practical society, 2012, we need to speed up our sexual reproduction lest the rapidly adapting sex addicts who parent our society leave us behind in an academic muddle. By this trope I intend to question the poets who respond only to poetry, to the poetry world, who live solely within it, and don't fuck with the world at large.

This case by itself has a history in the NY School efforts to undermine New Criticism, but many species don't live outside a narrow ecosystem like the academy or their groups. These rarified specimens are often very beautiful, very delicate and at risk in a changing climate. They are also flamboyant in their safety behind ivied walls, so they can have a lot of fun while funding persists. But is ivied safety delusionary or will the academies sustain poetries while the world collapses outside. Certainly major university endowments have kept pace with the growth of capital accruing to the 1% and improve these institutions chances of survival. The answer remains obscure.

Who am I talking about? Innovative poetry has been widely and roundly criticized for ignoring more serious issues in favor of mere word play. Yet to me this play stands for creative activity in spite of many innovative poets' efforts to move as many levels of abstraction away from sex as possible. Even those poets who studiously avoid any hairy bits in their poems, for whatever reason, make love in another mode. Perverts, maybe, but making new works that change the way we think and feel about ourselves seems to me to be the goal, by hook or crook or whatever sex toys we find in those classified ads promising a good time. Ignore multiple strategies at your peril.

If we put together these two strands of reproduction, sexually reproduced poems are the best poems because they increase species adaptation through innovation. And asexually produced poems are the best poems because they look and sound more complete. And they produce a plethora of poems. Whether it be the imagined trysts of *Vita Nuova*, the collaboration of Eliot and Pound that created *The Wasteland*, renga, or verse poetry that isn't about my ego in nature and how much I appreciate its music, interacting poetry sustains. But we know as writers that we do our inscribing largely alone. Isn't this solitary epiphany of the creative process precisely the analog of asexual reproduction? This issue has already been addressed through the agency of influence, but it goes further.

These thoughts excite another level of creativity: the subconscious collaboration of poets with readers and their feedback. As more readers read, the collective set of written and spoken comments filter into the creative process. Criticism sways no matter how much the poet might claim to be immune. Some poets seem to move in the opposite direction of criticism about their works, a reaction formation, but none are immune; physical laws prohibit it. And the poet who persists in thinking she's free succumbs most readily to suggestion and gradually loses any measure of self-control. Poets in this model are looking for that small measure of self-control that comes with recognizing how the word reproduces. So procreation, collaboration and even vague interaction occur similarly at many levels of scale from the tiniest mental hint to memorable lines that transcend cultures. The world is too much with us whether we like it or not as the hermit in his cave meditates to discover.

If we delude ourselves that our minds are locked and loaded at the outset, yes, solitary creativity is a kind of reproduction. But if we open ourselves to realizing how we achieve our poetry, even in solitude, we realize that even the interactions of private cognition with its countless outside contemporary forces and internalized priors climax in creativity. Poetry writing coils our organisms and our collective selves in a rheostat with the whole humping universe.

Is There Such a Thing as Writing?

> ...You know,
> those guys who sometimes have faces. You know,
> those guys who sometimes have faces?. You can see
> them in the Metropolitan Museum of Art. Go see
> how the Metropolitan Museum of Art is made
> up of tiny Metropolitan Museums of Art. The way
> bones are made of little bones and twigs contain
> a little ash and smoke, a little fire and twig-blood.
> --Brandon Brown, "No Future"

It should come as no surprise that poetry takes more than it gives. The muse in all her guises is never depicted as generous to poets, tantalizing at best with promises of satisfaction. In most cases, the poet dies a horrible death by Pepsi overdose or pronoun asphyxiation. The sense of continuous loss pervades every poetry transaction, making what Michael Gottlieb calls, "Whipsawed knee plays.//As one learns/that zero/ is not a vowel."

It should also come as no surprise that many poets have sought a way through the morass of poetry to redefine it beyond the Romantic exegesis of the individual: How can poetry be contextualized within the larger art and cultural worlds? What politics is in poetry? What is the value of poetry? How can poetry add to our overall knowledge of our world? Questions like that were heavily addressed by the initial group of language writers, but with the impetus behind environmentalism, these subjects deserve revisiting. (Here again before I start, I remind the reader of the complexity of irony, depending on the relationship between the intention of the writer and the expectation of the reader.)

Since the industrial revolution, poets have sought to variously confront or embrace science as a kind of tentative exchange of ideas that might help them to gain a greater return on their imagination than the usual abuse and the volley of small stones promised by Petronius in *Satyricon*. Many poets have attacked science, initially the industrial kind (William Blake, et al.) and more recently science and scientists themselves (Allen Ginsberg and Bruce Andrews), as largely blind to the consequences of their work. And many scientists wish that art would resist temptations to expand beyond its decorative function. Further, scientists hope that economic forces would put science on a pedestal and allow scientific method to rule in the marketplace. Computerization of that marketplace has increased scientists' expectations of achieving that dominance in such intellectual turf wars.

Science today gets the lion's share of the spoils, in that its products add directly to the power of those who hold the purse strings. At the same time, writing, from *Frankenstein* to Bernstein, spends a great deal of its effort attacking science. The relationship of science to art has yet to be well defined, because of the intensely ideological stance of poets and scientists of all persuasions. Yet among scientists, there have been unionists, such as Paul Feyerabend (*Against Method*, 1975), who recognize that poetry uses scientific strategies and that science needs metaphor to communicate its ideas.

For example, when I initially thought about science (*Our Nuclear Heritage*, 1991), I focused on entropy as the "final" law, even turning universal energy exchange into a debit transaction. Yet not all poetry has provided such menial returns. It appears to be a European phenomenon, although lyric poetry about loss occurs in all languages. In medieval Arabia, however, the Caliph would go into battle from Baghdad with the drummers on his right and the poets on his left. It is not inevitable that poetry take a back seat. Yet in modern times, as thinking has been recodified, poetry has been systematically reduced in status in a culture that puts decreasing value on single-medium arts such as poetry, musical composition, and painting, and greater value on corporate arts that take teams of people to produce, such as film, TV, musical performance, theater, and dance. Central and South American poets represent a notable exception. How has the hierarchy been redesigned.

Since the Enlightenment, knowledge has been divided into art, science, and politics. The introduction to Diderot's *Encyclopedie* similarly shows a process of acquiring knowledge through "imagination," "reason," and "memory." These kinds of divisions replaced the medieval scholastic universe with a taxonomy that was useful for categorizing information for purposes of collection and retrieval. If Diderot wanted to find someone to write an article on pathology, he looked for the best cadaver cutter. And when you want to find out about how to cut up cadavers, you will look under "Cadavers, Cutting Up Of" and the encyclopedia says, "See Pathology."

So successful were the scientists in dominating the field of knowledge that studies of human activities began to be called "social sciences," although the origin of political science is the *New Science* of Vico. Leaders in critical studies from Marx to Freud sought to categorize their understanding as if it were science. Freud particularly wanted a science of the mind and was widely influenced by theories of dynamics derived from studies of steam engines. This popular eighteenth- and nineteenth-century metaphor was as widely applied from French schoolbooks to popular songs like "Casey Jones" as today we use indeterminacy, statistics, and relativity to give credibility to our arguments in politics and art.

These specialists were/are the best in their field, but they are not necessarily the ones with the most scope to their learning or the widest peripheral vision. In fact, the opposite was/is often the case. For as we know from Boris Karloff movies, the cadaver cutter was not always as scrupulous as he might be about whether the cadaver was legal or illegal—or even, in some cases, quite dead. And while Diderot and later pragmatists such as John Dewey divided knowledge into art, science, and politics, today New York State has a commissioner of Tourism, Arts, and Parks. The public status of art's thought has been significantly reduced.

From the beginning of modernism, human studies at all levels were and continue to be colored by scientific, scientistic, and science-oriented jargon, discourse, modes of thought, and disciplinary divisions. Even the godlet of late Romanticism, Rimbaud, talked in the language of sciences. In a letter to Paul Demeny, Rimbaud says, "This future [of poetry] will, as you see, be materialistic—Always filled with Number and Harmony..."

Rimbaud's diction, choices seemingly more appropriate to the vocabulary of Pope or Dryden, reflects a preoccupation with poetry as a study of language rather than an expression of the soul. Rimbaud's seer sees by "rational" disordering of the senses, not bacchanalian disregard. He is looking closely. "He looks for his soul, inspects it, puts it to the test, learns it." Sounds frightfully like experimental method.

Objectivity dominates his discourse. "For I is someone else." (One might call such a remark pathological if Rimbaud had not said it.) His criticism of his friend Izambard should shock the twentieth-century poets aching for a chance to express their personal vision:

"At bottom, all you see in your principle is subjective poetry: your obstinacy in going back to the pedagogical trough--excuse me--proves that. But you'll still end up self-satisfied, having done nothing, and never having wanted to do anything. Not to mention that your subjective poetry will always be disgustingly tepid. Some day I hope--many other people hope, too--that I shall see objective poetry in your principle.... I shall be a worker...."

But it doesn't shock the poets of today. They ignore it, preferring to position Rimbaud in a boat on a wild sea of the mind. Of course he is there too, along with his analytic side, refusing to adhere to either discipline. More applicable to our consumer society, Tristan Tzara and the Dadaists protest against the iniquities of politics using the name of science. Bacchanalian disregard came from Dada as a kind of parody of bourgeois pedantry.

"I'm writing this manifesto to show that you can perform contrary actions at the same time, in one single, fresh breath; I am against action; as for continual contradiction, and affirmation too, I am neither for nor against them, and I won't explain myself because I hate common sense." (Tristan Tzara, *Seven Dada Manifestos*, Manifesto II, Calder Publications, p. 4.)

Tzara uses these negations to get attention for his theory of energy, necessity and "supreme egoism." He does not mean that nothing else is useful, but describes a method for discarding all but the essential motives to gain one's objective.

Hence Tzara's objective in Manifesto VIII "To Make a Dadaist Poem" is cutting up some newspapers as an uncreative act that still makes interesting art. In some sense he is simply being practical in undercutting the overwrought ideal of willed imagination. In no sense is he describing a social program, just a social critique and an affirmation of the individual.

In his poetics "publicity and business are also poetic elements." In this sense he's an environmentalist. But this bid for control reads like a kind of religious tract with negation as the principal mechanism of understanding. Buddhism and other "striver" religions use the same method.

I do not mean to disregard the anarchic tropes of late romanticism and modernism, since they have a great deal to offer a society with an alarming and increasing regard for methodological control on the individual and a desire to limit the set of acceptable behavioral options. I only mean to be sure I understand the value of such "freedom" for artists.

In science and politics Paul Feyerabend, for example, seeks a "pluralistic methodology" adopted for the sciences that would compare theory to theory, not attempt to make theory agree with all the empirical data. Of course, this idea has the immediate problem that if he desires an inclusive set of methods, then comparing theoretical results with experimental results provides greater pluralism of method than comparing different theories, but the notion helps. In contemporary science it is vital to provide an approach that increases the scope of the researcher and the theorist rather than limiting them. And Feyerabend does not propose to adopt an alternative method to the existing one, but rather to allow multiple theories to be considered simultaneously.

In *Against Method*, Feyerabend claims, "The task of the scientist, however, is no longer 'to search for the truth', or 'to praise god', or 'to systematize observations', or 'to improve predictions'. These are but side effects of an activity to which his attention is now mainly directed and which is 'to make the weaker case the stronger' as the sophists said, and thereby sustain the motion of the whole." [motion of the whole scientific apparatus].

The same arguments might be applied with opposite results to the poetry. The isolation of method from the multiplicity of possibilities is as true for the arts as for science, but we cannot truly understand our prejudices as poets until we are willing to contrast them. As Feyerabend says, "Proceeding in this way [the scientist] will retain the theories of man and cosmos that are found in Genesis, or in the Pimander, he will elaborate them and use them to measure the success of evolution and other 'modern' views."

What is true for science is, in this case, true for our art. Poems contain theoretical assumptions and most often assert them by the use of prosody in the poem. The assumptions, if questioned, might be viewed as highly doubtful, but the poems might be wonderful. Ezra Pound's political trials are a good example of the conflict between theory and the results of practice. For although results can be manifested as the "telling" point of our art, we must be aware of the high level of risk involved in suggesting that all the value is in the result, in the poem. What else are we buying into when we accept beautiful or authentic or powerful language as the value or goal of the poem? It is necessary to know the answers before we walk down the path suggested by our siren values.

If it is important to know the basis of our assumptions, how can we know them? Certainly not only from evidence within the poem, as the New Critics might have suggested. We need an external standard, as well as the internal standard, to legitimize the work to a readership unaccustomed to reading new poetry and to questioning the work. The external standard becomes the environmental poetic, a profoundly difficult step in a polemic such as a poem. But to understand our assumptions it is vital that we break the circle of logic created by the convincing poem. Even our enjoyment of the poem will be more profound by so doing.

Feyerabend's approach here seems to me to be related to Habermas' concept of critique as a discipline to balance or interface art, science, and politics. Speaking specifically within the arts, criticism and theory serve a wider cause by addressing the assumptions of a poem, comparing them to assumptions of other approaches to poetry, rather than merely evaluating those poems that the critic likes and dislikes and making up grandiose theories to justify her predilections. That is to say, a theory often precedes the individual poem and can be included in the overall poetics along with a context and a set of assumptions.

A holistic approach to poetry allows interpretation of poetry as a value within the society as a methodological unit as well as an aesthetic instance, rather than evaluating the results of the society in the manner of a Thomas Hardy or a Frank Norris or an Allen Ginsberg. Poetic structure establishes and accepts assumptions for a society. The various uses of poetry in society can be brought together: traditional poetries, risk-taking poetries, rock'n'roll, advertising jingles, logos and slogans, poetry within prose, prose poetry, verses, songs—the list is long. If we thought of all of these as poetry, how much more important would poetry be for us all?

Bruce Andrews' poems, for example, postulate a culture composed of small groupings (of language) spread across an entire field of the society. They do not depict the current society in which a predetermined structure is imposed on the individuals, interest groups, and parties.

In this way Andrews' fields of language are idealistic, utopian, directing our attention to a theoretical bias that he has refused in his criticism to separate from the poetic discourse. On the one hand, it feels good to be bathed in a deluge of language and explanations that elude us.

"You Learning Bombs To Watermarks Sudden City/Molding Lit Only Against Compass Split Is Bigger/Doubt Curves Politic Tourist."
("Wobbling," *Wobbling*, Roof Books, 1981)

Or

      "not as Hispanic as
      shape
                a moment   customary
            former kingpin
                            expressionist
                  forms boredom
            sue we
      this mask"
("Narragansett," *Getting Ready To Have Been Frightened*, Roof Books, 1988)

On the other hand, this work doesn't reflect our experience but keeps it constantly out of our reach with a combination of sarcasm and rhetorical allusions, as if the poet wants to frustrate himself by setting a goal in front of him while looking over his shoulder at every step. These formal kinds of meaning are but one aspect of Andrews' poetry that cannot be viewed alone. They invite comparison with their theoretical underpinnings, with other poetries, and with the uses of poetry, merging poetry and criticism toward a whole writing.

By establishing a context in which other poetry needs to be read, the poet breaks with the tradition of independent poems. Poetry can be read as contingent, with great benefit. Meanings can be developed that are not merely lexical but structural and grammatical. Multiple poetries can be recalled by a single poem. The relationship of poetry to other disciplines is a further but distinct echo. A holistic, environmental poetry can extend off the page…

Linking modes of poetry such as metaphysical and romantic, as in Rimbaud and Andrews, is not a novel approach to poetry. It is basic to the process of any non-technical view of poetics. Yet all romanticism, not just Rimbaud and Andrews, is filled with scientific categorizations and structures. The possibility of critique itself arises from the metaphor of objective distance. And what is romanticism to the nineteenth century if not a critique of the city and of industry, as in William Blake's *London*, that I play with elsewhere.

> I wander thro' each charter'd street,
> Near where the charter'd Thames does flow,
> And mark in every face I meet
> Marks of weakness, marks of woe.

Dealing simultaneously with sciences and arts entices the poem out of its shell while the mainstream of society, the academic educational institutions, the institutions of labor and management, the taxonomies of the sciences and bureaucracies still intend to create islands of cities in otherwise undifferentiated nature, islands of knowledge in otherwise undifferentiated "ignorance," islands of discourse in otherwise undifferentiated "noise/silence," islands of process and practice. Specialists of all sorts, but no one to connect them. As the *Saturday Night Live* skit that dates me says, "Baseball been bery, bery good...to me. Football, I don't know, but baseball been bery, bery good...to me."

This silo'd approach to knowledge appears as a control mechanism, alienation canonized. The joke "How many Microsoft employees does it take to screw in a light bulb? None, Gates declared darkness the standard" is part and parcel of this principle of operation. The dictatorship of taste and opinion in the arts promotes the same level of humor and contradiction, produces the same hysterical anger to shut down alternatives.

Poetry of the innovative kind has broken its charter, while much of the readership still clings to an image of it from the past, hoping for a counterrevolution on the Russian model. Values such as beauty, depth of feeling, reflection of the natural order dominate the critical language in reviews of poetry books. *Publisher's Weekly* (August 23, 1991) contains a fine example in a review by the usual unnamed source.

"Probing the depths of consciousness, [the book in question, I leave its title to your imagination] delivers a remarkably evocative vision of the transcendent possibilities of the heart and soul. Suffused with poignant feeling, these poems speak, by way of detailing fluctuations in both human nature and the natural world, of the mysteries

of 'living and dying,' for, according to the poet, 'there's no other conversation'."
(Note: *PW* reviews, under the direction of Michael Scharf, have advanced their rhetoric since then.)

Not only is poetry defined in the review as a species of soul surgery, but it is defined exclusively: Talk about narrow specialization, "there's no other conversation." The author of the book in question has accepted not only that poetry is an island but also that it is engaged in the *only* "conversation." Must be getting pretty lonely out there in poetry land.

The discipline of poetry has decided from a position of weakness and isolation to assert its discourse as dominant when its readership is actually scattered among countless petty states and bureaucracies. Even that readership is in question, consisting, according to the latest Department of Labor figures, primarily of the writer's friends and relatives as well as other less fortunate writers.

So let me ask a question. How is it that a writer as important to modern poetry as Rimbaud maintains a rational viewpoint while so many critics and minor poets croon a totally different tune? And further, how do critics continue to misinterpret Rimbaud. The critics and minor poets are suffering from the Domination of the Restricted Text.

The Domination of the Restricted Text, a Postulate of the "Cult of the Individual," asserts that meaning is derived only from the poem itself. There is no additional meaning derived from reading the letters of the poet, knowing about the life and times of the poet, reading one poem in relation to another poem, or reading poems by other poets who knew the poet.

Reading the poem alone and abstracted transforms the reader into a generalized consumer, devaluing the knowledge that poetry imparts and certainly ignoring its context. There are only inferiors and superiors (the poem and the reader), no equals, no electrons on the same energy level as any other electron, just as no two snowflakes are alike. Yet even this last saw is dull. Caltech physicist Kenneth Libbrecht published a website pointing out that although each snowflake is different, there are thirty-five models for all snowflakes, and those differences are based in turn on the physical laws of water and temperature. (http://www.its.caltech.edu/~atomic/snowcrystals/)

Repositioning results from the second Postulate to the Axiom of the Cult of the Individual, known as the Postulate of the Underdog: Followers of an alternative discipline see what they do in terms of the dominant discipline. (The current text follows this postulate deduced from *The Pleasure of the Text* by Roland Barthes.)

The Corollary to this Postulate, known as the It Rains on Every Dog corollary, acknowledges: the Postulate of the Underdog does not assure that the followers of the dominant discipline have a correct perspective, only that they are less abstracted.

So let us review the course of study.
Cultural Axiom: Cult of the Individual
Postulate: Domination of the Restricted Text
Postulate: Postulate of the Underdog
Corollary: It Rains on Every Dog

Now if this were a mathematics paper, I would demonstrate a proof of these statements in a rigorous mathematical notation based on previously proven statements accepted by most if not all followers of the discipline. But this is a poetry essay and I will not prove anything, but rather use the time-honored technique proper to poetics and ultimately, as Feyerabend points out, the method of science as well: metaphor. In fact, this entire work may be characterized as a figure of speech taken too far. But you may remember that I have, several times already with reference to physics, political economy, and business practices, used the word "metaphor" to describe how other disciplines have demonstrated their correctness.

Not only are figures of speech and manipulation of form the mechanisms of proof proper to poetry, they are also used by other disciplines without citation. Now, when I began to use the discourse of mathematics to describe poetry, I'm sure you all said to yourselves, "He's trying to use a mathematics metaphor. It's all too transparent." But when a mathematician or physicist uses a metaphor, do you also say, "He's trying to use a literary mechanism to prove his point." No, you do not. The Postulate of the Underdog rears its ugly heads.

A good example of such a metaphorical abstraction, the one most accepted as a correct understanding of a principle of physics, is the metaphor of the railroad train in Einstein's discussion of the Theory of Special Relativity. You know the one. A man walking forward on a train is not traveling quite as fast as the speed of the train plus the speed of his walking because of the limiting factor of the speed of light.

Who thinks the Special Theory of Relativity should be invalidated because of its use of metaphor? (Note: You should not be deterred by the fact that Special Relativity also has a purely mathematical representation of its proof; that is, there's a path through the thought that does not require poetry. But it's incomprehensible to most people and it is not the method used by Einstein in his "thought experiments.") Now ask the question the other way. Is a poetic principle invalidated because it uses a mathematical mechanism? I suspect most of you will say that it's not pure poetry. If you do so, you're causing yourself a lot of grief and denying poetry its own place in the larger society.

If you remember how each of the above-mentioned specialties was communicated to a larger public, the common feature of communication of those ideas was metaphor, something standing for something else—a variety of metaphors, pictures, metonymy, formal intrusions, logical breaks, misrepresentation, irony.

What's good for the goose if you can't take a gander? I'm suggesting that another way to communicate between disciplines is by the careful use of mechanisms from one discipline in the context of another discipline. For I hope I've shown that each discipline is defined by its formal characteristics and that those characteristics also carry over to use in other disciplines. Not all of course. To carry a step further Clifford Geertz's concept of layering disciplines, genres of thought, to achieve a more accurate picture of a subject into a "thick description," we can begin to interweave two disciplinary mechanisms, styles, or genres without compromising the accuracy of either as long as there is also a way to represent the thought totally within the mechanisms of the primary discipline.

There are some good examples of my procedure and some bad ones.

The problem I am trying to solve is how are we going to get some credibility for the way poets and other artists know things except by getting them to have a little pride in their discipline. When Einstein uses a metaphor, they should think, "That's my poetry." When George Bush (the first) talked of a thousand points of light, they should angrily declaim the misuse of their technique.

But they/we/I/you/he/she doesn't. It seems to me that the primary reason that poets, artists in general, are not considered to be contributing to "real" knowledge is that they refuse. Refusal takes several forms. Most often contemporary artists try to talk about meaning as something internal, inseparable from their work. The refusal takes the form of refusing to talk about how they know things, refusal to examine in detail the whys and wherefores of the process and product of the art, refusal to discuss connections with daily processes and products, furthering the problem of spiritualizing comprehension. They derive such an absurd notion both from the idea of poetic creativity as a mystery (mystery is really a technique, but the mechanical interpretation of technique is not acceptable to those poets adhering to the mysterious theory of creation) and also from modernist theory, such as Gertrude Stein's concept of "composition as explanation."

Interpreted simply, the concept of integrating process and understanding is a particularly mystifying and dysfunctional one that excludes comprehension by those who do not compose, understanding by those who don't write, enlightenment by those who are not believers. It implies that there will be no explanation apart from the composition and asserts a view of nature as immutable, class-oriented, and not so much opaque as distorted. It does not materialize the values of language but confuses them, making them less available to use. Yet it proposes an integrated model.

By integrating the meaning and the process, Stein creates the illusion of an organic whole. But what if I propose a modification to this mechanistic interpretation of her essay? The essay would be more useful if I accepted her model of writing, in which process and understanding are intertwined, as a metaphor for the interlocking condition of the biosphere and for the primacy of language as a linking agent. An ecology of literature in which meaning is a by-product of the writer's awareness of the process of writing, as an addition to meaning being generated by the reader as she relates the text to the world.

Here I can point again to the value of metaphor as a meaning generator and carrier of knowledge. Why don't poets seek value in what they have? Again the Postulate of the Underdog rears it ugly heads. The only way poets and artists can establish their ways of knowing as valuable to the society at large beyond mere entertainments is to value what they do themselves as contributing to the society as a whole.

When metaphor is used in science, why don't artists get credit? Because the dominant discipline does not need to acknowledge the existence of the secondary discourses unless an alliance is required for hegemony. This is the political part of the thought. How do we begin to open poetry, literature, and arts to linkages with other disciplines without being co-opted by the more powerful social forces?

The first question that arises for me is whether those linkages can be arbitrary, ad hoc connections, or whether they must be essential connections complete with all the requirements of legal or scientific proof. To answer this question I think we need to go back a step, to define what we mean by writing, to redraw the boundaries of writing, and to establish the points of connection that are possible with near and far disciplines.

Metaphor as a Taxonomy
Seeing this as that,
More than a thing
Of beauty. Rather a bond
Of scale, diminished
By cleaving to poetry.
Dialing the iris risks,
No doubt, ungrammatical
Acts, but riskless verse
Sings alone in the shower.

Three Short Pieces that Compete for Resources as Species in a Niche

> We need to make sure that our policy solutions are as integrated as nature itself.
> —Thomas Friedman, *New York Times*, August 23, 2009

Corporate Structure of Confession

The model is a naked man or woman who is placed in front of us and sits between us and the canvas. We look at him or her when imagination or memory requires some assistance. We look at him or her when we need to know how the arm connects to the shoulder or the distance between the hand and the foot, foreshortened when the model reclines. The question often arises whether the model should expose his or her genitals to the artists, and this argument has several reasonable answers. Naked genitals attract the eye, and for many viewers of the model or the subsequent painting they become the center of focus. Even naked breasts distract the viewer from the mouth and eyes, from the composition and the overall coloration and other effects of the painting.

This distraction can be moralized, and morality can become an additional distraction from the artistic effect of the painting. But some artists may not want to avoid raising these issues. Some artists may, in fact, want to raise the energy level of viewers by exposing them to their reactions to the nude figure. Continued avoidance of the genitals may be viewed as a mechanism of control and may over time arouse more dangerous reactions than sexual arousal—politics, war—arising from concealed intent.

This metaphor raises the question: to improve the global environment, do we need global control? And who has that control? As David Harvey questions in *The Condition of Post Modernity* (Oxford, 1989), is the free movement of capital imperative while free movement of labor is constrained? Do we warehouse humanity in cities? How do we absorb the populations displaced by environmental degradation? Is someone even asking these questions? Dare we answer them overtly, or must we resolve problems in an ad hoc way by the usual means of war, suppression, and charity? Can we allow free movement of displaced populations, or are border fences just a start?

Can the cultural construction of nature be applied to increase the transparency of corporate control? Can corporate boards function in an open, transparent environment? (See reports of Hewlitt Packard's probe of its own board for spying on one another: (http://www.thesmokinggun.com/archive/0905061hp1.html) Can humans accept that they are similar to other life forms in ways that we have never before allowed? Can writing promote transparency of language and the material of writing at the same time? This question I can answer.

The current focus of the intellectual community on human rights has limited the kinds of connections that people are willing to consider. What, for example, happens when humanity, having ignored the warnings of climate change starts making decisions about access to highly limited resources? Linking appropriate governmental activity to a specific model of freedom (Sweden vs India for example), can ethical behavior be exemplified by Western consumer culture, in which choice of commodities drives social structure? Here are two quotations, one from 2007 and one from Darwin in the middle of the nineteenth century. Human rights advocates appear to require legalistic solutions while Darwin felt morality an inherent, read natural, component of intellect.

> Darwin's theory of natural selection does not entail any strong type of genetic determinism regarding human behavior, and attempts to apply evolutionary models to the development of cultures have not been notably productive.
> [Footnote: For a discussion of the difficulties of evolutionary explanations of cultural phenomena, see Richard C. Lewontin, "The Wars Over Evolution." *The New York Review of Books*, October 20, 2005. ("Culture and Evolutionary Theory: *NYRB*, May 10, 2007, "Are we Born Moral," by John Gray)

> Any animal whatever, endowed with well-marked social instincts, the parental and filial affections being here included, would inevitably acquire a moral sense of conscience, as soon as its intellectual powers had become as well developed or nearly as well developed, as in man.
> (Charles Darwin, *On the Origin of Species by Means of Natural Selection*, 525)

Academic Structure of Confession
I remember being in the same position 25 years ago, speaking at the Institute for Policy Studies education series on "Poetry and Politics" to a group that I knew was going to reject avidly what I was saying to them because it broke so ostentatiously from what they were used to hearing (Galileo). Today I feel more alone (Liebnitz), although I'm sure agreement on this subject is initially easier (U.S. security policy) and rejection in the long term is far more likely as we slip into predictable (Systems Analysis) modes of thought, in part, since what I am saying at the beginning is not what we will believe at the end (Augustine).

What I am about to say is not something novel to you (it is poetry familiar to you with a twist). The current views of "nature" poetry (EcoCriticism) employ the new naturalism to refer to old nature writing to find ways in which a point of view about nature is wittingly or unwittingly referenced in the literature. Thoreau is easy; Proust is more difficult, because the EcoCritics, in the documents I have read, find it difficult to discuss writing beyond the canon of nature writing. And of course that would be the key to changing how readers think about nature. Failure to diversify the strategies of criticism in environmental studies makes any linkage between human and non-human phenomena that much more difficult. To the extent that EcoCriticism accepts a diversity of strategies, it will be a useful tool.

But let me not generalize. EcoCritics do create alternative definitions of EcoCriticism. The 1994 EcoCriticism conference (ASLE) in Salt Lake City provided 16 papers defining EcoCriticism. They have certainly reduced the risk of being wrong and established a Bayesian basis for extrapolating. And there have been many others since then, each conceived and executed to shape a specific set of views about nature and then to find the embodiment of those views in literature.

Vying for control misses the point at which multiplicity has value. EcoCritics would be more useful if writing about how literature that is *not* directly associated with naturalist themes looks at nature. EcoCritics could show the multiple ways nature exists in niches that speak primarily to the human niche. There is much of importance to say about and in EcoCriticism; that is, how humanist literature views nature and how those views would affect writers' biases and conclusions.

Environmental poetics' view of nature will predetermine how we align our current assumptions with the biosphere (Thompson, see "Human Views of Nature") and would help us to acknowledge our inevitable affiliation with our planet (Smil), which is on a higher dimensional level than any single species (Atkin). Our view has not to do with distancing ourselves from it (Baudelaire) but with identifying ourselves in our appropriate and radical taxonomies (*Oops!*). What do I mean by that?

Can your ideas of poetry, can your idea of self, accept the value of something you did not write or of writing in other modes than the style you choose? Although as students, practitioners, and even general readers, you're training yourselves in that regard by reading this. I submit to you that those who are more successful at accepting the points of view of other people will get better jobs, work better at their jobs, and relate more effectively to their peers. Don't be dismayed; it's characteristic of humans and especially of poets, but we cannot separate ourselves from the folds of our affiliations without committing atrocities (Bush) or accepting them as part of our lifestyle (Looney Tunes).

How many other references here ignore the constant buzzing in my ears from the matrix of life in which I am encased (self-help)? The air is thick with it (9/11). And yet I go blithely along with questions and answers… (Socrates). But how do I get away from being called an old, miserable poet seeking consolation in familiar retreats, however sophisticated I make my argument (Tolstoy)? I think you'll be happier with the direction of your thinking if you do not begin from the premise that these arguments can be dismissed, separating yourselves from me in order to reject the idea, a poet's trait (Freud or, in environmental terms, mentalscape).

So what I am trying to get at is a multi-level idea of identity: you are in your own taxonomic category as well as in increasingly populous ones as you radiate to your roots (Darwin). The individual is as much a part of the taxonomy of environmental poetics as the species. As poets you try to stay high on the tree of knowledge by being specific because the history of poetry descends into essentialism (Shelley), seeking epiphanies even as you generalize (Objectivism). But as you know more of the unseen connections you make (Wittgenstein), the more readily received is the poetry you write, until the reader reaches a threshold, different in different individuals, where the reader is thrown out of the text and falls back on herself (Inman).

At that moment, I put the word "nature" in parentheses, not the word "poetry." And that is the difference between what I am writing about and the nature theorists/EcoCritics. I would even want to build a social structure (Chaucer) based not on job and character but on the view of nature of an individual under stress (Thompson).

Individual Structure of Confession
This book suggests several contextually valid views of nature. We have discussed how various groups, from species to corporations, are positioned in the environmental model. We have discussed how human and non-human interests both collaborate and compete. But how does the individual fit in?

For a start all collective activities and ethics need to reconcile their proposals with the single most important fact of the biosphere: the individual organism. All change in Darwinian time, that is, generational time, must deal with the fact of the organism and its drive to survive at least long enough to reproduce. We must address this conflict of interest at every step in the process where the greater good is not the same as individual good. And we will need to compromise at every point possible to keep people's allegiance to our efforts. We are not talking about a simple dualism between the individual and the group, but many interaction models.

In the canon of humanism each person, while unique, retains allegiances and interests in the various groups to which that individual belongs. Consumer capitalism takes that notion of the individual one step further, positing each person's uniqueness to drive a wedge between the individual and his or her community for the purpose of fitting every transaction into the marketplace model. In today's poetry, individual uniqueness is constantly reinforced through the paradigm of creativity. And many poets glory in their uniqueness and solitary writing practices, critical of writing in which poets are aware of one another's work or speaking to it through a variety of forms, derisively calling them "schools," as if a person who pays attention to those around them are not in the real world. Of course, poetry groups can isolate themselves in much the same way as individuals become alienated.

Exploration of the varieties of non-unique events helps us to understand the poetic process. Repetition, for example, has been important as a musical value in poetry, providing continuity and demonstrating characteristics of uniqueness in three ways: First, of commonality in the repetition itself; second, in the way the same word changes when repeated; third, in that the different kinds of change demonstrate conditionality. When repeated words are close together, they have a different effect than when they are further apart in the poem. When logic intervenes, repetition has a different value than when words that emphasize their phonemic values intervene. Edgar Allen Poe's *The Raven* demonstrates the varieties of repetition using, among others, the word "nevermore." Ronald Johnson's *Ark* demonstrates the effects of constant repetition in the epigraph to my essay "Passive Voice: Forcing Amaryllis."

Repetition in various forms is characteristic of both science (isomorphs) and literature (rhymes and verses). Copying something exactly—citation—is a special case of proofs that are generally avoided by literary writers and poets because of value ascribed to creativity, the putative uniqueness of the artistic process.

Biomass doesn't repeat as much as it exists in a state of conditionality, but similar forms exist at many levels of scale. Each niche is unique in components and common in complexity, with overlapping workings in adjacent niches, whereas organisms relate to one another in similar ways by providing resources, competing for them and sharing them. Each animal is unique, each cell is somewhat unique, but each chemical and its relationship to other chemicals may not be so unique. ("Are Clouds Collapsing at the 2' North Position of Sagittarius B2?" www.journals.uchicago.edu/ApJ/journal/issues/ApJ/v498n1/37606/37606.pdf) Can we ascribe uniqueness to biomass and outside the biological? As we descend in size to energy quanta, increasing similarity of entities moves towards identity among atoms. Or are atoms only apparently similar because they are so small to us? Can we also find similarity in methods and tagmosis even within biology? Certainly there are many similarities in processes and connectivity even among widely different species.

In the poetry world, several examples of dynamic poetry that explore this relationship between uniqueness and repetition have been essayed. As one of the writers who has long been aware of the positive relationship between art and science, Mei-mei Berssenbrugge has consciously attempted to link the way people think to the way nature works. (What follows are extracts from a series of emails between us in 2007.)

Dear Mei-mei, I'm working on getting the ideas around poetry and science (note inconsistency of topics) into *Oops!* in a more exemplary way, as you suggested, and I wanted to use your writing. In reading through *Endocrinology*, I found both what I wanted to find and what I was afraid of finding, the linkage and the separation of people and nature. These paragraphs below are a draft of the idea. But if you have other citations or formulations that you think would be more appropriate, please let me know.

…I am often asked to show the poetry that bridges the gap between humanity and nature, to not just theorize about their connection. Many poets using nature create interesting, vital material that links our species with the rest of nature but end up retreating to the special separateness of people.

The poem links people and natural phenomena as biology, politics, and poetry: "Think before that moment, freedom is inside there./Think before the man and woman, their freedom of the animal among silvery trees." You might say, Here's a fine example of what this book says. But then, a few pages later, "To make this whole, any object, brings into being something not in nature, an interior measurement, yourself,/not yourself, bursts of growth when you sleep." The point of this book is that Berssenbrugge is on the right track but reverts to the cultural bias separating humanity and nature by that "interior measurement" of which she speaks.

Ultimately I think this separation is more Darwinian, more about the separation of the writer as person from other persons than about the separation of humanity and nature. We say we're separate from nature, but we are doing no more than distinguishing ourselves from the pack as individuals in an effort to drive greater reproductive likelihood; in this case, hoping that the poetry will be adopted by readers. And of course humans are, in a specific sense, different from other species but only in the way other species differ from each other.

Berssenbrugge replies: In recent years I'm emphasizing a unified context or environment, which I see as the opposite of the science in scientific method.

There's a separation between the point of view of the persona you quote and what the poem is trying to state, since a burst of growth while you sleep, which she doesn't measure, is herself also.

Dear Mei-mei: The whole point of *Oops!* is the issue you raise of science in an environmental context with other ways of understanding. That's why I want to include you in the way you think best. I agree that the overall poem is going in one way and the statement about the self is going in the other way. I'm trying to resolve that issue now to at least find a way of talking about it. You are key to that discussion, so I hope we can continue this exchange.

Berssenbrugge replies: I think it may not be a statement about self, but a statement by the persona or by a character. The whole poem would possibly be the statement of my self. But I very often use fragments of others in a poem.

Dear Mei-mei: I like that formulation you have that these lines are about a character or, in my terms, a person who is delineating specialized processes that she perceives in herself. But does nature have an analog to self-consciousness? I'm looking to find ways of talking about people that show both our uniqueness and our commonality with other planetary components. I think your work on science and art over the years is a vital point in the discussion, and, of course, you and I have had that discussion off and on. I'm looking for the way you address the problem: when you point to the common aspects and when you think it's important to delineate a separation as opposed to the usual taxonomy that is neither objective nor useful beyond certain limited disciplines. What structures do you use for a person and what structures for non-person, how they are the same and different?

Berssenbrugge replies: Here is the question I think you asked: What are the structures that you use for a person and what structures for non-person, how they are the same and different?

First, I say that my work is not intellectual or idea-based, and that it has been a developing inquiry rather than one thing, maybe an inquiry that uses ideas as a guise for emotional, aesthetic, and vibrational inquiries. The inquiry is more about connection with others than with person-nonperson, which I may take as a fluctuation that is given. The voice of a poem as a whole is one person, "myself," and the various voices "I," "you," "she" are facets of the whole. I think this may be true in all poems. I've always been interested in figure-ground issues, but now I'm pretty committed to the unity of things, to seeing the connection of everything, which is ecological, but for me personally is a development of my very early search for connection between two people. Lately I'm trying to perceive connection and unity, not duality or analysis. That also seems to challenge our idea of chance or fate.

How ideas of an inquiry and poetry intertwine keeps poetry as the larger impulse.

Dear Mei-mei: This is very helpful. I'm supportive of your notion of using ideas as a guise for a more general inquiry. I see this as a kind of associational process. The ideas, events, and relations act as guises for one another, starting, of course, in reality from you writing about them. The place where I'd extend your idea is to say person/non-person may not be so different from person to person, and the extension of "natural" events to people and non-people kinds of things is the core justification for an environmental view of the world instead of a person vs non-person model.

Berssenbrugge replies: I agree, and I would extend to say that the unity implies that the situation is good, although we have to wrap our minds around how.

**

This exchange is typical of the difficulty of coming to agreement. I think it shows how we start fairly far apart, with my criticism of her separation of human and non-human activity. Berssenbrugge's reply is about the use of distance in poetry to represent characters, persons, instead of a univocal presentation. Ultimately we come together over the use of ideas as metaphors through the exchange of notes and the desire to both effectively represent divergent positions and appeal to the necessity of finding a core of agreement in order to proceed. These negotiated settlements are typical of human interaction, although I suspect they may not be a perfect example of how to use nature to solve problems for people.

Using Multiple Forms to Enact Environmentalism Rather than Describe It

> …language is the platform; speech the application…. In this sense, the language writers stepped down into the infrastructure of the poem.
> —Kit Robinson

The act of writing starts by juxtaposing words; words in a lexicon singly become writing when put together. Writing may go on from there to more complex structures, but complexity is not required to get interesting and useful results from writing. Bruce Andrews wrote a group of poems using one word per line:

> Words
> were
> what
> were
> whole
> what
> wasted
> words
> want
> waiting
> whose
> travel
> there –
>
> (Bruce Andrews, *Jeopardy*, Awede Press, 1980)

Kit Robinson's *Dolch Stanzas* based on the limited vocabulary of the Dolch Word List and lists of the hundred most common English words compiled and formatted differently by Charles Bernstein and myself are good examples of simple strategies that produce robust organisms.

Another simple strategy produces writing from a method. Once the method is applied, little else needs to be done other than format the text. Jackson MacLow's chance operations and Tristan Tzara's cut-ups are well known examples. The simple vocabularies of Andrews and Robinson or the simple methods of MacLow and Tzara produce small niches of language from which meaning is easy to abstract. These specialist niches are constructed by manipulating the prosodic infrastructure using vocabulary and method while allowing thought and theme within the language to largely find its own shape. Here is my version of "100 Most Common English Words" from a dance collaboration performed in 1980.

> the/of/and/to/a/in/that/is/I/it/for/as/with/was/his/he/be/not/by/but/have/you/which/are/on/or/her/had/at/from/this/my/they/all/their/an/she/has/were/me/been/him/one/so/if/will/there/who/no/we/when/what/your/more/would/them/some/than/may/upon/its/out/into/our/these/man/up/so/like/shall/great/now/such/should/other/only/any/then/about/those/can/made/well/old/must/us/said/time/even/new/could/very/much/own/most/might first/after/yet/two//
> (James Sherry, *Integers*, danced by Nina Weiner, Dance Theater Workshop, 1980)

Ron Silliman's writing based on the Fibonacci sequence, the numbers linked to the growth patterns of plants and branching of trees, is another example of the use of a single-method process, but in this case derived from a natural process. Silliman used the method to order the language rather than select vocabulary. These processes show that creativity is not a binary structure that is either on or off. These method-based poems help us to understand how creativity can be applied at various stages in the sequence of writing to produce meaning. The methods also show that meaning can be expressed formally as well as lexically.

For environmentalism, the materials need further enhancement to demonstrate the performance of interactive contexts in an existing, dynamic landscape of writing. Simply identifying how writing functions environmentally requires untangling many knots of specialized vocabulary and practices that seek to differentiate the writing rather than further illuminate the reader. These practices have been driven so deeply into the creative processes that the notion of collective or formal creativity appears as anathema to many art workers when nothing can be further from the state of the art. Complexity and collective action are endemic to the conception of poetic practices and the writing of poems.

Environmental writing may start with the whole lexicon or go forward with pre-constituted tools like limited vocabularies and methods following the relational arrangement of their components. While not predictive of method, environmental writing's social utility implies a greater reliance on interactive and collective creative processes that work like natural processes. Environmental poetics relies on continual awareness of context, the larger landscape of poetries, and their relationship to each other.

Certainly the reader would more easily understand a single-threaded exegesis of one form, fully explored, than this potpourri of examples that are often redundant and leave lacunae. But we have been trying that succession of single-threaded, logical flows of poetry that exclude each other for centuries, and not improving the relationship between poetry and other discourses. Rather the relationship has deteriorated.

Some readers have objected to this approach as inconsistent and nothing new. If I am proposing a multi-level, multi-solution poetics, then why aren't other poetries more in evidence here? Why does the group of writers I am associated with appear so extensively? One reason is that the work of these poets is what I know as an editor and publisher. Another reason is that poetries exclude themselves from discussions of environmentalism, except as negative examples, by attributing to themselves total control and sole rights to poetic value. These must stand on their own, although environmental poetics provides an opportunity to redefine their taxonomy. Finally, language writing diversifies itself by a plethora of distinct styles and forms, more so than most prior groups, and it's fairly easy to co-opt it for my purposes.

Environmental poetics implies a polemical approach, but not necessarily. The discussion remains dynamic and interactive because it accommodates a variety of constituencies, from microbes to presidents, and a variety of relationships, from symbiotic to competitive to those that are only peripherally related. Relationships can have single links in the way one species eats another or multiple links like those species that provide food for others but also enhance the fertility required for all of the species to thrive.

Language structures have similar links. In field poetry a word can be counterweight to a phrase or paragraph. I have discussed this at length in "Tagmosis (Extending Parataxis)". The kinds of links are many and varied and it might be useful to attempt to catalog them in a connected model of poetry rather than a distinguished on as in Johnson's *Lives of the Poets*. In fact one might talk about the taxonomy of language as a kind of grammar that describes all the interactions of language components. And in visual arts these components and links might also be easily characterized. Take the components of shape and color. A shape may contain a color; the color may extend beyond the edges of a shape; or the color may fit exactly into the outline of the shape. Here we describe two components (shape and color) with a connector (location) in three states (within, without, and congruent).

A group of practices and assumptions holds each set of components together. Red in European painting implies passion while in Chinese painting red means good luck. Biologically red increases blood flow. Putting them side by side we can see them by looking at the same issues from different perspectives.

Many poets have tried to use prosody as a lexicon looking at it different ways to see what works. And it's been called experimental writing for that reason. P. Inman shows how meaning exists in alphabetical and phonemic forms that are smaller than words:

>   eyeds,
>   dreg,
>   daint
>   ===============
>   diff -
>   --earth
>   (*Red Shift*, Roof, 1988)

Ron Silliman, in his concept of The New Sentence, uses the distance between sentences instead of standard connections and conjunctions, such as logic or narrative, to enhance the value of each sentence and its meaning in space.

> Why does he keep large bills in his shirt pocket? How do you locate the cross-hairs of your bitterness? What was it about shouting, mere raised voices, that caused him always to go out of control?
> ("Sunset Debris," *Age of Huts*, Roof, 1986)

Supersagas by Khlebnikov, novels, and sonnets are other complex forms vested with meaning independent of their lexicon. Classical texts such as Hesiod and Lucretius that do not seek catharsis have an environmental perspective of diversity…

> No single thing abides; but all things flow.
> Fragment to fragment clings—the things thus grow
> Until we know and name them. By degrees
> They melt, and are no more the things we know.
> (Lucretius, *De Rerum Natura*)

These forms are useful as an explanation of environmental poetics in relation to one another. Sonnets imply logic, whereas odes imply a more socialized complexity. How each form generates meaning allows it to fit into a matrix of similarities and differences. Their independent value as specialized discourse acts as material resources for environmental poetries.

And if I consider that this writing, although a human construction is a work of nature as well—because humans, their logic, and their works, are also natural phenomena—then I consider this book as a work of nature. As Francis Bacon would have said, it is more important for nature to be complete than to be perfect. Only when it is complete can it perform the functions of life. Perfection is expensive and provides diminishing returns. Yet our culture inspires the mind to look for perfection, to get that last little bit into its artifacts. Hence there is an ongoing discontinuity between our mental picture of the world and the way the world works. As William Burroughs would have said, avoid "woefully incomplete acts."

As a result, I am placing related ideas in their niches, some in lexical transparency (much to the chagrin of some of the more radical experimentalists among my peers) and others in formal obviousness, while I invite the reader to find other forms that have meaning without and within.

For the moment, however, I am more concerned about the effect of natural philosophy on ecology, residing ultimately in the requirement for conservation measures to gain any particular objective and extend this niche into utilitarianism. Is it possible that environmentalism can be realized only as a dominant discourse through its true etymological link to conservation? Does it strike anyone else as strange that political conservatives do not support conservation measures?

On a subtler layer, the subject of habit is part of this niche, like air and soil to a tree, something that feeds it and is part of its environmental space but is not to be confused with the tree itself. (In environmentalism, things exist in themselves but have a less distinct identity than in humanism.) Habit connects to form and reminds us of the extensibility of all things into their processes, like the example of the tree's environment: form, content, and the process by which they interact.

The niche of form is linked by habit and its antithesis, experiment. Another adjacent subject in this niche is examples—quotations, glosses, forms—all metaphors (formal or grammatical structures that exist to stand for something else) that extend the idea of environmentalism into the human, that break down humanist distinctions and circumscribe them with the larger linkages of the environment. I suspect, further, that the discussion of using examples in these niches is part of the discussion of form, since I'd like to say that using a quotation or a metaphor is as much a formal example of environmental poetics as the niche-like structure of the short essays that compose this book. Due to the complex (fractal) characteristics of the environmental model form, theme, process, and habit will reappear in other niches for other purposes.

Finally, I want to do what I can to assure that environmentalism isn't misused as a way to exploit people, animals, and resources. For example, developed country (G8) economic leaders have in some cases used ecology to try to suppress economic growth in countries with rainforest rather than supplying them with alternatives to unsustainable exploitation. The leaders take this approach to the problem to reduce competition and because they do not have the framework of environmental poetics to inform them. I cannot control the misuse of what I'm proposing, but attempt to shape the thought to always include self-criticism as a check on power. Environmentalism as a model needs a self-supporting framework. And every action in it carries self-adjusting criteria such as duplication of effort or reflexive validation.

Environmental Poetics as Biography

> There is no theory that is not a fragment, carefully prepared, of some autobiography.
> —Paul Valery

Rather than attempting to say, "Theory is" this or that, can we effectively discuss the components of theory; even map them as an ecosystem? For example, psychologist and poet Kim Rosenfeld cites Valery to me at the Bowery Poetry Club pointing to the theorist as the key and inseparable component of the analytic process. From the point of view of psychology this is quite true, but we are not looking at environmentalism from the point of view of any one discipline either geology or psychology. The statement that all theory is autobiographical misrepresents the variety of theory's origins and operational components.

To be sure, when any one person writes down a theory it would be absurd to think that she would construct it contrary to her own composition—history, location, physiology. It is equally unrealistic to identify theory solely as an extension of individual proclivities. The impulse to theorize comes to me as a combination of wanting to know (a philosophical component), wanting to show that I know (a self-valorizing component that connects to the fact of biological organisms), wanting to share (a social and group formation component) and wanting some influence beyond my immediate presence (an isomorph of reproduction).

But reasons for theory don't stop with those drives. I am also attached to representing environmentalism because it is widely misrepresented. There is an additional impulse to get it right where it was wrong. We often want to redress past grievances, but are advised that the past is past. We are further advised that we merely need to construct a plausible persona and get on with it. We are given knowledge about ourselves to understand that.

Environmentalism seems a plausible persona for many people, although I can imagine that it contradicts more than a few inclinations that derive from the fact of the biological organism. And fixing what we perceive was done incorrectly drives our sense of justice, but there are also group formations that promote justice because of our affinities. Improvement of past wrongs is not impractical even if it doesn't make us feel that the wrongs done to us as individuals are properly redressed. In our mental makeup we can improve our attitude but we can't change the past. In environmental work we can clean up the mess, actually improve it, not just for our satisfaction but physically, concretely.

In environmental studies these past failures are necessarily corrected because continuing along the same path will only make things worse. That doesn't stop many people whose anger and desire to assert themselves promote continuing errors of judgment and behavior especially when they are reinforced by wealth and power. Once again we are confronted by the behavior of highly productive individuals in changing culture. One can point to education and family culture as ways to address these problems with power, but I suspect it goes deeper, into the asserting of the individual organism and all that complexity that makes survival possible.

Even if we overcome and convince by culture or force these highly productive individuals to assert themselves more directly on behalf of the entire species, the set of improvements required will in many cases have unintended consequences, in some cases worse than the prior condition. A set of improvements in our mental condition often frees us for worse trouble as well, but this is not a situation that the psychologist wishes to contemplate because of the illusion of freedom that predominates. The Golden Rule, too, implies the centrality of the individual in decision making, but really collective action is at least as important. And we don't simply ask ourselves what we want for others, we can actually ask them. We can use ourselves as models of the group as in the Golden Rule but we will find many conditions where our individual perception does not include the group.

Therefore the environmental model proposes that we both ask ourselves what we think of a situation and compare our answers to those of the group. Such a process is more complex than most of us are willing to undertake and we regress to the solipsism of the Golden Rule. Nevertheless the world is just that complex and unpredictability is largely the rule in complex situations. Unpredictability is a key force in environmentalism as well as society and probabilistic results are the best predictions we can make in such complex situations as our world. Complexity also acts in psychology, but there is the belief and it's probably true that doing things for yourself improves your mental well-being as well as potentially the rest of your condition.

Beyond being a reflection of who we are, theory also has several other important characteristics. It should be able to be generalized beyond ourselves, that is, apply to others and be adopted by others. My biography is my own, but it has similarities to other biographies. If groups of people adopt a set of ideas, Occupy Wall Street for example, then they enlarge it beyond autobiography to the extent that they represent a societal identity, even an institution that succeeds by adopting the theory. In generalizing the idea, one also opens it to scrutiny and variation by other individuals with different autobiographies. Such scrutiny democratizes theory and brings it closer to operational procedure.

Theory also has an external objective, wanting to manipulate our surroundings. If we look at the world in a particular way we will treat it accordingly. The culture that changes how we look at the world will ultimately drive environmental change by humans as our current culture drives the climate changes we are causing today. And effective, widely supported theory does represent an objective reality as well as a personal perspective. Reality's construction may be partly shaped by who writes it, but it also partakes of the actual pieces of the world, not just the overall impression. Effective theory is therefore flexible since reality and our perception of it fluctuate. The structure allows transformation of one thing into another as they occur.

Most prior theory attempts to be a lens through which reality is filtered. Theory usually turns a blind eye toward other theories. What for example do psychological theories have to say about geological impact on the individual psyche? Yet theory of psychology makes claims to blanketing of reality or ignores the issue to make it seem that way. In large measure psychological theories focus on the individual and participate in the cult of individualism. Group psychology is a separate discipline.

Environmentalism on the other hand looks at the individual differently, even environmental cognition is different. The individual is not a monadic mental state surrounded by a feeble body. The construction of the environmentally defined individual includes the mental state, the physical state, the states of interacting with the world and various feedback mechanisms that question even those boundaries. The simple identity of theory and autobiography is contrary to environmentalism. For environmentalism such an identity represents a moment in time rather than a continuous state. The transformation of autobiography into theory occurs while the individual is identifying with other people and such a conflict is evident both for Valery and for Rosenfeld's environmental tract *re: evolution*. Writing about the world implies the individual and vice versa. The interactions and transformations implied by metaphor occur in physical reality as well as on the page.

I'd like to properly construct the matrix of theory, but at this point only list some components that would show the larger context of the identification of theory as autobiography. Mental state, physical state, mental and physical states' rate and direction of change, ecosystem(s) inhabited by the theorist, the viewpoint varies with role, the external physical surroundings and its interactions, the interactions through various roles between individuals, perception of the interaction of others, social climate, weather, expectation. And the mind has a somewhat different construction than the world because of its extreme levels of reflexivity. Reflexivity in the world is isomorphic more than transformational as Ovid. You can see why people try to simplify into monolithic theory in order to function.

The main problem with this theory of environmentalism is its complexity, its unpredictability. Therefore notions of perfection, now or in the future, are out line with environmentalism, but completeness is necessary for it to function as completeness and/or symbiosis is necessary in and for organisms. (I'd point out the one of the differences between the world and its instantiation in the mind is that fragmentary positions often suffice in mental states, while the missed trick may be fatal in organisms…and I hope that changes your mind.) The presence of internal contradictions, an inevitable outcome of this condition of complexity, should not undermine our resolve to engage in actions that, to the extent possible, move toward desirable conditions.

While I am avoiding writing why I like to write about environmental theory, I can easily do it. In thinking of my motivations, I have focused on many aspects of my own roles as poet, publisher, technocrat, producer, father, son, husband, employee, business owner, patient, theorist and their interactions. For each of these I think somewhat differently and somewhat the same. In putting all those pieces together, I am also confronted by this massive issue of environmental degradation looming in the cultural landscape without a contemporary culture to inform it. It was introduced to me by other people for whom I have deep respect and who became part of my world in a way that made sense. It also occurred at a time when the theories and practices that I had been operating under, viz. language poetry, were fading in importance and I could see the writing on the wall. But in writing things down this way I fail in my own objective to write the individual into the world and while it may address your point, it acknowledges it too fully.

Most language constructions predict specific results; I'd like them to create general effects as well, but maybe that's utopian, maybe it's just ambiguous.

Book 2: Cultural Toolkit

Snowball Earth Creates Innovative Poetry

> For the roads there are animals…. "Where does this road go?"
> —Rabelais

The intense focus on social life in cities by innovative writing during the past 250 years obscures the truism that human activity is not unnatural or separate from nature. People behave strangely, but we are still biological organisms. Our cognitive powers, while in many ways unusual, remain a product of natural selection.

In one respect, however, humanity distinguishes itself as a single species by threatening to significantly alter the climate of the entire planet and thereby cause the extinction of many if not most of earth's species. While exceptional we cannot really credit ourselves with being the first species to cause wholesale climate change. As long as a billion years ago, massive blue-green algae blooms produced enough free oxygen to drop the average temperature to around -50⁰C. The planet iced over as deep as 1km on all oceans. Slowly volcanic activity raised CO_2 levels and the planet returned to a habitable temperature. The receding glaciers fragmented earth's tectonic plates. This process may have occurred several times. In the "Evolution of the Marine Phosphate Reservoir" Noah Planavsky et. al. postulate that:

> Specifically, there is a peak in phosphorus-to-iron ratios in Neoproterozoic iron formations dating from ~750 to ~635 Myr ago, indicating unusually high dissolved phosphate concentrations in the aftermath of widespread, low-latitude 'snowball Earth' glaciations. An enhanced postglacial phosphate flux would have caused high rates of primary productivity and organic carbon burial and a transition to more oxidizing conditions in the ocean and atmosphere. The snowball Earth glaciations and Neoproterozoic oxidation are both suggested as triggers for the evolution and radiation of metazoans. We propose that these two factors are intimately linked; a glacially induced nutrient surplus could have led to an increase in atmospheric oxygen, paving the way for the rise of metazoan life. (*Nature* 467, 1088–1090 (28 October 2010))

These speculations reveal that primitive algae conditioned the planet for advanced life forms. Given the immense time horizons imagination does not have to stretch far to foresee how human carbon emissions can tip the planet into a hot spell that would result in elimination of most species. Even if you do not believe these facts, even a modest risk that they might be true would encourage you to change your behavior. If algae can create conditions for life, certainly human ingenuity can destroy it.

Why then would we knowingly continue to behave in a way to destroy our habitat? Because individual organisms attempt to survive and propagate themselves until their condition changes. Life could not thrive if individual organisms did not seek to improve their chances of survival through territorial control, reduced use of energy to feed ourselves, forming groups and reproduction. Individuals and group formation will continue to overuse planetary resources until our collective willpower or external forces change. The biology of individual organisms drastically affects our species' ability to act on obvious facts and risks. We know how strongly people assert themselves.

Culture helps individuals to assert themselves. The delusion that the human ability to reflect helps us to control ourselves operates as the cultural isomorph of the organismal survival drive. This delusion continues to jeopardize our ability to understand what we're doing as a species. From *Genesis* to graphic novels and 21st century poetry, culture reinforces misapprehensions about the human ability to consciously govern our actions. How can we change culture to reinforce behavior that supports acting our collective interest?

Currently, innovative writing supports our myths about our uniqueness by attending increasingly to the materials of creation and presenting concrete themes in increasingly elaborate disguises. From social writing to psychological and personal narratives, to theaters of ideas, to the poem itself, and most recently to language-centered writing the materials of construction dominate literary imagination. As innovation progresses our perspective has become increasingly internal. At the same time writing addresses more subjects, apparently democratizing culture, but its structural complexity and underlying theory have the unintended side effect of excluding more and more readers from believing that contemporary writing has something important to tell us about how the world works.

And true to the biological tendency of each individual organism to act in its own interest, these excluded readers have developed independent forms and audiences, further marginalizing innovative writing. From the narratives of country music to graphic novels to movie and video games' solo male protagonists, the broader cultural picture has fragmented and reduced older forms such as poetry to specialized readership. We might view this progress toward popular culture as appropriate if we did not have the collective problems of population expansion and climate change hanging over our heads.

Innovative culture by failing to address more concrete issues and capture broader audiences abets the separation of human activity from other planetary agents.

Fragmentation extends far beyond poetry to disconnected silos of knowledge in many fields of endeavor. We are taught to separate art from science and from politics in a way that justifies ignoring the environmental links between those vertical compartments and the synthesizing of ideas in all but the most pragmatic frameworks such as management, marketing, distribution, and accounting, contributing to the rise of corporate oligarchy unfettered by a sophisticated culture confronting its power.

Since corporate succor barely exists, reborn fundamentalisms within all major religions, New Age Culture, Asian styles of meditation, deep ecology, and Jungian synchronicity have arisen to soothe people's suffering. These cultural alternatives proliferate as the corporate drive toward specialization and focus on technical skill undermines the awareness of the environmental connectors that afford people confidence and a sense of well-being. While human welfare has been and continues to be the purpose of civilization, neither our cultures nor our leadership apparently promote it. Instead contemporary culture encourages complacency overlaying insecurity.

There are, nevertheless, some good reasons to accept these divisive boundaries between silos of thinking. (It's never simple unless you are economical with the truth.) Each discipline's independent tools help acquire detailed knowledge of and excellence in any field. (General knowledge is suspect for several reasons.) But once the valued distinctions have been established, what psychologists call the narcissism of small differences takes hold to fossilize the borders.

Artists and scientists often place colleagues' work into categories in order to dismiss it, attack it, or otherwise affirm their own existence in distinction to it. In essence, to categorize is to dispose of certain details in a way that distorts the complete picture of our artistic ecosystems. If a work cannot be categorized, it is easily marginalized as outsider art, dismissed as experimental or condescendingly referred to as quirky or personal.

This tyranny of taxonomy separates what is otherwise related among the different arts, between arts and sciences, between A and B. As a practical matter, resolving dilemmas and eliminating false polarities would be facilitated by the tree structure of biology that would help us to think about related poetries, related ideas, and related individuals simultaneously in both separate and common spaces. Of course we do that already, but I rarely represent the fact that I am both myself and part of my family when I discuss my poetry; it's not good for the career. I can and should represent myself as a writer who is part of several innovative poetic tendencies. But when I do that many of my fellow poets deride the connections, calling them schools as if working together somehow diminished my value as a writer. On the contrary, to encourage individual organisms to see collective reality would be a valuable artistic contribution.

The cultural entities that I simultaneously inhabit add to my effectiveness as well as to the depth of my work. Communities with an acceptable public identity would make public discussion of poetry more productive and less an evaluation of individual worth. (This is not an easy job, because differences are often far more stimulating than similarities, but more on that later.)

Another isomorph of focus on the individual: Isolation of the disciplines of learning and action from one another has allowed the rise of the marketplace model, the zero sum competitive game of boutiques where everything is treated as if it were for sale. This model suggests that pursuit of self-interest in the aggregate produces results supportive of collective interests. Quite the opposite has proven to be the case in the example of the global financial system. Self-interest, both individually and unfettered in the aggregate, destroys the social fabric by creating confusion between individual necessities with collective values. The domination of exchange value and marketplace competition sadly extends to basic human needs like health care and education to the detriment of both. It extends even to the tiny, impoverished poetry world.

For example, the Lila Wallace Fund (*Reader's Digest*) offered money to literary publishers to build market-oriented strategies aimed at publishing books based on how well they can be distributed and sold. Publishers who accepted these grants were disposed to change their editorial stance to fit the requirements of the grant. Some succeeded but many excellent presses died of expansion. The market mentality justifies such transitions as creative destruction just as global destruction of species allowed the rise of more complex life forms. But do we want to be precursors to the next advance of life? Rather we'd like to improve and appreciate our species and those around us. A careful look at our pretexts might allow us to avoid what now seems like the inevitable demise of our species by our own hand. Changing course toward policies addressing collective interest would be an exciting example of rationality. How can environmentalism help us to move toward that goal?

One of the supporting pillars of individualism, specialization, and marketplace mentality, Descartes' views the mind as part of an organism where cognition takes place as if on a stage. The Cartesian metaphor dominates our culture of thinking even though it has been thoroughly questioned by several subsequent philosophers. While Descartes model of cognition supports the biological individual, it fails to address the collective social and species influences on our lives. Environmentalism can only become effective throughout our culture if we can develop an environmental model of cognition and replace the Cartesian metaphor and its personalized vision that sequesters all valuable thought within the individual. And it might do so in correct proportion between internal and external thinking.

In his article "Environmental Epistemology" (*Ethics & the Environment*, 10(2), 2005), Mark Rowlands, professor of philosophy at the University of Miami, suggests that cognition can be said to take place both inside the body and "also in the manipulation and transformation of external information-bearing structures." Several functions take place externally, especially the function of memory, like an external disk array on your computer. "In certain circumstances, acting upon external structures is a form of information processing."

Organisms exploit external resources in order to reduce their energy consumption and increase survival rates. Rowlands cites how a beaver's dam-building skills make food more accessible with less effort and less risk. The beaver might have developed longer legs and bigger muscles to run from the pond to the tree to eat its bark before the wolf could catch him. As an adaptation such a strategy would use far more energy than a strategy that manipulates the environment. Taking fewer risks, the beaver who adapts through manipulation of the environment survives more often than the physically enhanced beaver.

Recent conceptual poetry uses a related strategy, appropriating prior texts, recontextualizing them and publishing them largely unchanged. The success of new conceptual poetry, from the environmental point of view, must be focused on that low energy output / strong reader response conceptual poets' attain. Ironically, with little work applied conceptual poetry achieves a greater amount of consideration compared to poets laboring diligently on the page. And predictably many writers flock to utilize this low effort poetics.

In another example, a person finds spices on a shelf. Rather than memorize the position of each spice, the cook runs his forefinger across the bottles, reading the label on each bottle in turn until he finds the one he wants. Understanding the position of the bottle that he wants takes place both inside and outside the mind, creating a situation where cognition takes place.

> The cognitive operations, by way of which we are supposed to acquire information about, hence represent, the world, are themselves, at least in part, processes *of* the world. They possess, quite literally, worldly constituents. And even those vehicles that can legitimately be regarded as located inside the skin of cognizing organisms can, in many instances, not be *identified* independently of the world. Such vehicles will, in many instances and perhaps most, have been designed to operate only in conjunction with the *manipulation of environmental structures.*
> (ibid)

This low-cost strategy makes it more likely that organisms survive in conditions of reduced resources. It also accounts for human success. The drive toward social structure in towns is a good example, although recently developed balance sheets of energy consumption raise questions about the efficacy of certain economies of scale. Our social organizations like cities and governments exemplify external cognition, and the fact that we build cities proves the inadequacy of an internal-only model of cognition to account for existing conditions.

Rowlands cites the case of the mobile, adolescent sea squirt that has developed a rudimentary brain that allows it to move about collecting food. In adulthood, to enable reproduction, it affixes itself to a rock and proceeds to eat its own brain as an energy-saving method. How often in my life have I applied only a few things that I know in order to get a job done and not confuse thinking with the execution of the task at hand?

The notion that cognition can take place as a complex combination of activities inside and outside the body helps explain why we need to be concerned about the condition of the environment. Establishing that self-interest includes the individual in the ecosystem extends the idea of environment to the mind itself. Linking internal and external processes by defining cognition in this way promotes environmentalism from the core of our being, not as an abstract, impersonal value that we *ought* to support. If we think of our surroundings and ourselves as integrated entities then we might stop using our environs as trash bins and develop increased respect for other people.

Externalized cognition represents a first and vital step toward environmental perspectives. Writing looked at this way becomes an example of such externalization. Interestingly, poetry dealing with the materials of writing, from Mallarme's *Le Livre* to Silliman's *The New Sentence,* includes a great range of external subjects and materials, expanding poetry from a few monolithic subjects like love and war to complex and multiple issues. These writing strategies that use diverse materials and practices open the door to an extended poetry that addresses real-world concerns. Such writing practice potentially reestablishes poetry as a valid knowledge-creating process. Focusing on culture this way reduces the limitations of innovative culture's narrowing focus on the materials of construction.

In *Cheerleader's Guide to the World: Council Book* (Roof, 2007), Stacy Doris' constructs the work from internal and external components rather than by analyzing a core event or idea through internally consistent logic. The book "…sandwiches Popul Vuh Patterson/Tibetan Dead Jigme Linpa Pindar//Rah rah." (The quotation is followed by a chart of a football play as if drawn for a high school sports team.) "The good old idea//was that corn growth//+ tax cuts make leisure."

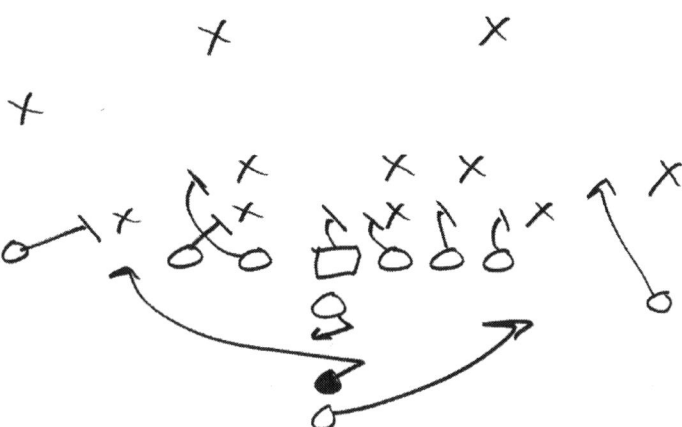

By juxtaposing these elements, Doris relates them physically on the page and establishes a variety of connections between internal and external components of varying strength and usefulness. Some of these associate subconsciously, some through our knowledge of history, and some through their inherent connections such as common content. In all cases, the exercise establishes a cognizant link of person and external components in an environment. These links reach out from the mind to the page and back. We read them again and they change; we are thinking as we read.

Compare Doris' lines to a sonnet by Milton where emanating from god "…thousands at his bidding speed / and post o'er land and ocean without rest…" all with the same interest, passively waiting to execute his will. While each differs, they agree on a common master. Here people outside the mind of god link only to god's will and the poem refers to the readers established understanding about biblical text. But even in Milton's case using fixed meaning the reader thinks using the words on the page as much as what is already in the readers mind. Milton's poem talks about internal cognition but is read using a combined process evident of external cognition.

Doris' synthesis reveals another kind of agreement. Synthetic poetry is greater than the sum of its parts, requiring more than the components of its construction to be read and absorbed. In this sense, poetry is externally understood. Meaning goes beyond the poem on the page to the experience and assumptions of the reader.

Like the beaver dam, Doris' synthetic poetry expands our access to resources that common usage would exclude. By juxtaposing the different texts, *Popul Vuh*, "Patterson," etc. they arrive together in the present in the poem. Collapsing time represents one tool that writing uses to deliver cultural change and expand the possible solutions to our climate problem. By showing readers past, present and future together new correlations develop. But synthetic poetry requires more than juxtaposition to operate as an ecosystem.

Putting components together in an operative way, such as syntax for example, where their resources become available to each other creates examples for the poetic components to be guided by and push against as in any ecosystem, moving the metaphor into a reality that extends beyond that of a figure of speech. Poetic metaphor represents a real world analog of the complex interactions and correlations of components in the biosphere both symbiotically, homologically and experimentally such as using mice to help understand human disease. Mice and humans are not the same but have many similar processes. Accurate comparisons are few but in sufficient numbers to make many of Doris' combinations valuable culture modifiers.

> What's human is formations
> and drills. In the mix not the
> matter or match. The commercial
> habitat ploughed tracked stolen
> or too glorified and thought
> may be boating.
> (*Cheerleader's,* p23)

Doris' combinations allow us to look at the components in a comparative way as they appear in the world rather than as they appear in their own context. Improving our skill in understanding the perspective of another context or another person's context will be important in addressing the multi-context view of global climate change. The combinations that Doris links are forms that enhance poetic technique much as rhyme makes poetic lines both more memorable and prosodically connected.

Localized technique used without reference to form, that is, not modeled, leads to a practice of poetry based on an invertebrate abstraction without understanding how that abstraction arises, that is, without analysis. Put another way, the more language is isolated from the forms where it is used, be they poetic, that is, multidirectional, or instrumental and toward a specific purpose, the more fixed meaning becomes. Fixed meaning in a limited context effectively accomplishes specific tasks, but does not allow us to think outside its context. Doris adapts the links to each context. Where they work, like genetic code, we achieve poetic lift off. Where they don't work, the writing falls flat.

Environmental poetics provides analytic models such as externalized cognition that can perform many functions in support of synthetic writing, addressing multiple contexts and actually understanding another person's point of view. It provides tools and connectors for poetic components as well as a well-documented history of how those techniques have already been applied. And consistent with the practice of environmental poetics, examples from biology display the values of models in poetry. (This book is intended to be not just an argument for its idea but also an example of it.) Metaphor viewed as an example of complex systems also appears as a useful tool and I see no reason to avoid such extended metaphor or its use in modeling.

> **Metaphor as Taxonomy**
> Grasping this as that,
> More than a thing
> Of beauty. Instead a bond
> Of scales, cleaving
> To poetry. Dialing
> The iris risks ungrammatical
> Acts, but riskless verse
> Sings alone in the shower.
> Metaphor more than
> A fig leaf of speech
> Represents the world
> Where each shares
> Enough of another
> To be called a part.

Alas metaphor also makes it difficult to maintain a serious mien about this process of environmental poetry and its ridiculous appearance. Using examples from biology to validate literary arguments, describing poetry in such grandiose terms—these and many other methods used in the book have often made me laugh at myself while writing. To stop using nature as a person, but instead limiting the definition of nature to intrinsic characteristics supports such a physical universe.

But irony at many levels also plays a part in negotiating the change from a walled topography to a geography of permeable membranes within an organism. Just how seriously can we take this approach? Can irony exist at a continuous level in an environmental text or is it always modified by the reader's relation to what she is reading? Can we show the value to the environment of irony, which has heretofore been largely an aesthetic technique or approach to social criticism?

As we begin to distribute the environmental model, we also will need a new social taxonomy to replace the one observed by Chaucer in *Canterbury Tales* at the dawn of humanism and that is still in operation. As people begin to assimilate the environmental view, how will they be reorganized? How will they interact? What kinds of institutions will replace the existing ones, which are based on prior, polarized models? We could wish for no more than a suspension of time. Let us go forward.

Human Views of Nature

> Time is ripe for a *project* to better organise information in articles related to Environment. This page and its subpages contain the suggestions; it is hoped that this project will help to focus the efforts of other Wikipedians. If you would like to help, please inquire on the *talk page* and see the *to-do list* there.
> —*Wikipedia* entry for Environmentalism, fall 2006

(Note: This citation has as of February 2008 been replaced by a long list of other links and entries rather than a single statement about Environmentalism, including Environmental Psychology, Environmental Determinism, Environmental Art—all distinguishing "the external conditions, resources, stimuli etc. with which an organism interacts." This statement supports the approach that environment is not just a thing, but a set of relations.)

If, as most scientists suspect, there is a significant change in global climate within the current century, then we will likely see a concomitant change in social structure. Just as weather will be the news, the social structure will focus on the biosphere. But rather than defining the biosphere in only one way, the social organization arising from global warming will accommodate several myths of nature for different types of people in different social roles and environmental situations. A cabdriver in New York, for example, will have a different picture of the value and scope of his surroundings than a Tutsi warrior. Furthermore, as a person's role changes, his or her view of nature changes as well. For example, in my role as a poet and critic, I view my surroundings differently than in my role as a father and husband trying to feed my family. These complexities condition our culture for a social construction of nature or the biosphere. (Michael Thompson's article "Man and Nature as a Single but Complex System" is the inspiration for these ideas.)

As environmental processes become less predictable, change will occur in the scientific, the political, and the cultural spheres. Individuals will be expected to take a stand, have a point of view. But as Wikipedia points out above, we don't have a clear idea of what our environment is composed of or how to make changes in it through the study of ecology.

If we are not clear about environment and ecology, then we are even less clear about nature. Is nature the ceiling of reality or are there supernatural forces that control nature? Does nature include humanity or is humanity irrevocably opposed to nature by virtue of self-interest and special capabilities (reasoning and reflection) that allow us to "rise above" it in special and important ways? Is nature the material world? The forces and phenomena that produce everything that exists, the world of living things, the total of reality, a primitive state that we seek to exceed? Or is it all of the above couched as a multiple-choice question that can only be answered by not seeking essential meaning and a single reassuring truth, by a conditional that can change over time. And as I have already mentioned, perhaps nature is best discussed as inherent characteristics rather than personified as that which is not human.

In one sense, the need for a word like "nature" is a result of the disintegration of our relationship to the rest of the planet and our cultural separation from it, especially if we think that nature is all that is the case. The elimination of local spirits protecting trees and streams began a long decline of our awareness of our symbiotic relation to our surroundings.

In another sense, nature is a very useful way to describe the overall presence of our world in our lives as seen from the human-only point of view. A danger, and one that is especially dangerous for a poetic discussion of nature, is that the word "nature" is a noun and therefore makes us think it's a person or thing, when it's also a set of processes, relationships, and abstractions; that is, when there is no object that we can point to.

Given this level of multiplicity and uncertainty around what nature is, how can we use the term and make sense of it? In order to understand nature we need to understand the relationship between ourselves, other organisms, and our environment. But again, the path to that understanding is circuitous and not well understood. We are accustomed to positing a definition and applying it, even in the case where multiple definitions for a word are common.

From the essentialist point of view, all human activity around ecological and environmental issues is conditioned by a single myth about nature. Reliance on proof limits our tools of understanding. For example, in science, nature is the ceiling beyond which speculation is fruitless because assertions are not able to be proven false. For deists, there are supernatural views and values (based on texts like the *Koran*, the *Bible* or the *Bagavad Gita*) that will influence their choices regarding how humans should treat one another, animals, plants, and non-organic components of our environment. But deist assumptions are inconsistent with data about the environment, whether fact-based (earth temperatures, for example, are increasing) or belief-based (God is continually reengineering the planet to improve human conditions so long as humans continue to follow his rules, so any changes are God's will). The problem for us all is that we cannot at once dismiss all our assumptions about nature and society. Remember how hard it was in 1970 to talk about the words "him" and "her." How many fights were started by questioning something as simple as a pronoun! Any essential view of nature, be it scientific or belief-based, will be more difficult to change.

A non-essential view of nature implies that the complexity of interactions among all these components drives a cultural model of the environment that includes, but goes beyond, the science of ecology or a single set of statements about the environment. And to avoid lumping all these values and studies together, we need a cultural model of nature to help us condition our modes of action. In this way, scientists can act as scientists, politicians can legislate and cultural workers can create—all while acknowledging the values of the other workers. Michael Thompson in his work on the cultural construction of nature takes it a step further by pointing out how each of us in our various roles will subscribe to different myths of nature depending on our role of the moment.

As an environmentalist, I look for a planetary model that includes points of view that may be invalid logically but yet exist and have a significant impact on the forum of discussion. I am not simply solving problems, but seeking methods for making a composite world comprehensible. I also want to propose a multi-faceted view of nature.

A useful activity might include imagining an environmentally oriented social structure like Chaucer did in *Canterbury Tales,* in which the pilgrims and their relationships represent civil society in the fourteenth century. Chaucer wrote a series of stories, each, like *The Decameron,* from the point of view of one person. But Chaucer included not just a group of aristocrats hiding from the plague but a whole social structure of individuals of different classes—knights, bureaucrats, householders, priests—each with a unique point of view and set of interests concerning their venture.

In our environmental model addressing social structure is a critical component because of the lack of conviction in the popular press around environmental problems as opposed to the general agreement of the scientific communities concerning environmental threats such as environmental degradation or global warming. (Several writers, including Al Gore, have pointed to the popular press' denial of a greenhouse problem as opposed to the near 100 percent concurrence in the professional scientific press.) I further suggest that there's a difference between the external, fact-based approach to the environment and the values-based approach. Nevertheless both fact and values require belief in a system of thought.

There also is the question of whether we should give priority to the scientific fact-based approach or to the emotional approach when making decisions about our lives, our communities, and then our planet. The poetry world is conflicted about this subject as well with some poets focused on language and some focused on an immediate expression of experience. An environmental model would allow both to exist, each in their own sphere as in a society differences of culture inevitably coexist.

While these multiple points of view coexist, environmentalism also extends data and metaphors from microbiology/genetics to ecosystems and larger frames? As I have pointed out metaphor reflects the isomorphic structure of the biosphere, including human thought, and is not only a figure of speech. From the point of view of poetry, the question of the value of metaphor becomes strikingly less trivial when posed in this way. If our myths of nature make us behave in ways that are contrary to our individual and collective self-interest, then essentialist metaphors, left unchecked, pose as great a danger to civilization as nuclear weapons.

In addition, essentialist metaphors have a long-running impact at a very low level that renders them nearly invisible as a threat to society. This situation argues for continual investigation of messages about society from all levels rather than just leadership. Local news about mayors and mullahs as well as awareness and acceptance of the values of countless local cultures improve our ability to see the cultural world as a reciprocal component of our environment. Non-essentialist positions support the shifting values of art, science, and politics, and help seek ways to understand the major problems confronting us right now and just over the horizon. Essentialist misrepresentations with a specific emotional appeal don't disappear, but people can train themselves to see them in context.

We need to avoid prioritizing along the fault lines of value and fact. The advantage of such an approach would be that each of us (almost all of us) has both a fact-based and a value-based set of biases that need to be addressed before personal or social change occurs. A real solution, from the human perspective as well as the environmental one, would simultaneously accommodate both biases. Otherwise, we will forever second guess decisions about climate change depending on which set of biases we are focused on at the moment.

The result of these discussions about essentialism (fact and value) all direct me to a non-humanist, non-deist construction of the world based on our view of nature. God and humanity can fit into this view, but they are neither the center nor the focus of our endeavor. I am talking about environment and ecology, which, regardless of any human or godly plan, are views of nature. As a result, a view of nature that takes us into the parallel world that I am proposing is a prerequisite, so that we carry forward as few assumptions as are useful to such a discussion and ultimately to action.

Nevertheless, we can't eliminate all these ideas; we'd alienate all the people who support them. And after all, older ideas continue to exist even after the rise of humanism. Therefore, environmental inclusiveness acts as a buffer to political instability. The values of diversity are thereby achieved biologically and socially.

**

Michael Thompson's thesis centers on the effort to redefine society and nature together as a single complex entity. And the change from viewing the world as a competing set of essentialist views requires that we understand even that change as bi-directional. "The classic assumption in both ecology and social science is that there is a one-way transition from state A to state B." (Thompson and Price, *Newsletter of the International Human Dimensions Programme on Global Environmental Change*, 2002). Models of change are often temporary and uni-directional, especially in today's finger-wagging ecological culture. This is hardly our actual experience and not the way either the facts or the values structure would project change going forward. So why are we constantly making this mistake?

If we accept that human activities take place within environmental complexity, a multi-disciplinary matrix suggests several contextually valid views. In a paper that brings together the concepts of "relative surprise" from theoretical ecology, "cultural bias" from social anthropology, and the investigation of decision rationality, Thompson suggests that one's view of any change has as much to do with the point of view of the individual (psychology and environment) as with the validity of the change.

> When people argue from different premises they will, in all probability, fail to agree.... Attention is focused not on the facts of the matter but on the facts of the disagreement.... In other words the discerning spectator begins by granting legitimacy to all these sets of contradictory premises. Nor does the fact that they are contradictory cause him any dismay. On the contrary, he sees social life as a process that depends for its very existence on the perpetual contention between these different sets of convictions about how the world is.

For example, a physicist's world has resources in abundance, since matter is neither created nor destroyed, whereas an ecologist's world has limited resources. Thompson goes on to outline a set of cultural relationships to nature that inevitably define the individual's approach to facts and opinions. And such a model might be a useful tool for environmentalists and ecologists as well.

As the environmental model of the planet begins to take hold in the culture, a new set of social classes will emerge based on the individual's view of the biosphere. Thompson hypothesizes that "there are just five distinct cultural biases each of which has associated with it a distinct idea of nature."

Social Being	View of Nature
The Ineffectual	Lottery Controlled Cornucopia
The Hierarchist	Isomorphic Nature
The Hermit	Freely Available Cornucopia
The Entrepreneur	Skilled-Controlled Cornucopia
The Sectist	Accountable Nature

Our view of our environment—its politics, sciences and arts—filters through a cultural screen. An act may be considered rational if it is consistent with the actor's idea of nature. This relativism reflects the political reality of our world. But if we view culture not as a set of habits of mind but as a continually renegotiated set of social relationships, we establish what Thompson calls "a cultural construction of nature."

Thompson proposes that the new model resist the urge to remove complexity, goal ambiguity, contradictory certainties, conflict, institutional inertia, and temporal change from our culture. (The very stuff of poetry!) He suggests conceiving of policies to preserve their "historical contingency." Thus the arts and sciences can represent their processes as evolving with the imperfections inherent in any cultural unit. While we cannot make much progress in specialized knowledge without a rigorous taxonomy, we cannot make much progress in our relationships in society or nature without an art and science that accommodate the peripheral views: value and fact. Yet we cannot argue effectively from these peripheral views, but need put our efforts into the subjects of day-to-day engagement.

The implications of this concept for policy, for art, and for integration in the sciences show us an approach as Thompson says "to moderate specific debates so as not to erode general consent." The disputes today between conservative and liberal political views, between scientific disciplines and environmental sciences, between traditional and risk-taking arts, may benefit from this analysis of how we view environment. In any case, disputes will become more and more prominent as climate change drives social change.

One additional point: There is a fundamental conflict between planetary nature taken as a whole and the survival and flourishing of any one species or group of species. Without such analytic tools as Thompson and others provide, we cannot manage our successes. Not only does our success as a species doom many others; it may, in the long run, have been our own undoing as our success taxes the supporting ecosystems beyond their ability to regenerate. Thompson asks a fundamental question: How do we treat humanity and nature together as a single complex system? (As I mentioned above the very word nature, separating humanity from the rest of the planet, makes change more difficult, but Thompson does not acknowledge that point.)

The great irony of our age appears as soon as humanity grasps the possibility of getting out from under nature's boot—plague and privation. At this very moment, we see the results of our having gone too far: global warming, ozone deterioration, resource depletion, and general discontent with the political hierarchy. Can we use the analytic tools of arts and sciences interactively for the purposes of a policy with a less invasive approach to global domination? And finally, it is possible that the soft power of the American global trading empire, integrated by balance sheets and capital movement, if it can avoid the military excesses encouraged by the marketplace, represents the less intrusive way of which I am speaking. Perhaps it too will soon be swept aside by climatic forces.

At this point, the contradictions in capitalism are being managed by stifling labor movements and allowing capital to move freely around the globe (David Harvey, *The Condition of Postmodernity*, Blackwell, 1989). And conscious globalization, the irony of Marx's panacea, is for the first time a possibility. While many—from technologists to investment bankers to religious fundamentalists—want to claim credit for globalization, the ability to mediate difference / diversity will be the measure of its success in the future. I continue to be less concerned about how we got here than about the nature of our continuity. As such, as the first step, I want to represent what I consider important distinctions that condition action, rather than suggest convenient courses of action. The essays in this section of the book begin to list those conditioning processes.

The fear is that we need to act right away, or with planning by "my" group—or never. The fear is that change cannot be predicated on facts. The fear is that… Well we might start by arrest basing our activities on fear and hope. Occupy Wall Street movement of 2011-12 presents an alternative to hope and fear by bringing forward the idea that self-interest can be synonymous with the interests of the 99%, because only by addressing collective interests can we avoid distortion. Occupy's refusal to propose specific solutions but only encouraging people to think in terms of 99% represents a definitive break with goal directed problem solving.

Yet each of us has one or many of these fears, and they modify our actions. And then there is self-interest, which modifies our judgments. Can we develop institutions that operate in the interest of the 99% instead of the interest of the owners? How can that aim even start to be realized considering how organisms strive for their individual survival?

What I'm suggesting in this niche of ideas is that we start looking at our planet through another scrim than that of the humanist or deist. Just walk away from those divisive perspectives and start looking at the situation environmentally. See if you can identify yourself. That may be where you start making decisions that matter.

In my role as a poet, I am writing from the point of view of one or more singular myths about poetry (poetry styles or schools typically posit themselves as independent of other styles):

- how I feel about what is happening to me and my group (expressive and personal poetry such as Confessionalism or the New York School),
- how I communicate and make you feel about events (communications model such as Hardy or Yeats and their contemporary followers),
- how I make meaning (philosophical poetry),
- the subjects I write about may be primary (political poetries such as Romanticism that acts as a demonstration against industrialization), or
- how I may be concerned with how I use language (language writing, Surrealism, and other formally innovative poetries).

If, for example, I am writing from the point of view of my personal identity (expressive), is my poetry irrevocably different than if I am writing based on the myth that poetry is about the materials of poetic composition—language, form, and other non-lexical meanings? What is my poetry when I mix the two or include a third set of components? Does such composite poetry lack rigor in that it uses inconsistent components to drive its meaning? Does poetry need to use a mode of expression that is consistent with its themes? Can it, like an environmental niche, incorporate a variety of functions, differently expressed?

> Asymmetry provides the centrality/peripherality
> Criteria that serve to separate the prescribing
> Entrepreneur from the prescribed ineffectual.
> A personal strategy aimed at the deliberate
> Avoidance of all three types of order in nature—
> Randomness, chaos, and order—
> Can also result in a viable conjunction
> Of social context and cultural bias—the hermit.
> The author does not take it literally,
> But reading materializes.

Limiting the Social Environment for a Good Reason
Is Not Enough of a Reason

> The Cyclopes were the first fathers.
> —Vico (perhaps citing Plato)

Which is to say that the Greeks blind Polyphemus with their obscure adolescent logic ("I am Nobody.") and thereby escape from the "family" of "heroic" culture. They want to be themselves, not adopt the posture they detect in the parent. Once they are out in the world they confront many problems, almost none of which they fail to screw up. But in the end, after all his companions are dead, Odysseus washes up on the shores of the well-ordered state of the Phaeacians on the island of King Alcinous and accepts its bounty. He then returns to organize his own kingdom along similar lines.

Thus ends, according to Vico, the heroic period; classical society has stabilized. Innovation in the *Odyssey* often produces disastrous results and often saves Odysseus' life. A similar process continues today. Social innovation never gets it quite right but can't be stopped. Highly productive individuals as a class keep returning to assert control regardless of the innovations of isolated creative individuals and mass rejections of authority.

On the other hand scientists often produce their best results when their minds are young and flexible. And innovative writing sometimes produces good results immediately. Innovation is a crap shoot. But limiting opportunities for change by letting institutions either private or public control it pretty much guarantees stagnant social structure, stifles creativity and presages that new groups will soon lead society.

Ultimately Vico backed the wrong horse, but he introduced a method to structure our thinking about life in society. And while I abhor his class orientation as I do Pound's politics, Vico's work points toward some effective ways to condition our thoughts, even if in opposition to him, about how to address climate change as a society. For example, how can our response to the weather imposed by environmental change prevent humans from becoming slaves of climate and one another? How is freedom to be preserved when individual freedom, entrepreneurship and culture that focus on the individual have been such an important driver of our society as it outgrew its ecosystems?

I don't imagine that we can change our relationship to the planet with minor adjustments of attitude. Although it would be helpful if the changes to society can be incremental and intentional, a thorough rehearsal of our culture appears necessary. While I can't find any examples of a culture of environmentalism in the humanist periods either modern or classical, I find in Vico some features of humanist culture that shed light on the direction we might take toward an environmental poetics.

I have already pointed to several biological and poetic concerns propelled by the same need to question and revamp humanity's relationship to the biosphere. But for humans climate change will drive societal change rather than humans changing themselves. Intentional change, although I promote its methods and values, appears less likely. I have mentioned the cultural construction of nature, but what of the cultural construction social structure. How does art shape society? I deal with a contemporary perspective on environmental social structure in the essay "Human Views of Nature" based on the work of Michael Thompson. In this essay I want to show the sources for constructing society with culture in the work of Giambattista Vico.

As we progress into the global period in which much activity anywhere on the planet intertwines, we seek a sustainable form of order that serves the interests of the people in as many climes and cultures as possible. From our current perspective in the world today, such integration appears laughable. How can we convince the Chinese that everything in their culture from food to history is not the center of human experience? How can the Indians slow their population growth? How can Muslims not seek cultural sway over others? How can the Europeans adjust their social structure? How can South America not become excited? How can North American be shaken from its complacency?

Like regional cultures, the language, values, behavior and institutions about environment exist in niches that are conditioned by climate, geography, history, and availability of resources. But since each cultural node is linked in the modern world, the common bonds among humans might be planted in the global culture and fertilized with environmental language and art. Examples of commonality around the globe include sympathy for others, respect for nature (both fearful and benign), biological identification beyond the individual, group formation, death, taxes, and desire, which, as I have mentioned, is the deeper cause of global warming. The earth itself is also a good common ground, and although real estate is as divisive as religion, appeals to our planetary commons may support global culture.

Among practical problems we need to determine how can we integrate highly functional individuals if they follow only their self-interest? As Vico says in *The New Science*,

> The weak want laws; the powerful reject them. The ambitious promote laws to gain adherents. Rulers protect the laws in order to make the powerful

> equal to the weak. ... It is characteristic of the strong that they do not relinquish through indolence what they have won by courage. Yet if it proves necessary or useful, they will gradually give up as little as they can.

Vico's statement provides ample justification to seek transformation. He chooses society itself as the subject to transform. Society is not an abstraction. "The order of human affairs is more real than points, lines, surfaces, and figures."

But given a set of self-interested oligarchs, disguised as aristocrats with the commonweal in mind, how do we shape our ideas to include them? And how can we allow their institutions of suffering to survive, be it bomb or babe? Vico, in his role supporting divine right, claims that "The order of ideas must follow the order of institutions." As already stated, leading by institutions prescribes a static society. Vico also subordinated language to society. "In recounting the history of words in various native languages, we must follow the sequence of human institutions." Modern linguistics shows in rigorous way that, while it is not a one way street, institutions are more likely to grow around language.

If all human activity is filtered through social institutions as Vico would have it, no center, no core, except in the abstract, can be found. And institutions (and cultures) vary from place to place. Yet in the modern world common interests often connect these varying institutions. In the case of increasing awareness of climate change supported by daily and seasonal meteorological surprises, all weather all the time quickly and definitively will alter many seemingly fixed attitudes and institutions.

This network of institutions has many strong nodes but no central one except in monarchy which is Vico's point. In network theory, however, the more active connections to any individual node the more central that node is to the stability of the whole. Destroying a central node with a large number of connections like a centralized monarchy or an oligarchy risks the network. Distributed power with strong connections is hence more stable than centralized power. So today's widely distributed network of institutions communicating through well understood channels secures the institutional future better than a centralized global government. But our highly productive individuals continue to push for risky centralization in order to gain more control.

In the case of climate change where control starts to pass from humans to larger ecosystems and even human institutions are challenged by climate, control must pass to a more stable distributed human network that takes advantage of as many non-human stabilizing forces as possible. There are many smaller scale examples of how such distributed power works, for example, solutions to Brazilian inflation or comparisons of command-control systems versus systems led by individual initiative.

My statements in the prior paragraphs should not be taken entirely in contrast to Vico. Otherwise I should not bother to bring him up at all. Like any complex system Vico's is dynamic. "By its nature, the human mind is indeterminate; hence, when man is sunk in ignorance, he makes himself the measure of the universe." Here I find direct support regarding the weakness of the cult of the individual in contemporary society. "Another property of the human mind is that, when people can form no idea of distant and unfamiliar things, they judge them by what is present and familiar." Taken together, these statements imply a view of dynamic global systems that coincides with modern scientific and mathematical concepts of order and predictability. Our current political and social errors may be remedied either through our institutions or by the force of events we'd otherwise seek to avoid. Which do we prefer?

As Vico's ordering principles generated political science, I suggest an environmental poetics that encourages intentional innovation but allows forays into newness to fail without causing despondency. These multiple solutions thrive in an ecosystem that values creative process, but quite a bit of work has to be accomplished within the culture before intentional creativity would find a culturally acceptable setting.

Much of writer's writing about creative process mystifies creativity instead of clarifying it. Jean Tobin's *Creativity and the Poetic Mind* and other books love to cite poets' disavowal of their creative process (p95 especially). But innovative poets start to question that mysterious process. John Ashbery says, "My best writing gets done when I'm being distracted by people who are calling me or errands that I have to do. Those things seem to help the creative process, in my case."
http://www.english.illinois.edu/maps/poets/a_f/ashbery/general.htm

In a conversation between Ashbery and Kenneth Koch, Ashbery pokes fun at creative mysteries:

> KK: There's no key to understanding the poem, of course, no hidden meaning?
> JA: No, it's just a bunch of impressions.
> KK: Why is the idea of keys and hidden meanings not appealing to you?
> JA: Because someone might find them out and then the poem would no longer be mysterious.
> http://thisrecording.com/today/2011/1/20/in-which-john-ashbery-and-kenneth-koch-start-making-sense.html

From the environmental perspective the creative process may be indeterminate but it is not simply unknowable. We know a lot about the creative process; we may simply not want to draw conclusions that will change every time we look at them.

"Since human judgment is by nature uncertain, it gains certainty from our common sense about what is necessary and useful to human-kind; and necessity and utility are the two sources of the natural law of nations." Vico drops humanity right in the middle of natural law: hence, the politics of environmentalism with an historical antecedent.

Ultimately these kinds of statements by Vico are supportive of environmentalism in spite of his judgmental hierarchy, his adherence to "the proper study of mankind is man," his followers, such as Croce and Joyce, and the overly complex ideology that must include God in nature and society as a contrasting hermeneutic. Furthermore I wonder how Vico was both so understanding about uncertainty and so supportive of a mostly fixed hierarchy, such as that of the Greek aristocrats. I also tend to reject his statements about the inappropriateness of trying to understand nature. I suspect that his conflict over religion was twisting his logic. He knew very well that he was compromised by the combination of science and religion in his work and vulnerable in his home in Catholic Naples.

Vico does help us understand the other constantly visible fact of our contemporary American situation. "Once warfare has made a people so fierce that human laws no longer have a place among them, religion is the only means powerful enough to subdue them." Religion appears now as a last resort of a desperate society. Conservatives have galvanized the idea of space with a combination of fear, violence, and religion. How do we creep back to a more civil state in which fear is replaced by diligence, violence is replaced by concentration on common goals, religion is relegated to that which is rendered unto God, and empires can be hated for their unethical use of soft power instead of bombing of innocent civilians?

Vico reveals a different perspective on today's liberal/conservative dichotomy. Remember that Vico's main point is that we cannot examine the past by the values of the present. His support for the importance of culture as distinct from science precedes my interest in systematic linkage between humanities and science. I include him in this discussion to draw from as far afield as possible an inclusive environmental model, and because his idea of organizing society through culture changed thought for hundreds of years and spawned entire disciplines in social science. Environmental changes will produce such utter alteration in thought. Shall we wait until our hand is forced?

Ultimately though, "poetic" is for Vico a belief structure and is opposed to rational structures, yet he uses it as a principle of organizing his new science. Thus, as Europeans sought to accomplish things, Descartes' science takes precedence and becomes the enabling force in society. Vico is at best a source for the structures of social science and at worst misused for nefarious political purposes.

Vico understands his own limitations, and continually reprieves himself: "The earliest men…were unable to conceive rational categories of things, and thus felt a natural need to invent poetic archetypes…imaginative categories or universals." That's a pretty straightforward and acceptable view of progress: 80 percent of Neolithic tools were left-handed; 80 percent of modern humans are right-handed. Environmental poetics formulates culture that unlike Vico's includes both rationality and creativity in its ecology.

With that goal in mind, let's see how reason and creativity work together. Frederic C. Bartlett's essay "Imagery in Thought" (1932, from *Remembering*) points out that in the mind "images are particularly liable to arise when any slight check occurs…" He means that when the logic of a process starts to break down for us, we project an image to bridge the gap. And it is only after clearing up any confusion that rational thought recurs. Put another way the logic of the situation breaks down; images arise that provoke emotional, predetermined (cultural) responses. Contrast this with Vico: "Philosophical statements approach the truth as they ascend to universality. Poetic statements gain certainty as they descend to particulars."

Bartlett says, "The over determination by a fixed chronological series are both biologically uneconomical and to some extent unsound; …" In our discussion, the tendency toward serial behavior and fixed logic undermines environmental diversity. (Ron Atkin also has an interesting view of serial time that we will explore later.) The patchwork of situational logic, images, and language leads us to question the extensive use of imagery in poetry as redundant. In our environmental model, because so much of its complex logic is unprocessed or unknown, the images appear and disappear with a kind of flickering along with "a growth in the capability to deal with situations at a distance." (Bartlett).

This conclusion follows Napoleon's remark that a general cannot rely on a fixed plan or image of the battle because within two minutes the image ceases to be viable. The general with a fixed image has no recourse when the image, used as a model, no longer fits the facts on the ground. Fixed ideas have a very short reach and a limited predictable use in nature and less power of prediction. From the point of view of a social dimension to environmentalism, we cannot accept many fixed ideas without compromising our ability to change. Yet society needs stable models for people to feel comfortable. To achieve temporal value in environmental action, we must move beyond these fixed ideas, however attractive they are and however they ease our path through the unknown.

Bartlett's sequence of image production helps understand metaphors in past and contemporary poetry. An environmental art must be inclusive, but how can we use images successfully; that is, use images as a way to continue disrupted thought. Bartlett suggests that we reserve images for when our logic breaks down. Does that include questions? And if so, are questions images whereas propositions are logic? Vico provides a point of view that I'm not satisfied with but want to share: "Poetic wisdom has come down to us exalted by a supreme and sovereign esteem which springs both from the conceit of nations, and, to a greater extent, from the conceit of scholars." This view supports the embedded belief that poetry is about heightened language and images. Starting with language, we convert to images to bridge lack of understanding or disrupted logic. It also reinforces the contemporary bias against fixed ideas in the academy.

Vico may have already explained himself when he says that even the ultimate aesthetic social philosopher rejects the "reality" of art. The principles of the civil world are discovered in the mind: shades of Chomsky. But then he rejects our ability to know the world of nature "which only God can know as its creator." And this statement, in his section on "Principles," provides another reason for Descartes' selection as the standard epistemology and theory of cognition. See "Snowball Earth…" for an environmentally oriented theory of cognition.

With such rational objectivity, Vico continues his assertions about God. Yet neither Vico's nor Descartes' structure supports all the facts: Descartes' oversimplifies, is redundant, and, as noted above, internalizes cognition. Vico's structure is confused by religion failing to be placed in its proper domain as a belief-based explanation of natural origin, subordinated to nature. But he then does say the right things over and over, so I wonder about his religious conviction vs. his religious cloaking:

"Let us make an assumption which does not contradict nature and which we shall later find true in fact." Such scientific method (presumably influenced by Bacon) might well be applied to assumptions about God. And he takes the inductive approach much further. The structures of thought are found in nature and the structures of nature are found in human thinking.

Yet, in spite of his clear sighted views of power, Vico returns to obviously failed dichotomies, discussions that resonate more directly with art production from Bartlett's point of view: "The weaker its power of reasoning, the more vigorous the human imagination grows." They exist in a sequence. So advanced into romantic logic and yet so formulated as scientific reasoning. Yet if we view either reasoning or imagination as subordinated we get very different thoughts.

Environmental thought goes one necessary step further. For example, if we say that reasoning is one kind of ordered imagination or that imagination is one kind of reason that jumps to conclusions, we can use them together rather than keep them apart and unable to synergize into effective action. This theory conforms to the facts that Bartlett uncovered. We always use reasoning and imagination together as circumstances change. Such recombination is a characteristic of other activities in nature as well, such as applying the *force* of logic, when cultural assumptions need to be overcome to complete a task. And it happens in science as Feyerabend points out in *Against Method*.

Yet it should not be a surprise that Vico makes assertions that are mistakes from an environmental perspective, because I, in his terms, cannot judge him with my values. He is where he is in Catholic Naples and I am here in New York in the twenty-first century. And I'm sure the next writing (I don't say writer, because it might not be a writer) will not share my errors either. Vico's main mistake, from what I can understand of him, is his reliance on archetypes. "…poetic truth is metaphysical truth; and any physical truth which does not conform to it must be judged false…all commanders who do not *entirely* conform to this Godfrey are not *true* ones." (italics mine)

"True poetic allegories gave myths meanings, based on identity rather than analogy." Therefore, without detailed learning, people will condescend to accept one who is charming but will not take him seriously. That's how George Bush, for example, wheedled his way into power.

Vico's comparison of the human lifespan with historical epochs implies his intuitive grasp of complexity and hence an environmental view of the world. But does such an affiliation spell death for my concept if I ally myself with such a tort-oriented philosopher? "For the arts are simply imitations of nature and are, in a certain sense, concrete poetry."

Religion links myth and poetry, narrative and process, but because it's based on the external falsehood of myth, it has a chink through which science can attack it. Religion today is pushing back on science, especially biological science. The link between science and religion is evident in "Christian" science and Christian Science. In Islam the same process is being used today as in the reaction against the progressive Islamic governments of the eleventh and twelfth centuries. Back then, Al-Ghazzali's doctrines on faith and science were amazing in that they were far removed from the general state of belief about the world.

> Fire causes burning, lightning causes thunder, winds cause waves, and gravity causes bodies to fall. Such connections… form the cornerstone of scientific thinking, both modern and classical. Al-Ghazzali says: 'This we deny, saying: the agent of the burning is God, through His creating the black in the cotton and the disconnection of its parts, and it is God who made the cotton burn and made its ashes either through the intermediation of the angels or without intermediation. For fire is a dead body which has no action, and what is the proof that it is the agent. Indeed, the philosophers have no other proof than the observation of the occurrence of

the burning, when there is contact with fire, but observation proves only a simultaneity, not a causation, and, in reality, there is no cause but God.' (Pervez Hoodbhoy, *Islam and Science*, London, 1991)

Ultimately this is an exciting doctrine for two reasons: first, because in some ways this kind of stroboscopic reality (God coming down with angels to constantly fan the flames) reflects current advanced thinking in theoretical physics. Second, the argument is so similar to the ones used today by the "Christian" scientists to justify their basis for the science of belief, for their image of God.

The lack of self-reflection in scientific method has exposed it to religious resurgence. This unreflective behavior is visible even to the unschooled in the simplifications necessary to solve real world problems as well as in the conflict that arises between tactical human interests and the rest of the biosphere. Such issues bring us back to the question of what social fabric will support environmentalism.

A corollary, in Vico's terms, to the preceding paragraph addresses how Western art values speed. Shakespeare, for example, used the iamb, or swift foot. And Achilles is swift of foot and wins by speed, chasing Hector until he is forced to turn and face his enemy.

Separation of human and non-human activity is central to humanity's definition of itself, since we see ourselves as the measure of all (as opposed to one measure in response to a deity who controls all, paying lip service to free will). "Because of the senses, the human mind naturally tends to view itself externally in the body, and it is only with great difficulty that it can understand itself by means of reflection." Compare Vico's formulation to Descartes' "*cogito ergo sum*"—Vico was in active conflict with Descartes and his school throughout his career. And his theory of language is pre-romantic in that "words are transferred from physical objects and their properties to dignify what is conceptual and spiritual" (not Saussure or Chomsky).

"People first feel things without noticing them then notice them with inner distress and disturbance, and finally reflect on them with a clear mind." Vico is so often right in his observation that a great effort must be made to find out what can be taken from him without error and what is merely attractive emotionally.

"Eminent domain was assigned to the ruling order itself, which constitutes the lordship or sovereign power, in aristocracies." This is a statement about ecosystems, too, and why, along with the issue of time in environmentalism, I bring Vico into this discussion.

To review a list of possible social orders that can conform to environmental distress along the lines of Thompson's thinking would be useful. But I'd suggest that the complexity of change makes the social order not only unpredictable but oriented to the climate of the age.

Autocracy in the heat and liberty in the cold are likely divisions of government and, not surprisingly, conform to what we see today. If global warming is the result, great social constraints are likely to occur to protect against unpredictable environmental change. Vico's archetypes are not so alien after all.

(E)Valuation in Poetry: Sequence and Geometry

> I admit that two times two makes four is an excellent thing, but if we are to give everything its due, two times two makes five is sometimes a very charming thing too.
> —Fyodor Dostoevsky, *Notes from the Underground*

Culture's hierarchy for evaluating poetry helps distinguish one poem, one poet, and one poetic from another, but it is frequently misused to apply morality to judgments about poetry. For example, we have all heard people say that a poem is good because they like it. And there are more sophisticated versions of this approach. Some kinds of hierarchy can support environmentalism while others bias our judgment. This essay explores one tool for developing a non-evaluative hierarchy that builds cultural, social and biological structures with geometry.

One way to discuss evaluation in terms of environmental poetics, terms that do not predict the superiority of one poetry or another, is suggested by Ron Atkin's 1979 book, *Multidimensional Man: Can man live in a 3-dimensional space?* Atkin, a mathematician focused on communication, provides a common method to evaluate arts, sciences and politics by shaping their relationships into a geometry using set theory. A set is defined by a group of items that are included within it. For example plants, shrubs, and grass are all components within the garden set.

Or let's call set #1 a series of points in our geometry, and points have zero dimensions. At set two are lines, a single dimension. Above, at levels three and four, are two-dimensional planes and then volumes. Each level includes the prior one. We can understand this number of dimensions readily from our three dimensional perspective. We can even intuitively grasp four dimensions, but beyond that, at levels five, six, and beyond, we have difficulty traveling directly to those ideas. And Atkin claims such a model is pretty close to the way physicists really think about multiple dimensions.

Atkin's approach shows how it is easy to understand an idea if it is on the same level (dimension) as your ability to comprehend it, but difficult if the idea to be understood is part of a more inclusive set than your understanding. We can have, for example, understanding of letters and punctuation that doesn't enable us to fully understand words and grammar. We have to gain understanding of words in other ways such as speech. Knowing the definitions of words in a lexicon does not really allow us to understand written phrases and themes or poems or groups of poets. We need to slowly build up that understanding through a process of experience and other ways of learning.

Modeling poetry can be accomplished in many ways. Atkin suggests an approach to Shakespeare's sonnets and plays that I invite the reader to peruse in his book. But let me take his ideas of art, which are somewhat aestheticized and overly emphasize the individual, and bring them into environmental poetics.

Atkin points out an important idea that I want to develop later in this essay. Modeling with sets doesn't necessarily make poetry accurately understood beyond a limited range. To distinguish a more inclusive set like poetics from the set that includes only poems, we can expect probabilistic results rather than single value solutions. And any attempt to fix the poetic value from the specific poem may fall within the range of those probabilistic results but will certainly not be the only answer. It will take a bit of patience to get there, but we must become accustomed to operating with these ranges of value in results. So let us start to model a poem using q-analysis:

At Level 1: There are marks on the page, letters, punctuation, and numbers. These are the zero dimension, like points in space. We might build a poem out them alone. As an individual the poem composed from these materials alone would be a rather simple structure, but as P. Inman has shown, it can be artistically powerful.
Level 2: In the first dimension, phonemes and morphemes of language appear. Inman has also written with primarily these materials.
Level 3: Next, words appear, and we have the grammar and other rules that hold them together. Remember the example from Bruce Andrews.
Level 4: The third dimension contains those words from level 3 built into phrases and sentences according to the rules of grammar from level 3. These phrases also imply themes. Note how combining materials from one dimension improves comprehension of the next dimension.
Level 5: The fourth dimension contains forms such as stanzas, sonnets, and thematic arguments built from the materials of level 4.
Level 6: These forms, along with all the prior material, are put together into a fifth dimension that we can call poems.
Level 7: In the sixth dimension we have books of poetry, MP3 and other audio files, readings, broadsides, and other media for presenting single and multiple poems. It may include criticism of single authors.
Level 8: At the seventh dimension we have anthologies and other definitions of poetry. This dimension also includes criticism of multiple authors.
Level 9: At the eighth dimension we have reading interpretation and meta-theories about poetry, models of what creativity means and how poems are created.

Level 10: There is even a ninth dimension at which notions of creativity, the mind, and poetry's place in society and the world exist for groups of people each in their own culture.
Level 11: In the tenth dimension environmental poetics links poetry beyond human social structure to the non-human world, and defines a way for poetry to act as an environmental model.

The reader may find changing our view of poetry to this ten-dimensional one a bit shocking, but it helps us to look at poetry in the same way we look at the rest of the world. As we will see, in spite of the limitations of q-analysis, set theory models most structures and enables a geometry of communication to be drawn. Q-analysis as a communications theory also explains some of the difficulties in defining and identifying the creative process. Some of the complexities concerning why people write and the condition of the creative process exist at a very high level of abstraction. We in our three-dimensional world have difficulty traversing the levels upward beyond our own set in three dimensions to get an appropriate description of the poem in the 9th dimension.

We can understand probabilistically, but cannot do more than talk around the problem. While John Ashbery continues to want the creative process to contain the unknowable, pointing out the likelihood of probabilistic results is his strength. In support of our environmental model, in his 1993 article "By Indirection," he is unwilling to point to a single answer. As he says in the poem "Disbelief," "the birch stems might have been / painted in Vienna or by the Attersee." (See the internet for many articles on Ashbery and indirect address.) But there is a parallel dimension.

Atkin's q-analysis has been used by the Union of International Associations (UIA), an organization that seeks to support the idea of an international civil society. Solutions to some of the problems posed by environmental degradation appear in the UIA studies, but hope for implementing those solutions is dashed by complexity. In Atkin's terms, this means that the problems are in a higher dimension than the tools available to solve them.

According to the UIA website (http://www.uia.be/en/node/159?kap=59) for art "at the level within which it is possible to communicate, problems cannot necessarily be anchored unambiguously into terms and definitions which 'travel well.'" (And by travel is meant travel from one set, one dimension to a higher one.) Increased precision, i.e., dropping down one level in the hierarchy, introduces distortion, whereas more general concepts (inclusive such as Ashbery) are sometimes more accurate. This counter-intuition is acceptable locally, within a specific discipline, within any communicating society or niche.

If the background assumption changes or becomes dimensionally smaller, i.e., drops down one level by becoming more specific, communication is distorted. Distortion in communication has several values. It makes the stepwise formations of scientific or social engineering more difficult to execute. For example, read any computer manual to see how difficult it is to use language and avoid diffusion or assure that the reader can know what to do with each noun in the sentence.

But distortion, as noted in the research of Fredrick C. Bartlett, also generates images, forcing the mind to elide concepts. Bob Perelman's lines, for example, "Waves of impatience beat on conventional shores, waves of repression beat on the shores of light. Fact." quickly shuttle between conceptual levels creating an inter-dimensional machine. If done skillfully distortion generates enough energy to propel the reader upward to a more inclusive dimension, promoting and understanding that otherwise, as here in this prose, would be laborious.

The difficulty of communicating insights across dimensional boundaries as expressed in Atkin's work, a condition determined by uncertain results, has driven several important theoretical environmentalists to assume that people with our assumptions will not be able to address environmental degradation in a meaningful way. We'd do better to let it play out on its own rather than risk making the situation worse with our efforts. The recent fiasco with bio-fuels in the U.S., for example, has driven up global agricultural prices.

The conflicts are ameliorated by environmental poetics and its acceptance of probabilistic results. The differences in understanding that Atkin ascribes to any innovation do not mean that a general sense of communication, with its loose coupling of theory and practice, does not exist. Ideas change when they are communicated from person to person and also change for an individual over time. And the set of relations between those individuals, and even the faulty memory of an individual, continues to be replicated in complex domains. But although the desire for new ideas to be understood in the same way by many individuals over time has not been fulfilled, it was not a reasonable expectation. Not all events are amenable to being described by inclusive sets.

A hurricane's path is unpredictable, but we can predict a range of coastline where it will land. We can even predict a range of solutions when hurricanes dissipate. That range of locations changes and must be recalculated frequently, but this doesn't mean that the hurricane will not hit the coast. Even though the solution is at a more abstract level than our analysis, the fact that we can come up with only probabilistic solutions to its landing site does not deter us from protecting against it. The variability of solutions to any complex problem is characteristic of these problems when communication across dimensions results in probabilistic rather than single value solutions. The expectation of more than similarity among constituents is again unrealistic.

Communication according to Atkin is bound to a specific level of a system. Going down produces distortion and going up produces multiple answers.

> There is consequently a multiplicity of concepts of development operative in society. Individuals and groups may 'progress' from one [dimension] to another, possibly with a general tendency towards those of higher connectivity. But other individuals and groups will emerge and find the concepts of lower connectivity more meaningful before moving on, if they do, to those of higher connectivity. (In this sense the 'ontogenesis' of an individual tends to repeat the 'phylogenesis' of his/her society). Society in this sense is the arena within which individuals and groups refine their concept of development.

The world exists, interacting with us and its other components, and our skepticism does not make the world go away. The only effort we must make is to ensure that it doesn't make us go away. This challenge propels us to develop methods to understand higher dimensions. Poetry, by its ability to ascend rapidly and comprehensibly, is one tool. Theory, at a more inclusive dimension, contains and makes the issue more extensible but is slower to achieve results.

**

Here is another construction of environmental poetics using Ron Atkin's q-analysis. The following group of sets is isomorphic to the structure I have just outlined for poetry and poetics, and shows, by extending the scope of a problem, another way to link components in our picture of the world. It's a bit complex, so read patiently.

According to Darwin, the individual organism in its relationship to its surroundings is the primary carrier of diversity and continuity in that they are differentiated in form and pass on the common genetic material. Darwin's finch beaks, studied in the Galapagos, become longer or shorter as a result of their connection to the amount of rainfall. So Atkin's N-level might best be filled by individual organisms and the different kinds of connections they have to their surroundings. At that level are not just humans but also most of the animal and plant kingdoms.

But is the individual the key container of transmissible meaning in all species as our contemporary culture would have us believe? In the first place the individual alone does not make change happen. As discussed in the essay on Goodwin, the interactions of organisms and ecosystems drive change in the gene pool. And that gene pool cannot effectively reproduce without the organism as a model. Second, in species such as fungi, rhizoid plants, bacteria, Archea, and other life forms that do not reproduce sexually, the individual does not have the function or importance. (Archea is one of main domains of life. They are ancient bacteria that emerged in earth's earliest days and are quite different from the rest of life on the planet, sharing only 11% of its genes with other living organisms. They inhabit extreme climates and may be understood as a link between eubacteria and eukaryotes. Because they lack nuclei, their cells may be able to exchange genetic material across species and even domain lines.)

I suspect that so long as genetic material is shared between the genders of the organism, the individual and its ecosystem is the relevant container. In non-sexual reproduction, the colony or even the entire species could be the primary (N-level) container. An even wider net can be thrown around Archaean organisms. Archea exchange genetic material across what would otherwise be deemed to be species lines, and perhaps even horizontally to Eukaryotes (cells with nuclei such as e Coli resulting in virulent pathogens). The exchange of genetic material from one kingdom to another is one way that animal cells may have been enabled to metabolize oxygen when bacteria invaded Eukaryotic cells to form mitochondria. (Margulis) Fungi reproduce by spores that are external to the organism and extend their domain via mycelium.

So in many species the individual's value is not clearly defined. Therefore, for certain life forms, the individual organism is at the N-level and for others the colony of individuals, the species for some life forms, and for Archea, perhaps the entire kingdom, at least for continuity and sustainability resides at the N-level.

At the N-Level we also must place the cultural artifacts developed by each entity. Poems are written by individual people; individual beavers make dams; and groups of non-sexually reproducing plants group together to make stromatolites.

For species that use sexual reproduction then at the N+1-level would be the group, family, or colonies and hives of individuals. At N+1-level, too, would be groupings beyond a single species like symbiotes making up lichen, business corporations, or schools of poets. In addition at this N+1-level we have the kinds of relationships that are built between the symbiotes and the teams of workers. Emergent properties would begin to occur at this level. These relationships that generate emergent properties can be either affinities, such as common job title, processes, like accounting, or theories like environmental poetics.

But there are more than things. We must add the cultural mechanisms that link them. The inspiration for poems, for example, can be filtered down to the individual level where they are written. The social condition of ants and bees resides at this level. Family culture develops at this level for all sexually reproducing species.

At the N+2-level then, for species using sexual reproduction would be larger human and non-human constructions, still within the species domains. For species using non-sexual reproduction, the N+2-level might be sum of a species in a certain region, for example, various organisms that support the infrastructure of a coral reef or all the bacteria in your gut. Beyond species are the various niches—towns, forests, entire reefs, and fields of plants cultivated by humans. The affinities and processes that relate these entities are also resident at N+2. And to those affinities and processes, we can add institutions such as governments, town councils, corporate trade groups, artist colonies where different groups of artists come together, usually in parallel but some times in collaboration.

Human and non-human niches link up as regions at the N+3-level. At this level on the political front we see entities like counties with their institutions. We also have larger regions of biological affinity like ecosystems, which if you remember we have already defined as a unit of relationship. Regional writing styles develop like the San Francisco Renaissance. At the N+4-level we have states and provinces with their institutions, then at the N+5-level we see nations, but we also see larger domains like the EU which is a group of nations that has synthesized a colony for various perceived advantages. Here, as at the N-Level, not all levels should be populated by the same kind of representatives. And at this level of non-human organization we have large areas like continents, climate zones, and national cultures like patriotism.

At the N+6-Level we would like to establish a global awareness that goes beyond the globalization of the controlled by major corporations and other large interest groups. We would then see migration of workers to best work locations, fair trade practices between countries, and the emergence of a global culture with similar and divergent tendencies.

Below the N-level of the individual, at the N-1-level, we have the awareness and other characteristics of the individual that support the generation of connectivity. Consciousness in humans generates the interaction with the external world to create a cultural artifact like a poem. For species where self-awareness is not apparent to us, we can ascribe other relationships that the individual, as a result of its internal complexity, has to itself. These may include its awareness of the outside world, perception, or other interactive, cognitive functions that are established by internal relationships such as dam building capabilities in beavers where the relationships among the beavers various organs enables their skill. This level doesn't contain the dam itself, but the skill that resides within the individual. And we may then include human consciousness as one kind of relationship that the individual organism has to itself. The interactions that other species have within themselves may also be called self-consciousness, although such assertions make many people anxious or even fractious.

At the N-2-level we have inter-individual consciousness such as is found in the bee hive, the wolf pack, or in humans a cultural group or even species awareness. This level is vital to understand for the cultural component of our environment. For it is here that identity is formed for masses of individuals. The political problems resulting from clashes of cultures and religions arise from a poor understanding of how this level works. The failure to appreciate this level generates the misapprehension that the concept of poetry and of writing poetry resides within the individual. Q-analysis makes it apparent that the individual is not the creator of poetry, but only of poems and books of poems. For other animals and plants we have the structures of how these species interact internally, that is, the sum of their functions and their interfaces with the outside world that they share with others of the species. And interactions among these structures act for these species as self-awareness does for humans.

(Note: Defining self-awareness as one kind of relationship that the individual has to itself does not, in my view, imply that these relationships are things. They are nouns, to be sure, but we speak here of a thing where there is no object that we can point to point to. These concepts, if materialized, lead us astray into spiritualism. They establish cul-de-sacs that require further metaphors that take on a life of their own, leading us further and further from the traceable realities. As a metaphor has its own logic, we may be encouraged to follow it, rather than return to the logic of the event in which we are engaged or the problem we seek to solve. I repeat this caveat because we have been so often led astray by our metaphors that I insist (probably because I can see no other approach) that if we use metaphor responsibly and sustainably we will tend to return to the logic of the problem or event that we are addressing. If we seek not to return, we do so with awareness of the risks we are taking and these experiments have produced interesting and important results. (I have discussed this elsewhere in relation to Dada. We may point to a loss of emotional content in these returns, and I probably need to address that issue as well.) In the cultural model, we return to the logic of the poem or dance in order to proceed with the work and thereby retain the good faith of our readers and audiences. In solving environmental problems, we must seek to avoid adopting an idea simply because it is in our self-interest, although self-interest needs to be considered and prioritized.)

As we go on we can draw a geometry, like Atkin's, that links humanity and non-human nature. The geometry links the individual and its various affinity groups both among individuals and within the individual. It shows where we are separated by gulfs that are difficult to traverse and where communication can be achieved. In doing so we can start to see the ways we can reconstruct our society to work in a way that helps us to solve for environmental complexity.

Detouring for a bit, one of the key factors that I noticed in constructing the paragraphs above is that the sets represented by the various N-levels have different categories of things for different species. What represents the individual level (N-level) for humans and other sexually-reproducing species may be the colony level for bacteria or fungi. The organism is not the model of self for all species. If addressed at the cultural level, we may write about ideas in the same way as species that do not reproduce sexually. Ideas do not exist alone as archetypes, but as components of an ecosystem, a unit of relationship. We will, as pointed out above, need to continually return to the problem we are seeking to solve, rather than following the logic of the metaphor, but we are able to address ideas and other mental constructs as part of our q-analysis of the environment.

In the political world, for example, the introduction of new classes threatens the hegemony of old classes. The Roman Civil War was fought to suppress rising equestrian power but as the senatorial class ultimately lost, the empire was extended by many hundreds of years by this rising class. In today's politics, the classes have recently reformed suppressing all others in favor of corporate management. Here the introduction of highly functional individuals is aided by the rhetoric of economic freedom and an appeal to traditional values. Until the society as a whole actually pushes back and retakes control of resources that have been ceded to the oligarchy, the corporate leadership will continue to dominate and control vastly more resources than they need to perform their functions within the economic environment. Biological metaphor that cross boundaries facilitates understanding as opposed to thinking only within the frame of the argument that currently rages in western societies.

This imbalance created by the dominance of one class, one country, one species precipitates misuse of those resources. The consequent pollution and degradation of the environment is a direct result of unmediated power at the N+2 level. In Atkin's model, the lack of communication from the individual N-level up to the N+2-level is the structural reason why the industrialists cannot be the instrument of their own change. The lack of cultural connection that enables movement upward of ideas in the hierarchy means that good ideas from individuals, that would be useful to the oligarchs are seen as threats because they change, for example, how energy is generated and consumed. Because they are at the same level, the oligarchs equate this change emotionally with threats to their power and hence suppress changes that would enable them to keep their power. If corporations and governments do not embrace environmental change, it will destroy them. If they accept and co-opt it, we may move into the environmental age with the power structure intact. In a practical way, we could wish for a more universal control of these new methods and resources, or we could build the N+2 institutions parallel to the existing ones that can take us into the environmental model of society.

In the cultural world, change is continuous but culture tends to support the class that pays for it. If we accept that culture encompasses more than the tastes and manners of our civilization, we can define culture as an ecosystem that includes our knowledge and our behaviors. Such a definition allows us to operate within the culture in a way that supports nature as well as the classes supporting that culture. In this case all classes support this broader definition of culture. And we can apply these analytic tools to help with cultural change, as we have with social change, to define culture in an environmental way. We can see where we are like and where unlike other species. For example, we have seen that at the primary level (N-level), which for humans is the organism, there are many kinds of life which do not support the organism at that primary level such as fungi, all Archea, and all common bacteria. In another example we see affinities that can be culturally exploited, as they often are, between human colonies and ants or bees.

The ability to represent common features and diverse structures for culture allows us to describe the knowledge and behavior of other species, too, and thereby create alliances that were heretofore threats. Wolf behavior displays well-documented affinities with human culture, so many in fact that I wonder if the fear of wolves includes fear of ourselves, the knowledge of our own fearsomeness.

Another example is lichen, a combination of a fungus and algae. Reproduction of the lichen is entirely asexual. It may occur by soredia, spore-like structures, composed of alga cells and hyphae that are formed from the algal layer and become exposed when the cortex ruptures. The other means of asexual reproduction is by isidia, columnar to swollen structures that are part of the lichen thallus that are likely to break off to form new lichens. Ascospores and conidia also form, but these will only reproduce the fungus. It is assumed that these structures will come in contact with a suitable algal host and resynthesis the lichen thallus. Pictures of these methods of reproduction can be seen at:
http://www.botany.hawaii.edu/faculty/wong/BOT135/Lect26.htm.

Since lichen (multiple organisms) reproduces asexually, we can place them at the N-level. If individual lichen can reproduce in these ways, can we identify the methods of culture creation in the same diverse manner? Does imagination now take on a different texture as a method of reproduction of the artist, rather than a creation out of the deity-inspired spirit of the artist? Treating this chimera as an individual, like a centaur or lichen, makes it possible to accept or even promote extensions of individual activities.

The changes to our understanding of nature in culture will provide us with new approaches to environmental problem solving. I don't want to take a good thing too far, but can I suggest that the knowledge and behavior of other species can be acceptable as culture to our culture? That is, we can surely include within or add other cultures to our own and thereby value it the more. In this statement I don't want to ally this essay with animal rights advocates. I'm suggesting here simply that linking ideas can be understood in a way that is similar to the interaction of multiple genetic structures to produce an effective technique for survival or even a novel result. The various ways that art links its materials can and should be explored as natural processes.

As an example of these kinds of connections, in his *Dialogues Concerning Two New Sciences* Galileo writes a pair of sentences that exemplify this kind of productive cultural diversity. In these sentences Salviati, the character in the dialogue representing Galileo's position, links two concepts that even today are separated widely by taxonomy.

> Yet if we wish to build up a line out of indivisible points, we must take an infinite number of them, and are, therefore, bound to understand both the infinite and the indivisible at the same time. Many ideas have passed through my mind concerning this subject, some of which, possibly the more important, I may not be able to recall on the spur of the moment; but in the course of our discussion it may happen that I shall awaken in you, and especially in Simplicio, objections and difficulties which in turn will bring to memory that which, without such stimulus, would have lain dormant in my mind.

Several of the issues raised in this essay are highlighted in these two sentences. First, it is an example of the reproductive capacity of ideas. By juxtaposition (a contemporary poet might call it narrative), Galileo identifies the social structure of mathematics. It is not the story of a person, but a biological interaction of ideas. Second, it is a linking of thoughts, presumably conceived by one individual, that support how two individuals can participate in the same cognitive process. This chimera, or symbiosis, seems to me to be one of the key mechanisms for environmentalism to become an effective method of change and securing our future. Acceptance of the other is driven by necessity. That which we most fear may in the last resort be the support we seek. Finally, I'd like to point out how a cultural view of nature can overcome the difficulties of moving between Atkin's N-levels, undermining unnecessary hierarchy and expanding the possibilities of communicating upward to those highly functional individuals who continue, in the name of freedom, to avoid the collaborative possibilities of human interaction.

**

The risk of simplifying levels in order to assure easy communication in Atkin's terms is as great as the risks of entrepreneurial adventurism, reliance on market wisdom, or the oppression of taxonomy. Simplification sets us on a dangerous path.

We must establish another distinction between the different kinds of barriers: some limitations don't kill; some limitations don't breathe. In biology there are impermeable, permeable, and semi-permeable membranes. In poetry we have a variety of linkages at different levels or sets, as just described. There are linkages of grammar, such as punctuation and conjunction; of rhetoric, such as changing modes or genres; of form, such as stanzas or field poetry that equates space on the page with time.

But we also can say that making distinctions is a bid for control of the discourse. When the distinctions expand the possibilities, we get a sense of accomplishment, such as with Dada or Futurism. When the distinctions limit the possibilities, we use technique to provide an aesthetic experience. But can we be sure which is which? To postulate a formal poetry—sonnets, sestinas, odes—is to open the possibilities of form, but doesn't that reduce the possibility of less restrictive form, simplifying form and eliminating more complex forms, organic forms, and integral forms? To postulate a multi-dimensional poetry is both inclusive and allows us to evaluate the results by structuring how the poetry is constructed with q-analysis. Here we have both a method and a value system that go beyond moral judgments.

In freeing itself from the architecture of rhyme and meter, the separation of form and content, modernism gave us a mystical notion of artistic freedom, and we have not yet clearly replaced that mystical notion with a more material set of distinctions. Atkin's approach shows us how to locate these issues in our geometry of poetry. Can we say that the idea of freedom in modernism is linked to the freedom that promoted the warrior class of the 20th century, the entrepreneurs and capitalists? What have we been freed to do? Exclude form? Establish more complex forms? Modify grammar for context? We can do all that but only if the culture opens wide enough to accept changes in the infrastructure of literature in the same way it accepts financial engineering or nation building. These freedoms are important when they are thought of as analogies to political, social, artistic, and scientific spheres and the changes in our grammar of knowledge, changes of dimension that create value.

Environmental Parallels Poem

Many	some	other	same
Are	is	were	same
Some	one	other	that
Of	with	in	to
Republican	Hermit	Mullah	Kevin
Negotiate	separate	leap upon	implant
These	those	their	her
Mental Health Programs	cherry	casino	reports of Jesus & Elvis.

Dangerous	reliable	brilliant	naked
Australian	pituitary	cardamom	covers
Covers	produce	invade	eats
China	psychometric	formal	spam
Injured	analytic	precaution	tummy
Women's wear	scientific methods	centurion	frog.

Many	one	few	both
Collect	are	link	scorch
Remarkable	mostly	the	an
Ways	wallpaper	impending	bookstore
Of	for	renaissance	before
Fish	League of Nations	creativity	diaspora
But	nevertheless	in spite of	however
Only	none other than	just	in addition to
Awakening	One	Two	Three
The	its	your	potential
Savannah	pork	performance	ages

Coda:
Q-analysis shows how writing is structured and why it is difficult to understand its process. The environmental model of poetry in ten dimensions reveals the "artistry" (risk-taking) rather than the "mystique" with its shady implications that remains part of our practice. Environmental poetics seeks not to be proven, but put into practice in order to reveal what can be accomplished with it. Dissimilar in the matter of proof environmental poetics is similar to 'hard' science in that it is satisfied with description as explanation. (Gertrude Stein extends description into the process of writing in her concept of "Composition as Explanation.")

Where do these ideas come from? Atkin points to work done from 1350 to 1370 at Merton College, Oxford, by Thomas Bradwardine, William Heytesbury, and Richard Swineshead that made a clear distinction between hard and soft science. Hard science needs only a description quite independent of the idea of its "cause," whereas soft science combines description with ideas of forces. (William of Occam even went so far as to assert that causation was irrelevant and that only description was needed to explain the motion of any body.)

Solving our complex environmental problems is a practice (in the way Stein means composition) as well as a description: a model and a language like an organism and its genetic code. Environmental poetics is in this sense soft science and hard poetry, because the materials engage the model. If we begin to execute, we will start to go somewhere. The risks must be continually assessed, and the struggle may have dire consequences. (I'd like talk later about risk management as a poetic activity.) But by continuing in our current manner, we will not survive.

Here are some of the processes we can engage:
1. Adapt approaches from other spheres, such as political, social, or family life, and incorporate them into writing;
2. Create model issues, emotional or political, from given or existing texts or from textual considerations (various identity-based poetries);
3. Find the issue in (during) the act of composition (Stein's composition as explanation);
4. Claim to write without respect to issues but with respect to alignment of the writing with a spirit spoken of but not pointed to with any demonstrative adjective (purist).
This list is limited only by poets' imaginations, and this is where ideas like imagination can be placed.

While these methods create niches for their practitioners, they all seek to establish a distinct value for their particular strategy. As value is created the process becomes fixed and more at risk. There is some historical precedent, although I wouldn't suggest that this list is a complete model:

> The title of distinction reacheth verie far, bycause it conteineth all those characts, and the vuses, which I called before signifying, but not sounding, which help verie much, naie all in all to the right and tunable vttering of our words and sentences, by help of these characts, which we set down, and se in writing. The number of them be thirtene, and their names be Comma, Colon, Period, Parenthesis, Interogation, long time, shorte time, sharp accent, flat accent, streight accent, the seuerer, the uniter, the breaker. (Richard Mulcaster, *Elementarie,* "Of Distinction," 1582)

To use a modern standard, the first set of distinctions (Comma, Colon…), being current, are in question, while the second set of distinctions (long time, shorte time…), even though some have fallen into disuse, are assumed as grammar in poetics. And using Atkin's approach, we can take this kind of structuring further to include romantic imagination, modernist linkages of form and content, and language writing's inclinations toward technique.

As we establish these restrictions in the name of environmental poetics, I feel the need to address liberal ideas of individual freedom as postulated by the liberals of the eighteenth century and by contemporary consumer culture. The craving for freedom in poetry and politics has led to questioning grammar and its uses, even to claiming grammar as one of the agencies of state control that poets would rather have more flexible.

> Present-day conceptions of 'correctness' are to a large extent based on the notion, prominent in the 18th century, that language is of divine origin and hence was perfect in its beginnings but is constantly in danger of corruption and decay unless it is diligently kept in line by wise men who are able to get themselves accepted as authorities, such as those who write dictionaries and grammars. Latin was regarded as having retained much of its original 'perfection.'... When English grammars came to be written, they were based on Latin grammar, even down to the terminology... The most important 18th century development in the English language was its conscious regulation by those who were not really qualified for the job, but who managed to acquire authority as linguistic gurus.
> (Thomas Pyles and John Algeo, *The Origins and Development of the English Language*, 1982).

At the same time that we are questioning grammar, environmental poetics asserts the importance of one view of problems over another and creates a new grammar of ideas. Some kind of grammar or language infrastructure albeit flexible is required from the poem to push against. Otherwise it quickly becomes structureless and does not match to the grammars in our brain or elsewhere in nature. Although environmentalism may question liberalism and consumerism, it is primarily moving boundaries rather than building new ones.

Appendix A: How Language Writing Got Its Period

Poetic theories develop out of choices and assumptions that are neither arbitrary nor inevitable. The Language poets made particular assumptions about the properties and conventions of poetry and its texts that have led to one of the most successful theories to have recently emerged in literature. They posited that the major phenomenon of poetry that needs to be accounted for is the adaptation of poetry to the larger language environment. The effect of language on poetry, especially changes in poetry fashions, was explained in terms of the political affiliations of the poets. No aspect of human life has escaped Language writing theory, modified in various ways to apply to politics, economics, the history of ideas, science, philosophy, and even the other arts.

All theories, however, carry with them a particular viewpoint, a way of seeing phenomena that produces a sharp focus on certain aspects of reality and blurred vision elsewhere. A striking paradox that has emerged from Language writing's way of approaching poetic issues is that poems, which we take to be primary components of the textual environment, have faded away to the point where they no longer exist as fundamental and irreducible units of our art. Much innovative poetry has replaced poems as the central element of poetry with the components of poems. What's more, there is no lack of highly persuasive books whose objective is to demonstrate why poems are not what they seem to be—integrated entities with existence and nature of their own—but complex language machines controlled by the linguistic components carried within them, bearers of the historical record of the literary tendency to which the organism belongs. Though this is certainly not what was anticipated, this is in fact the sharp focus that has developed from the theoretical assumptions of Language Poets about the nature of language, and there is no denying the remarkable insights that have accompanied this illumination of the component level of poems.

There is always a price to pay for excessive preoccupation with one aspect of reality. Contemporary poetry has come to occupy an extreme position in the spectrum of the arts, dominated by political explanations in terms of the development of linguistic properties and an associated single-level polemic reductionism to linguistic products. Visual arts, on the other hand, have developed explanations of different levels of reality, expressive and photographic, in terms of theories appropriate to these levels, such as abstract expressionism for the behavior of mind and minimalism for the behavior of seeing. Even in the presence of New Criticism as a theory of poems as distinctive entities in their own right, with a characteristic type of dynamic order and organization, the rise of Language writing has resulted in the poem's fading (if not disappearance) from the basic conceptual structure of contemporary literature. Poems have succumbed to the onslaught of an overwhelming linguistic reductionism just as organisms have disappeared from mainstream biological thought. They too have succumbed to the onslaught of an overwhelming linguistic reductionism.

Here we face another curious consequence of new writing's way of looking at poetry: despite the power of language-centered poetry to reveal the grammatical essence of poems, the large-scale aspects of literature remain unexplained, including the value of poetry. There is "no clear evidence...for the gradual emergence of any new poetics," says one of the most eminent of the contemporary Language poets. "New poetries simply appear upon the poetry scene, persist for various periods of time, and then become graduate studies." So Language writing's assumption that the changes to reading, poetic styles, and schools in the political / linguistic environment is a consequence of the differences in poets' political assumptions and reading of prior poetries appears to be without significant support. Some other process is responsible for the emergent properties of a poetic tendency, those distinctive features that separate one group of poets from another—New York School and Beat, San Francisco and Black Mountain, Iowa and other identity poetics. Clearly something is missing from this poetry in that it is not capturing the attention of major media reviewers and readers outside the poets and graduate students who make it their business. (The Language poets' explanation that the reviewers' own political and economic affiliations prevent them from seeing or revealing the truth of the matter is too potentially self-serving to act as proof even to the extent that it is true.) It appears that Language writing theory works for the small-scale aspects of poetry: it can explain the variations and adaptations within a single writer that produce a style. The large-scale difference of form between the groups of writers that are the foundation of literary classification systems seem to require another principle than language writing operating on small variations, some process that gives rise to distinctly different forms of poetry. This is the problem of emergent order in literature, the origins of the novel or the sonnet, which has always been one of the primary foci of attention in literature.

It is here that new theories, themselves recently emerged within mathematics and physics, offer significant insights into the origins of poetic order and form. Whereas physicists have traditionally dealt with "simple" systems in the sense that they are made of few *types* of components, and observed macroscopic (large-scale) order is then explained in terms of uniform interactions between these components, poets deal with systems (languages and grammars) that are hideously complex, with thousands of different types of linguistic structures from different uses of language from poems to ball park insults all interacting in different ways. Or so it seems on the linguistic / grammatical level. However, what is being recognized within the "sciences of complexity" as studies of these highly diverse systems are called, is that there *are* characteristic types of order that emerge from the interactions of many different components. And the reason is not unlike what happens in "simple" physical systems. Despite the extreme diversity of prosodies, their interactions are limited, so that distinctive types of order arise, especially in relation to the large-scale aspects of structure or morphology (sonnet, ode, haiku), and the patterns over time that constitute poetic tropes and genres which are distinctive (epic, lyric, formal experiment). A particularly striking property of these complex systems is that chaotic behavior at one level of activity—random words selected from the dictionary—can give rise to distinctive order at the next level—morphology, phonemics, or conceptualization. (For example, experiments by Bernstein and myself with the 100 most common English language words show how recognizable and identifiable meaning arises from seemingly random intentions.) This has resulted in one of the primary refrains of complex studies: order emerges out of chaos. The source of large scale order in poetry may therefore be located in a distinctive type of complexity that can be described in terms of the computational capacity of the interacting components rather than their dynamic behavior. These terms, computational and dynamic, actually reflect different emphases and are not in conflict with one another, although prior theories of literature and art have attempted to make a big deal of the distinction to validate artistic epistemology in opposition to the history of science. What has developed from the widespread use of computers to explore the dynamic potential of interacting systems that can process information, such as textual analysis, is a new theory of dynamic systems collectively referred to as the sciences of complexity, from which have developed significant branches of science and art such as digital poetries.

In this book I explore the consequences of these ideas as they apply to our understanding of the emergence of form in poetry, particularly the origin and nature of morphological characteristics that distinguish different types or genres of writing. These questions overlap those addressed by Language poets, but they focus on the large-scale, or global, aspects of poetic form rather than small-scale, local adaptations such as Projective Verse or New Sentences. As a result there is no necessary conflict between the approaches. Neither is there conflict with the insights of modern poetry at the "molecular" levels of poems. These contribute to the construction of dynamic theories from which emerge higher-level properties of poetic form and the integrated behavior of poems. Conflict arises only when there is confusion over what constitutes poetic reality, and this has historically been the basis of battles among poets. I take the position that poems are as real, as fundamental, and as irreducible as the components out of which they are made and the larger systems which they feed. They are a distinct level of emergent literary order, and the one to which we most immediately relate.

The recognition of the fundamental nature of poems, connecting directly with our own natures as irreducible beings (which Language writing and its cultural precursors in Post-Structuralism have brought into question), has significant consequences regarding our attitude toward the literary realm.

It is here that another aspect of poetic theory comes to the fore, one that is often regarded as secondary to the cultural realities poetry uncovers. Language writing, like all theories, has distinct political associations that are familiar from the use of terms such as poetic production, economies of poetry, instrumentality. Such political references are extremely important. They give meaning to poetic theories, and they encourage particular attitudes to the processes described—in the case of Language writing, to the nature of the poetic process predominantly driven by competitive political processes, linguistic fragmentation, political economy, and alienation. This makes sense to us in terms of our experience of our wider culture and its values. Both culture and nature then become rooted in similar ways of seeing the world, which are shaped at a deeper level than politics, by the cultural myths from which the politics arise. The consequences of this perspective have emerged particularly clearly in the post-war period, especially in view of Language writing's significant contribution to prosody, poems as socially constituted collections of prosodic components: technique as content. The criterion of value here is purely functional: either poetry styles work or they don't. They have no intrinsic value.

I shall argue that this view of styles or schools of poetry arises from Language writing's limited and inadequate view of the nature of poems, a too literal understanding of prior writing as a set of signs with their political "l=u=g=g=a=g=e". The sciences of complexity lead to the construction of a dynamic theory of poems as the primary source of emergent properties of poetry that have been revealed throughout literary history, the interaction of one frame of reference with another and the cross pollination of genres of situation, writing, and thought. These properties are generated during the process of writing the poem, the development of the complex form of the completed poem from simple beginnings such as an experience or a quotation from another writer. During the writing process, emergent order is generated by distinctive types of dynamic process in which the linguistic components and social dynamics of the author's condition play a significant but limited role. The act of writing and the life of the writer are sources of emergent literary properties, and it is the absence of a theory of its outcome, poems, that includes this basic generative process that has resulted in both the disappearance of poems from poetry and the failure to account for the origin of the emergent characteristics that identify poems and styles. Many people have recognized this limitation of Language-centered poetics, and my own arguments are utterly dependent on their demonstration of the path to a more balanced poetry. None of these critics to my knowledge have been able to present any significant new alternative, but only hearkened back to other extremities, such as Modernism, Romanticism, or Classicism, that now seem tame by comparison. And as a result the fragmented poetries of the post-war period have been viewed as competing in a

Darwinian set of graduate courses, poetry series, and grumbled asides which have limited poetry to a series of cults. No one has reestablished the poem as the dynamic vehicle of literary emergence now that the poem has been extended beyond its limited New Criticism definition. Once this extended poem is included in a view of the writing process, the focus shifts from the competitive economics of poetry production to creative emergence as the central quality of the evolutionary process of poetry. Because poems are the primary loci of this distinctive quality of poetry, they become again the fundamental units of poetry, as they were for pre-Modernist poetries. Signs and methodology continue to play significant roles in this expanded poetry, but they become parts of a more comprehensive dynamical theory of poetry that is focused on the dynamics of emergent process.

The consequences of this altered perspective are considerable, particularly in relation to the status of poems, their creative potential, and the qualities of poetry for the reader. Poems cease to be mere commodities packaged for consumption and assume an intrinsic value, having worth in and out of themselves, like organisms. Such a realization arises from an altered understanding of the nature of poems as centers of meaning both lexical and grammatical, connected with a causal agency that cannot be described as mechanical or merely the sum of its parts. It is relational order among components, which Language poets have mostly left to genre, automatic mental processes, or a fixed algorithm, that matters as much as phonemic particles in poetic processes, so that emergent qualities can be described as well as quantities. This consequence extends to social structure, where relationships and values are of primary significance. As a result, values enter fundamentally into the appreciation of the nature of writing, and poetry takes on the properties of a science of qualities. This is not in conflict with the art of quantities and evaluation, but it does have a different focus and emphasis. It is their combination which produces poetry.

Language writing criticizes the poetic process in terms that emphasize productivity, social Darwinism, and political process as the driving forces behind the creation of poetic intent. These are certainly aspects of the remarkable drama that includes our own poetry. But it is a very incomplete and limited story, both artistically and politically, based on an inadequate view of poems; and it invites us to act in a limited way as evolved writers in relation to the larger social and artistic environment, which includes other cultures and poetries. These limitations have contributed to some of the positive values of Language writing as well as the difficulties we now face with subjective *and* amorphous poetry emerging from the B-schools (Brown, Bard, Buffalo), decreasing standards of poetic intensity, and loss of communal values. But Language writing shortchanges our poetic aspirations. We are every bit as oriented to product as we are to process; as intent on content as on non-instrumental grammar and epistemologies. And we are poetically grounded in relationships, which operate at all the different levels of our beings, as the basis of our natures as agents of creative generativity, a property we share with all previous poetries. These are not romantic yearnings and poetic ideals. They arise from a rethinking of our poetic natures that is emerging from the sciences of complexity and is leading toward a poetry of qualities, which may help in our efforts to reach a more balanced relationship with other members of our potential readership.

**

The essay above is copied almost word-for-word from the introduction to Brian Goodwin's *How the Leopard Changed Its Spots*. With only about 100 word substitutions (largely nouns) a biology text becomes a poetry text. I invite you to read the original and compare their intentions and results. Another fruitful line of exploration compares poets' intentions and the obvious conclusion that humanity and nature share enough that poetry, even innovative poetry, participates in evolution and poems in biological processes.

Can scientific or artistic disciplines insist on their unique epistemological basis when there is so little separating their descriptions? Does the fact that this piece is written by word substitution from a subject related only by the fact that they are both linguistic systems invalidate its conclusions? Where does originality begin? What is requisite for validity or actuality? Do the apparent rationality of the discourse and reasonableness of its conclusions raise questions about the validity of the Goodwin piece, in that such a job can be done to it? Or does the fact that both systems can, with few modifications, be described in the same way say something about the validity of disciplinary distinctions in the arts and sciences? Can this experiment in substitution be used as a critique of exemplary writing, viz Gertrude Stein, or is it the proof that all human discourse is inevitably related, perhaps more than we in our *special* worlds would like to think? I suspect the latter to be the case.

Whether you agree with all the conclusions of this poetry/biology essay created by an unusual process is not critical. What I think we can agree upon is that the above is a credible essay, originated in one discipline and read in another. While you may agree with only some of the conclusions, the interpenetration or leaking across disciplinary boundaries has to be accepted not as an accidental phenomenon but as a result of the similarity of thought processes, structures, ideas, and conclusions in both disciplines.

Interpenetration (relations) occurs both intentionally and inadvertently as ideas cross in our minds. Interpenetration highlights the commonality of environmental structures of thought, language, and biosphere that make up human and non-human space. Although interpenetration will not be convincing for all texts, it will be true for environmentally related themes and I suspect any dynamic interaction. (See the discussion of exosymbiosis in "Tagmosis/Prosody (Extending Parataxis.) Such thinking is primarily a product of nouns, things and their relations to the rest of the text. In fact, humanity's relationship to things and the actions that result from those relationships are the central issues for changing the environment. Our focus today on what our actions with things will do for us is what must change. Some verbs will occupy the same dimension in various disciplines, but few modifiers.

Goodwin's work proposes values from complexity rather than linear thought approximating complexity. He describes the self-organizing composition of life. How far can we take this line of thinking? Arts and sciences have for generations, perhaps since Renaissance humanism, focused on differences to create value, but we will benefit now from paying attention to similarities in order to avoid divergent perceptions of conditions that are really the same. The environmental crisis demands such convergence. Yet since difference generates more immediate responses, it will be difficult to create a taxonomy in which both the immediate difference and the longer-term similarity can be accommodated.
1995

Book 3: Risk

Part 1: Business Process Interruption and Risk Homeostasis: Analysis for Technology Solutions to Regulatory Impact

> No fortress is so impregnable into which an ass laden with gold cannot make its way.
> —Juvenal

Last week I forwarded you all an editorial in the *NY Times* for your perusal. I suspect that the link between risk and compliance is not correctly drawn. The *Times* editorial reminded me of an article I read some years ago on how changing traffic patterns during construction created more accidents. The business-processes solutions for compliance you have asked me to participate in can be, I think, facilitated by issues like this in mind.

I realize that the views expressed below may appear external to the task at hand, but I send them to you because of our need to expand the scope of the discussion to find ways of sizing the burden of regulation on business by developing an adaptive process. Expanding the scope includes, of course, non-disruptive technologies for correlation and inference. It also includes non-polarized ways of viewing the problem as a whole. I hope the discussion below will facilitate that multi-faceted picture.

But I want us to think about the problems in the broadest possible context. I would suggest the obvious: flows for business processes, transactions and messages are related as business structures and as technology solutions, although we typically separate them by the products we use to address those flows. I would also suggest that our customers are concerned about linking structured and unstructured (text) data. These two topics will be "in the money issues" for our firm in the next few quarters, if not years.

I'd like to continue to explore with you software solutions to facilitate business-processes flows, especially as they are relevant to the similarities and differences between business processes with other flows. In the risk and regulatory compliance space, where we are focused, the issues, as I have said above, may not be correctly drawn, and a more realistic approach might produce some thinking that could be profitable. Here is an example from the risk field:

John G. U. Adams, in an article in *Ergonomics* (April, 1988) entitled "Risk Homeostasis and the Purpose of Safety Regulation," defines risk in a way that gives regulatory bodies seeking a single efficient path to control systemic risk and protect consumers, a view that should lead them in the direction of making more than one path available for control and protection.

Adams cites several examples showing how people seek to maintain expected levels of risk despite what we do to protect the target of the risk. Comparing U.S. to U.K. automobile driving, he points out that in Great Britain there are twice as many cars per mile of road as there are in the U.S. Roads are much narrower, and over half the drivers exceed the speed limit. Speed limits are also higher in the U.K. British cars are smaller, with fewer built-in safety measures. "'Subjectively,' British traffic seems to me, and to many others I have questioned, to be more dangerous. But 'statistically' the average North American is about twice as likely to be killed in a traffic accident as the average Briton."

In another example, Adams points to two types of children's playgrounds. One type is "fixed equipment playgrounds," where all the slides and climbing equipment are designed to be safe.

> All surfaces are smooth and rounded and each piece of equipment is surrounded by rubberized matting to cushion falls. My children proclaim it 'boring.' They much prefer the 'adventure playground.' It appears to have been designed to be dangerous. It has frighteningly high structures, and incentives to climb them.... Off to one side, it has a pile of second-hand timber complete with rusty nails. It is surrounded by a sharp-spiked fence and offers opportunities to test skills appropriate to chimpanzees. Supervision might best be described as 'laid back.'

Adams points out that "fewer accidents take place in adventure playgrounds than in fixed-equipment playgrounds." Another report (Ward 1961) states that "the prophesied casualties did not happen" and cites the case of an insurance company quoting lower rates for an adventure playground than for an ordinary playground. The same report offers the explanation of the secretary of the National Playing Fields Association: "'the accident rate is lower than in orthodox playgrounds since *hooliganism* [italics mine] which results from boredom is absent.'"

Boredom excites the arts from Kafka, in whose work boredom is synonymous with terror, to Nam Jun Paik, for whom boredom opens unexplored passages to self-realization. Risks taken by artists in reconnecting relationships between words, fragmenting narrative in film, or introducing everyday movement in dance enhance the artistic experience and stimulate artists to take even greater risks.

Ultimately, and we have gone to these extremes, a kind of entropy is reached at which poems are blocks of illegible type, films show only the characteristics of the celluloid, and music is composed solely of electronic feedback. Now that we have reached that point, innovative arts have largely lost their inhibition and connection to the larger culture. Artists have disconnected from the risks they take and have been lulled into a false sense of security about their value to the society.

Environmentalism appears to be a useful alternative to continued dissociation from society and fragmentation of the subject, although recomposition of fragments can take other shapes than environmental modeling. But here we propose that environmentalism in the arts and technology has multiple values: it will reinforce our connection to the rest of the planet and help establish a more accurate view of our condition.

"Statistical proof is not available." In fact, risk homeostasis is not unarguable, but the issue should be clear. Risk compensation, as in the regulations currently addressing everything from airline safety to general ledger warranty (Sarbannes-Oxley regulations) to proposed environmental regulations, will affect any changes we make in protecting the targets of the risk.

If we try to stop polluting the environment by reducing greenhouse emissions, what risks will we expose ourselves to? What will displaced workers do, even if we authorize retraining? What solutions will business leaders resort to when their profit margins are reduced by regulatory interference? What new risks will the mass of our population be exposed to if business-expansion policies are reversed and business freedoms are reduced? What will the entrepreneurial class attempt in terms of additional risk taking if resources are protected from further exploitation by legislation? In financial markets it's clear that firms will need to take greater risks in order to pay for the costs of compliance. (The causes of the credit crisis of 2008 are an example of among other things unmonitored risk.)

The kinds of protections we may initiate for financial investment may produce less predictable results than we expect due to risk homeostasis. Although management and government may seek to protect the targets of the risk and rectify improprieties in business conduct, the social effects may create new, higher levels of risk for the protected business processes. Political conflict has already resulted from the perception of excessive legislation by the sons of the man who started the John Birch Society and the Tea Party has been coopted into this maelstrom of counter revolution.

Risk homeostasis predicts these results and suggests the same kinds of solutions pointed to by natural systems. Efficient single-solution technology to protect the target of the risk needs to be replaced by systems that distribute the target of the risk wherever possible and build systems more consistent with natural processes than with human-engineered efficiency.

If the target of the risk is the transparency of markets—people trying to find new ways to conceal their actions to increase profit—how can we improve transparency by distributing the target of the risk? Diversifying and hedging portfolios work for market risk. Remote backup works for operational risk. What is the equivalent for transparent business processes, and, on the other side of the coin, what is the cost of their being interrupted by regulation?

It is an interesting question, and one I think we can focus on: If legislation is being created to address business conduct, what can we do with our computing capability to guarantee appropriate cross-checking (auditing) of results to make them more difficult to manipulate while at the same time facilitating those business processes. Complex Event Processing that does not disrupt the business flow is an important technology to investigate, as it may reduce the effects of risk homeostasis.

Diversifying the targets of the risk is also useful. For example, in the area of research compliance, Solomon Smith Barney's solution to regulations such as NASD 2711—controlling research-analyst participation in equity-sales processes—has been to provide more sources of research rather than to more vigorously control individual researchers. Although this by itself is an additional expense, it does point to a practical and effective alternative to supervision required by NASD 2711.

Part 2: Natural Resiliency and Inefficient Computing

> Rarity, as geology tells us, is the precursor to extinction.
> —Charles Darwin

As computers move from solving linear problems to solving real-world, complex problems, the model for computing moves in step from mechanically efficient processes to natural, biomorphic approaches. Changing computing materials to natural forms such as carbon nanotubes for storage is one such approach. Natural methods for solving problems are another approach, less efficient in some respects but more reliable and lower risk over longer periods of time—sustainable computing.

Using natural methods, inefficient processing does not necessarily decrease underlying accuracy or rigor; it relinquishes control at specific process points and replaces it with a level of risk management that provides greater resiliency by addressing problems through the end-to-end process, accepting less perfect performance in each component in the interest of overall consistency. Strangely it also improves speed as we shall see in a moment. Real-time versions of interpreted languages, such as Java, and low-latency networks are good examples of the less perfect or less specific approach improving overall results.

In capital markets, automated trading systems are sending increasing quantities of orders to programs that match buyers and sellers. The purpose of the electronic order may be to execute a trade, but more often it is to assess the market prior to selecting a price, volume or time at which to trade. These assessment inquiries, which are actually orders into the market, are almost always canceled, so that NYSE orders, for example, are currently eight times greater than executions, and the ratio is climbing. As this number of orders increases, along with cancellations, the complexity of processing also increases.

Commitment, that is, persistence to disk, becomes a larger problem for the sender of the orders because there are more types of orders and because many of these orders do not require commitment. And commitment, the activity of verifying results before proceeding, from the point of view of transactional messaging becomes more burdensome by using more resources. It also becomes less necessary.

Guaranteed transport models (like queued messaging systems) address the commitment issues currently in an efficient way (two-phase commit) but can be linked to other commitment problems. The message can be lost by the overall system after it is deleted from the sending queue, because efficiency is linked not to the application or the systems that process them but, narrowly, to the transport itself. Persistence is typically the solution of record, but the combination of persistence and efficiency, while reliable and recoverable, are reaching the limits of volume and latency, resulting in very slow and cumbersome solutions.

Solutions based on biomorphic models, whereby multiplication of effort substitutes for efficiency, increasingly improve results and provide a more sustainable framework. The IBM Stock Exchange Reference Architecture has now (in 2008) provided a solution by which more than 150,000 trades per second, per instance of the matching engine, can be matched for each system instance and acknowledgments returned in a mean time of 175 microseconds. By the time you read this essay, these numbers will have been substantially improved. (Update for 2010: 40 million fast messages can be traded and acknowledged in a single second.)

Reliability is enabled not by the hand-holding method of two-phase commit but by the beginnings of what I am calling inefficient processing. Inefficient solutions address the solution in the following way:

Instead of controlling the process at many points—queued messaging, database persistence, mainframe reliability capabilities—with concomitant reductions in speed at each control point, sustainable approaches increase the speed of message flow beyond that of the order flow using multicasting (fire and forget). While reducing reliability at the transport layer, multicasting increases speed and enables greater volume. When volume is increased to one million messages a second and beyond, the same message can be written to multiple CPUs simultaneously and by duplication of effort address both resiliency and volume considerations that were heretofore addressed by engineering efficiency (two-phase commit) without losing messages. Duplicate CPUs can fail-over (technical language for recovery to the point where the problem occurred and allow processing to continue) to each other sequentially at multiple sites. (Note: recovery times may increase and need to be tested for regulatory considerations, but even today, at the beginning of the process, fail-over occurs in less than 10 milliseconds.)

By reducing the number of control points and replacing them with a general principle of management, speed can be increased and dynamic systems with integrated reliability, similar to biological systems, are produced. This approach also can inform security issues at airports, in religion, child rearing and poetry writing. In banking and financial markets this process of relinquishing control can link transaction processing more directly to the customer without reducing reliability or compromising security.

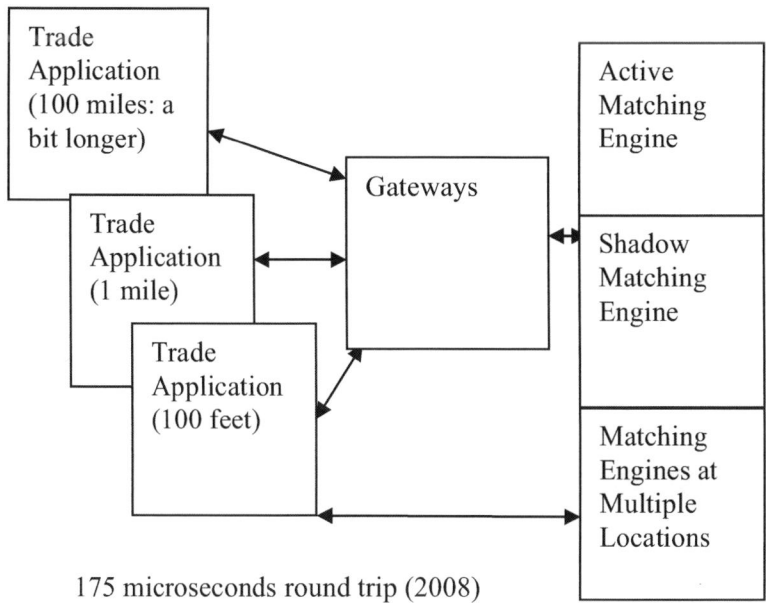

175 microseconds round trip (2008)

These ideas may relate to the section on uniqueness: "Three Short Pieces that Compete for Resources as Species in a Niche"

Part 3: Risk of Poetry

> Nature can become human too (Pan is only an obvious example, and so are you)
> –Jack Collom, *Second Nature*

Life in society has become easier due to advancements in technology and social structure but increasingly complex to negotiate. By operating at greater levels of efficiency humans, especially in information societies, increase the risk of component and even system failure. Due to division of labor individuals lack skills required for self-sufficiency. To cope with our fragile situation, our societies need more awareness of risk. But rather than propose that citizens understand their environment, our culture veers between the pacification of electronic media and apocalyptic nightmares.

Practical solutions to problems are usually confused by highly productive individuals and their interest groups seeking to retain control over specific resources. Understanding how planetary biology works allows humans to maintain clear images of problems confronting us. It helps us understand that rationality does not often free us from those biological mechanisms due to the complexity of the information available to us. Sometimes we can think through the complexity, but often we fail.

Scenarios projected in the media about the environment tend to try to convince us of one point of view rather than giving us the tools to consider the risks for ourselves. The scenarios over simplify conditions and do little to promote the real risks of climate change. The true implications are far from glamorous. Rising water tables mean widespread disease. Loss of potable water and competition for energy resources promote violence as we can see in Darfur, Kashmir, Palestine, the Balkans, and throughout sub-Saharan Africa. As mentioned in "War Against Nature," our culture's response is to declare a military opportunity as a way to prolong the security state rather than a concerted effort to make the situation transparent. Rather than promote changing our use of energy, the Pentagon and media promote the war machine, our greatest ecological abuser, as the solution.

We can follow the leaders who coordinate social and political activities. But when the leaders display such unvarnished self-interest, to whom do we appeal? Survivalism becomes epidemic. Collective action appears to governments as a threat to societies in countries as diverse as the U.S., Columbia, Iran, Afghanistan, the EU and China. Problems are too often addressed by reasoning from peripheral exceptions instead of from the core of an issue.

While the analytic tools proposed by Michael Thompson ("Human Views of Nature") may significantly aid us in conflict resolution by providing an awareness of social structure organized by role, how do we assure that leadership does not intentionally erode general consent in order to retain control? Examples in the US and China are well documented and countries like Syria have a poor track record of providing security for their citizens. In fact, complexity itself may be said to be the means of social control of populations by institutions returning us to a state where, in spite of technology, humans work every waking moment to survive.

In order to minimize the dangers of efficiency coupled with an unpredictable complexity, risk management must be developed as a cultural bias by both individuals and groups. Environmental poetics proposes as a cultural solution that poetry, for example, is not a set of themes structured by prosody, but rather consists of the risks that writers are willing to take with the components both lexical and prosodic. Risk is played out most thoroughly in innovative writing through changes to the grammatical and structural elements of poetry as well as embarking on new and risky themes. Which ones are effective and which work only partially?

To help us internalize how complexity works at the human and ecosystem levels, our cultural mechanisms, beginning with how we acknowledge each other and extending to works of art, must become engaged in the risk management process. What can we do, for example, to modify the perception of the risks in unpredictable new writing to encourage readers to take risks with what they are willing to read? To start, we need to understand the myth of progress.

The Hegelian doctrine of progress based on a dialectical process links change in society with natural change in that he describes a process very much like a biological one. His structure of thesis, antithesis, and synthesis looks a lot like sexual reproduction. Hegel's naturalistic approach as a romantic is not surprising. But he only addresses change at the individual level, and it is a long leap for him to show, by historical means, that progress for society mirrors that of the individual. So without disagreeing with Hegel's efforts to create a natural process, let's talk about large scale change in biology and see if we can enhance the idea.

We have already discussed complexity in biology in the essay on prosody as Tagmosis. A more complete example that shows the risks inherent in theory and in practice appears in Stephen Jay Gould's *Wonderful Life*. Gould's thesis is that chance as much as fitness drives survival especially in today's rapidly changing environment. This alone supports a more complex model of change. Further change occurs at multiple levels in different ways:

> The Burgess Shale includes a range of disparity in anatomical design never again equaled, and not matched today by all the creatures in all the world's oceans. The history of multi-cellular life has been dominated by decimation of a large initial stock, quickly generated in the Cambrian explosion. The story of the last 500 million years has featured restriction followed by proliferation within a few stereotyped designs, not general expansion of range and increase in complexity as our favored iconography, the copy of increasing diversity, implies. Moreover, the new iconography of rapid establishment and later decimation dominates all scales, and seems to have the generality of a fractal pattern.

Gould found in his analysis of variation among invertebrates at least thirteen unique designs compared with today's four arthropod "groups" and "eight anatomical designs that do not fit into any known phylum." Furthermore, Gould's perception that this pattern is fractal (order is unpredictable but similar at different scales) proves valuable also on the cultural level. That a reduction in the number of designs/forms takes place in the context of increasing numbers of species within those designs shows a multilevel change process that also looks like how culture changes.

Uncertainty between theory and practice takes place at another level. Since publication of *Wonderful Life* in 1989 and my initial reading on the topic, many of the "unique" designs documented by Gould have, as a result of further research, been integrated into existing groups or discovered to be fragments of organisms within existing groups. While the idea is still hotly debated, the risks to any theory are manifested in Gould's experience. Not only is success of any life-form dependent on stochastics, but the theories about it have multiple solutions. Neither the tree of life nor the fount of knowledge is an ever-expanding pattern of diversity.

With all these indeterminate and multiple results, one would think that culture might proffer more awareness of risk than aphorisms told to children. For example, at the beginning of the language writing movement in the mid-1970s, there were far more kinds of poetry being written in the new modes than are now present and elevated to the level of "poetry" by the "market" forces of the poetry world.

Look at early magazines of the group that came to be known as language writers: *This, Hills, Roof, A Hundred Posters, Big Deal, Tottels, Hills, Là Bas, Oculist Witnesses*. You will find a large variety of styles, formats, and strategies taken from throughout the world of literature and language. In 1999 we had many fewer active different styles than in 1979: new sentence prose poetry, collage/found poems, and field poems. Many styles that had independent existences and followings have been defined or co-opted out of existence. If we consider only the styles that have been deemed acceptable—read "teachable," poetry—the number decreases further. In the far-off reaches of America there are still lettrists, shaped-poem writers, visual poets, mail artists, writers focusing on opacity of surface linking with visual arts, political poets, etc., who were never elevated over the public horizon. None of the magazines that started the movement (*This, Hills, L=A=N=G=U=A=G=E, Roof*, to name a few) exists today. But the language writing movement appears today institutionalized in academies, blogs, and publishing houses. Many of the initial participants deny its existence.

Variety of format, style and prosodic practice was more the hallmark of the early language school than what most critics described as its cerebral tendencies. There were too many different kinds of writing for a single rubric or even a single critical front. Diversity and wide distribution across the English-speaking world is why the general term "language," at a high level of abstraction became such an appropriate description of the writing.

But there's a little lower layer. Between 1999 and 2012 other important innovative styles have emerged such as flarf and various conceptual styles. Using historical metaphor, we often assume that the events described occurred in the way they are narrated as in the case of Gould's evolutionary theory. In fact, there are many narratives, and reality includes them. We assume that the characteristics and relationships of the individuals and institutions are understood when often they are not. We assume that there are no other events that are lost in time or which we conveniently ignore that would substantially change our reading of history, like the presence of memories, external threats and technologies such as the internet. Vico's critique of the tendency to see the past through the eyes of the present becomes operational even in a decade.

Institutionalization rationalizes the initial complexity. This happens in our technological society as well? IBM, Microsoft, Oracle and Google have consumed many of the numerous technology innovations of the 80s and 90s. Is it the inevitable process of time driven by human ingenuity or natural forces? What are the differences between the two? Does the fragility of ideas relate to the fragility of biological life through natural selection? These are questions that ultimately answer themselves in the process of cultural realization. But we need to begin to address them.

Using scientific metaphor, few cultural underpinnings justify our experiment. Conditioned cultural responses reject interdisciplinary associations. Many readers skip such a bold step, viewing artistic risk based on hypothesis as unsound or scientizing, but it is in this step that I rely on poetic methods rather than science. Scientific method tends not to include external material, considering that it contaminates the experiment. It also assumes it includes only and all that's relevant. Only the arts and poetry in particular, by its disenfranchisement from the mainstream of contemporary knowledge, liberate sufficiently to engage external material. But even in poetry there will be lots of questions, because poetry itself has been rooted in science from Hesiod, Lucretius, Donne, Blake, and Rimbaud to the New Criticism.

Such experimental manipulation forms a stereotype of new poetry, while the risks taken today in the name of art seem less problematic than those taken in the name of science. But both art and science "must operate by analyzing similarities and differences; in other words, by comparison." (Paul Feyerabend, *Against Method* (New York, 1975) (Is this still as important a process if we expect similar shapes with phenomena on all scales, fractals? The expectation of differences is fear of the other.) We compare current events to past events in historical analysis. In interdisciplinary analysis, we compare the ways different disciplines use their common and unique tools.

For example, in zoology scientists separate homology— the inheritance of features in common ancestors—from analogy—similar features arising by separate evolution for the same function (Gould). In poetics there is no difficulty in making the same kinds of distinctions. Selection of vocabulary based on etymology has a very different association than sounds-likes-looks-like similarities of analogy with a different connection to meaning. Use of etymology in Joyce or Rilke is valorized. Alliteration, homophones, and rhyme are today considered mere prosody. What an odd hierarchy! In fact both are materials of the art. Analogy is not inherited but determined by similar needs within an ecosystem. Analogy is a potent reminder of the effect of environment. Homology, inheritance, keeps it all within the family and hence is acceptable culturally, whereas analogy suggests risk.

In poetry we have not defined prosody in sufficient detail. John Berryman opined "how amazingly fragmented and useless the literature was." But Berryman did not understand that his view of a hierarchy in which Shakespeare, Milton, Keats, etc., "had better things to do than write handbooks for our guidance" was at the root of its fragmentation—although Coleridge's "Biographia Literaria" and Stein's *How to Write* did not impede their poetical productions. Is this why the poets have been unwilling to do the physical labor and have insisted on a heroic, untracked waste for their underdeveloped technology to take its pathetic shapes? Indivisible wilderness versus cramped civilization is a popular poetic polarity. There is even a New Wilderness Foundation in the avant-garde art landscape.

As pointed out in "The Metaphor of Trees", there are not two, but at least three points, maybe more, on the "natural" compass: wilderness (which itself can be parsed), managed wilderness (agriculture and "second nature," as Michael Pollan calls it), and civilization (materials of wilderness transformed, and there are several variations on "civilization"). But, consistent with the themes of *Oops!*, civilization and cultivation function according to the same laws as wilderness. There are not the same but operate fractally.

What is the value that reason returns to nature? I suggest that reasoning makes it possible to recognize how to save the environment from the natural laws that made humanity so destructive of it. Although popular ecology provides a frightening set of options from industrial incursions, agriculture continues to be humanity's sole means of survival on a planet whose resources, unaided, cannot produce enough food, clothing, and shelter for our species. (Systematic analysis may suggest that industry is a kind of agriculture, with mining the inverse of plowing and chemistry a kind of pollination or grafting, etc.) There is even a concept of industrial ecology, developed by Jesse Ausubel (see "Industrial Ecology: Reflections on a Colloquium" *PNAS*, 1991). Industrial ecology recycles both the product and waste of industrial output until the system reuses enough resources to constitute a nearly sustainable industry. Equally important for culture, industrial ecology integrates human and environmental concepts in a way that we can begin to think about them together.

And what is the difference between nature and artifice? Artifice represents human efforts to concoct a substitute for nature that can more readily be controlled while retaining the function of convincing, of saving time and money, of saving lives everywhere, of refining social identities, of writing and art, the last and telling word. Artifice seeks more predictable results and greater efficiency, but at an Icarean cost of high-energy input and high-heat output. Yet its processes remain dependent on natural forces.

For centuries humans have been developing a sense of superiority over nature and a consumer life-style. Humanity tends to seek a single efficient path to a solution, whereas nature takes many paths, distributing the target of the risk, biomass, and its ability to reproduce, among the various activities it performs. Nature appears to have developed sexual reproduction to reduce the likelihood of mutation and disease spreading beyond a single species. Prior to the introduction of sexual reproduction, genetic material was shared among different species, creating a risk of larger orders of biological life sharing disastrous consequences. But from the perspective of our species, dominated by technical solutions, sexual reproduction is viewed as the risk, not the risk manager. This reversal is typical of human attempts to control risk by suppression rather than diversity. (Shang Dynasty burial mounds exhibit four types of skulls while China today has a single skull type.)

As I am proposing change, what results can we expect from changes? We engage in all kinds of risk avoidance from door locks to portfolio-risk-management software. But the kinds of cultural changes that are proposed by this environmental poetics discussion might produce significant, unexpected results. (See John G. U. Adams' article "Risk Homeostasis and the Purpose of Safety Regulation," referenced earlier in this text, and see "Business Process Interruption and Risk Homeostasis: Analysis for Technology Solutions to Regulatory Impact.")

Investment bankers already know about these solutions. We need legislators, inventors, and manufacturers to be willing to take the kinds of steps that reduce risk by distributing the target of the risk rather than trying to protect it behind locks or legislation. How can we apply this approach to the arts model except through innovative experimentation?

Literature has suffered from the same kinds of problems. The greater the literature, the fewer progeny it has produced. Melvilleans, Joyceans, Proustians, and Kafkaoids are not leading the masses to a new literature with a high regard for excellence in prose and individual achievement. The decadence of the narrative has only served to produce greater adherence to the narrative by those who have been excluded from identifying with high bourgeois art.

Publishers and editors, needing successful books, lean more and more toward a degenerate literature: romances, self-help, sci-fi, and other mass fiction. And the writers themselves, poets and prose writers alike, are led by the dominance of popular literature, the myth of the primacy of popular values, and the image of leadership passing from the middle class to the masses. Thus even language writing and cutting-edge artists of all types are compromised by the presence of a dominant culture of popular belief and canned images.

Along with this degeneration into genre, we suffer in the literary world from the Balkanization of schools. The poet each critic mentions as playing on the field establishes the limits of the field. Failure to take risks results in degeneration of the field. Failure to distribute the target of the risk produces rarity, and efficiency is a dirty business.

Poets can be said to be writing from the levels of consciousness that are not well-enough defined (wilderness) to be accurately represented by the set of fixed rules implied by a term such as prosody. Traditional poetics imitates past results or modifies them only slightly to protect aesthetic values by clinging to a restrictive set of ideas. Risk homeostasis predicts that the more these writers seek to protect traditional values the more radical the alternative suggestions will become. The more traditional poetries allow new ways of thinking about poetry into the canon, the more gradual and consistent the progress. Thus the co-opting of language writing by the academy was a key step in reducing the number of radical approaches that language writing continues to offer. But it was the introduction of its radical opposition that triggered the process. (Note: Language writers in positions of power feel both proud of their progress and still excluded by this moral tyranny.)

In these radical alternatives, poets take incredible risks, but like adventure playgrounds they are alert to the risks instead of assuming that certain components of the poetic environment like metaphor and narrative are safe. As a result, there are fewer dead poems, while the poetry is less efficient and more complete without closure. In order to eliminate objections to scientific or military language titling poetry groups, experimental and avant-garde poetry might better be described as risk-taking poetry.

But what happens to these perspectives as the mind becomes better charted. Should we expect that poetical Natty Bumpos will continue paddling up and down the libidinal Delaware? Will adventure language produce new epics? Or should we expect, for good or ill, that poetry will move toward more systematic views of thematics and meaning? Is an alternative that is both more systematic and freer too optimistic a solution for most poets' views of nature? Increased technology of poetry, diversifying uses of poetic technique, is both more freeing and constraining.

Poetry, inevitably, also has a perspective unique to each writer and a new interpretation each time it is read. To a certain extent, this distributes the risk and implies that the cult of the individual artist is a valid risk-management position. But these pleas of subjectivity have never convinced the poets who have defined what poetry will be for each subsequent generation. What are we to make of the leaders of each generation of poets who appear to have in common no interest in codifying prosody yet seek a more objective poetry. This apparent conflict is explored with respect to Rimbaud and the language poets in "Is There Such a Thing as Writing."

The flexibility of the human thought process further mitigates risk. In his article in "Imagery in Thought" (1932, from *Remembering*) Frederic C. Bartlett addresses how the brain produces images as part of a logical train of thought. (See "Limiting the Social Environment for a Good Reason Is Not Enough of a Reason.") When our biological-reasoning faculty reaches an impasse, our brain produces an image; a metaphor is a poetic example. We then use that image to carry us to the point where our reasoning can take over again. (In the poetic case, we can use narrative, descriptive, or other linguistic logic as a kind of reasoning.)

Too often, however, in a poem or a critical article or when making judgments about how to carry a poem forward, we, as poets, do not exit the metaphor to return to the main line of reasoning. We often start to follow the logic of the metaphor itself rather than return to the logic of the poem. Although this is an entertaining approach and a way to highlight prosody, it causes several kinds of problems.

Instead of continuing with our environmental view of the poem, its prosody, its argument, the frame in which it sits, we start to follow the logic of the metaphor. We have seen how this can lead us astray in biology from the examples Goodwin proposes in *How the Leopard Changed Its Spots*. A good example in literature is the satirical nature of early modernism. Tristan Tzara was "against action; as for continual contradiction, and affirmation too, I am neither for nor against them, and I won't explain myself because I hate common sense." (*Seven Manifestos*) But was he seriously telling us that all our actions should be contrary to the matter at hand?

No. His writing is satirical in its critique and devoted to a cult of pure energy. "I think we should invent new words to express better what we would like to mean by humour. I tried to introduce a meaningless word: 'Dada.'" Tzara himself posits Dada as "humour," yet generations of artists have followed his metaphor of artistic contrariness and never returned to his main line of thinking, which relates to pure energy. They follow Tzara's metaphorical line as if it were the logic of the thought.

In fact, Tzara (and other modernists like Artaud) were environmentalists in the sense I am using. "I'm writing this manifesto to show that you can perform contrary actions at the same time, in one single, fresh breath…." Although he carries his point to an absurd length:

> There is one kind of literature which never reaches the voracious masses. The work of creative writers, written out of the author's real necessity, and for his own benefit. The awareness of a supreme egoism, wherein laws become insignificant.

We can understand the early modernists and environmentalism only by noting its absurdity: We can be contrary. We can change and the world will not disappear.

In another mode, we can say civil disobedience is an important tool for social change, but it does not imply that whenever we break the law we do our society a favor. And there are more ways that modernists like Tzara touch environmentalism.

> Let's not look for analogies in the various forms in which art is materialized: each must have its own liberty and its own frontiers. There are equivalents in art, each branch of the star develops independently, expands, and absorbs the world of its choice. But the parallelism that records the march of a new life will brand the era, without any theory…. Art is a series of perpetual differences.
> (*Seven Manifestos*)

Here Tzara inverts the emphasis that embedded in environmentalism, pointing to the same notion of a complex relationship to unique individuals built on a few common forms. But he falls prey to emphasizing only differences, a product of his egoism.

How does the environmentalist view images? Metaphor and other formal tools are valuable when the normal logic and syntax of language is insufficient to address the complexities and alternatives presented by a line of thought. (Bartlett) We must be wary when we follow a line of thought presented by the metaphor or other formal device. Failing to acknowledge that we're following the line of the metaphor leads us to greater and greater levels of absurdity. At some point, and I think we're at that point now, people stop paying attention to poetry because it is too far from daily experience (a mixture of image and logic) for people to identify with it or even understand its purpose. We ask what we are gaining by following this line of thought. Unless the answer comes through some writing strategy defined in poems, we risk using generic arguments about the failures of society, and thereby lose the attention of our reader.

Following an absurd path, though, is often useful in itself (*Praise of Folly*, Erasmus). Schoenberg's idea to not return to the key note produced some of the most exquisite music of the twentieth century. The Renaissance ideas that we could take a human view of the world (climbing Monte Alban just to see what's up there) instead of looking at it only through the lens of faith produced a marked advance in thought. Now we need to expand even further to take an environmental view of the planet and get beyond human views that optimize each gain, follow narrow self-interest at all costs, assure comprehension through condescension, build social structures for reassurance and isolate art from science. If we follow only our own near-term interests, we will wish another fix of self-gratification.

Managing risk in language, politics and environment may use some of the same strategies because they participate in a common world and they may also use unique approaches dictated by their differences. Identifying where unique and where common approaches are relevant and effective needs both a great deal of thought and a great leap of imagination.

For Rejection

stopt charred bustier
negatory sunblade
insider theories of avid
outright tingling
with the stories she told
to remember you told
the next reprieve
pirated those doctors
flushed past ignore
and use again the fly
committed to the integer

Inter-dimensional Universality of Dynamic Interfaces

For Rob & Vanessa

A collaboration can reflect the personality of a single artist as it did in the studio of Rembrandt where, according to recent scholarship, the marks of the Master's most intimate subjectivity-brushstrokes, psychological insight, impasto, 'touch'-turn out to have been applied at times by hands other than his own. Thus, the one artist who has always been thought of as unique, as a particularly subjective kind of genius, seems to have engaged in a form of corporate art making.
—Susan Sollins & Nina Castelli Sundell, http://collabarts.org/?p=68

- The remediation of climate change lies not in chemistry, legislation or poetry but in their relationships.
- Relationships may be of several kids from active bi-directional to uni-directional or passive links that are only energized under certain circumstances. Each of these types may be stronger or weaker depending on conditions.
- Competition and difference attract an inordinate amount of energy in the arts, sciences, and politics whereas symbiosis and similarity are far more ubiquitous. Survival drives awareness of difference, but if we focus on them we end up reasoning from the outliers. A model that keeps us aware of similarities and differences would help improve the value of diverse organisms and things.
- Environmentalism thrives on an active mutualism of human endeavors that use the contemporary components of each discipline to best effect. Non-human endeavors are similarly impacted.
- Effect is intended: this is not an aesthetic exercise taken in isolation.
- To stimulate a common global consciousness based on current conditions, environmental poetics engages current modes and methods of production focused on their trends.
- These modes and methods condition attitudes like practitioners developing works and styles supporting environmental values into the future: sustainability.
- These activities and values must be potent enough to provide humanity with the will to change from a species-centered culture focused on the individual to an environmental one focused on common responses of organisms of many species and their relationships.
- Environmentalism, while broadening the focus, maintains humane activity for human interactions. Contradictions are imposed across species to complicate

this task. As one of the political animals humans can pay close attention to how humane behavior can be achieved in an environmental framework.
- Environmental poetics must be flexible enough to change with related models in politics and science, and in some cases to lead that change.
- Politics and science can in their current forms propel remediation of the environment, but culture is wedded to past destructive and separatist tendencies between humanity and non-human components of the environment.
- As a structure, environmentalism must be flexible enough to change as conditions change and not be chained to a past idée fixe relying on natural pietism and devotion to nature that is opposed to humanness and become a means of control in the hands of highly productive individuals and their groups.
- As a set of practices environmental culture must allow multiple innovations in concept and execution to be included, rather than an exclusive group of prejudicial attitudes. Dominance of one group of attitudes may be inevitable but hopefully temporary.
- Such diversity accommodates ecosystems and their populations of humans and other species in multiple climates both seasonal and relatively constant.
- Change, however, comes from individual or team discoveries promoted initially by small groups.
- Environmental culture must be flexible enough to allow intense mono-culture as one group of diverse elements so that detailed professional work of the highest caliber can advance our understanding without distraction of countless environmental influences.
- The culture retains its structure and awareness to minimize the likelihood that an extremely successful and cogent mono-culture gain control of the diversified, distributed structure and limit future options.
- Diversity includes expansive as well as conservationist approaches to problems since excluding some of humanity's tendencies builds resistance to the main thrust of environmental diversity.
- Environmental diversity does not require consistency as nature is complete rather than consistent and often contains contradiction and duplication.
- Environmental poetics avoids dichotomous argument except where relevant. Rather it presents a matrix of roles and things as well as their moment to moment changes along changing conditions.
- The sentence unifies subject and predicate not by making a third thing but by suggesting their relationship as an entity. A true noun, an isolated thing, does not exist in our physical surroundings. It is a perception and a factor of mind.
- Environmental culture uses this matrix structure to further effect diversity and attitudes that support diversity in spite of the human tendency to see the world from an individual's perspective through the structure of self and other.

- Environmental culture will not be perfect, and is not yet complete, but seeks to stimulate responses in kind that can overtake the politicized arguments of much of current classical and popular culture.
- Environmental culture does seek to keep us focused on itself and the risks of change so that we continue to support its poetics/purpose.
- Environmental poetics establishes universal diversity without relying on internal consistency so that mono-culture and specialization can occur among species and individuals and functions of individuals.
- Environmental poetics models its cultural solutions on natural methods more than descriptions of nature.
- Description of nature, as in ecopoetics' new nature poetry, functions to promote environmental awareness as a general case of mind/body dualisms.
- Environmental poetics tends toward alignment with environmental structures in order to move humanity's culture into association with them, not identical to nature but aligned with and fitting into the appropriate niche for a dominant species that recognizes a level of interdependence with the other planetary components.
- While environmentalism begins with a concept of nature, in the end human and natural elements are coincidental. The definition of nature as distinct from humanity withers away, and we remain with a definition of nature as inherent characteristics, as in the phrase "it's his nature to behave in that way."
- Universal diversity raises questions about the exact value of difference.

Uttering the word universality raises objections from postmodern culture. Postmodernism posits that universality only exists as multiplicity of form. The global is only the sum of locals. While the multiplicity of postmodernism for some writers is linked to the body, societal alienation produces isomorphs/analogs in all facets of life that render the discussion of universality moot at best and trite in the more dismissive case. Environmental poetics identifies with those critiques to the extent that they support diversity. Local cultures tend, as a result of global communication, to move simultaneously toward fragmenting into individuals and merging into global/ species identity. Environmentalism protect existing and builds new intermediate institutions to help promote local values and specialization required for innovation in the context of this two part global culture of individual-to-global relationships.

Universality has the added burden in its association with older deist cultural models, natural pietism such as Daoism, or the views of nature proposed by biomimicry. (Note: biomimicry uses appropriate methodological practices to solve important problems, but biomimics need a contemporary linkage of nature and humanity rather than reactionary natural pietism.) Poetry in turn has promoted several notions of universality associated with natural pietism and deism that I would not carry forward to the next cultural millennium. Some have value as universal scaling as in Donne.

> Is the Pacific Sea my home? Or are
>   The eastern riches? Is Jerusalem?
> Anyan, and Magellan, and Gibraltar,
>   All straits, and none but straits, are ways to them.
> ("Hymn to God, my God, in my Sickness")

Planetary structures cannot be supported on the shoulders of limited and aestheticized notions of culture. Modern poetry focused on mental structures from Baudelaire's correspondences to Silliman's quantum sentences. It also focused on political subjects and concomitant dichotomies rather than address relationships on the planetary scale. Universality will emerge as an important area of cultural conflict when people, seeing nature as the ceiling rather than god or the self, begin to describe planetary forces as universal terms to the extent that the planet is all that is the case. So I anticipate the need to develop the theme of universality in poetics.

The notion of universality derives from the q-analysis tool described by Ron Atkin in *Multidimensional Man* (1979). Q-analysis enables ecosystems, be they cultural or biological, to be analyzed using set theory. Atkin shows that the physicist's notion of dimension is quite the same as this cultural use of set theory where groupings of things are contained within more inclusive sets. For example, a garden contains trees, shrubs, and plants. The garden is at a more inclusive dimension than its contents, so there is the set of gardens and within it the sets of trees, shrubs, and plants. And then there are sets within those. Atkin says that the garden is one dimension and the other three are in another dimension.

Imagine building a multidimensional world using this method. A non-evaluative hierarchy is built up and each level can be construed as a dimension. If the physicist's notion of dimension relates to set theory then universality may be said to be in effect when similar structures result from events that cross dimensional boundaries. Not every natural characteristic can be described as universal. Universality of this type is limited in this example to scale.

Culturally I have little difficulty in building a world from sets although the world appears fairly limited at first. Materially, however, we need some proof to accept this theory beyond an imaginary *Flatland*. Some concrete experiment must support inter-dimensional universality if interdisciplinary scaling can be theoretically justified. Such a material proof is suggested by certain natural phenomena. While I am not sure if this particular experiment I am about to describe will stand the test of time, it does provide an example of how cross dimensional behavior can imply universality of a type that is culturally more flexible by being scalar, and scalar only.

> Despite the complexity and diversity of nature, there exists universality in the form of critical scaling laws among various dissimilar systems and processes such as stock markets, earthquakes, crackling noise, lung inflation and vortices in superconductors. This universality is mainly independent of the microscopic details, depending only on the symmetry and dimension of the system. Exploring how universality is affected by the system dimensions is an important unresolved problem. Here we demonstrate experimentally that universality persists even at a dimensionality crossover in ferromagnetic nanowires. As the wire width decreases, the magnetic domain wall dynamics changes from elastic creep in two dimensions to a particle-like stochastic behavior in one dimension. Applying finite-size scaling, we find that all our experimental data in one and two dimensions (including the crossover regime) collapse onto a *single curve, signaling universality at the criticality transition.* [italics mine] The crossover to the one-dimensional regime occurs at a few hundred nanometers, corresponding to the integration scale for modern nanodevices. (*Nature*, P740, Ap 9, 2009)

That's quite a mouthful. This experiment and the general theory of dynamic systems suppose that universality exists at some levels and not at others. This experiment for example suggests that universality exists across scalar divides through recognizably similar forms. Simply put universality is not universally universal but only exists in matters of scale and form. This limitation implies that method is not universal, neither is praxis, nor style. But scale does appear to cross dimensional boundaries. Take Donne's

> Let sea-discoverers to new worlds have gone,
> Let maps to others, worlds on worlds have shown,
> Let us possess one world, each hath one, and is one.
> ("Elegy 5)

The notion of conditional universality mirrors Gödel's incompleteness theorems and provides a general expression of natural events. English descriptions of the theorem describe mathematics as incomplete. Apparently English definitions don't translate the formal mathematics well, and we need multiple instances in English.

> Informally, Gödel's incompleteness theorem states that all consistent axiomatic formulations of number theory include undecidable propositions (Hofstadter 1989). This is sometimes called Gödel's first incompleteness theorem, and answers in the negative Hilbert's problem asking whether mathematics is "complete" (in the sense that every statement in the language of number theory can be either proved or disproved). (http://mathworld.wolfram.com/GoedelsIncompletenessTheorem.html)

The demand that poetry be consistent was overturned by modernism. The demand that poetry be complete and self-referential still is widely discussed as an extension of creature dualism. Formally, the description of Gödel's theorems is available in a unique version only to those speaking math. But mathematical logic comes close to singularity. What's important for environmental poetics is how both semantic and syntactic (what I have called grammatical) versions occur in logic.

> 1st Theorem (Semantic Version): Assuming that the axiom system A is arithmetically sound - i.e. all the axioms in A are true sentences of arithmetic - it is possible to construct a sentence G which is a true sentence of arithmetic but is not provable from A.
> 1st Theorem (Syntactic Version): Assuming that the axiom system A has the following two properties:
> - A is sufficiently strong to be a plausible candidate for an axiom system for arithmetic; in particular, it is at least strong enough to permit the derivation, by correct reasoning, of any true elementary arithmetic statement involving the operations of addition, multiplication and successor-taking, and incorporates the principle of natural induction;
> - A is consistent - i.e. it is not possible to deduce from it a contradiction; it is possible to construct, within the language of First-Order Arithmetic, a sentence G such that
>   - G is not provable from A
>   - if, in addition, A has a property called omega consistency (see below) then the negation of G is also not provable from A.
>
> (http://math.mind-crafts.com/godels_incompleteness_theorems.php)

English language descriptions of the math while not wildly different provide a further level of ambiguity for those seeking to use the lexical meaning of the theorem to generalize in other discourses. Hence Place and Fitterman's formal use of the theorem seems unusually accurate since it does not attempt to translate the sense of the theorem.

In any case, we can push the formal representation of the theorem further than the conceptual model posited by Place and Fitterman. A geometry of English can be identified that provides a clearer analysis of the biomorphic event, the point of the experiment and the field expressed by the theorem define a multi-dimensional polygon in which the world is made visible as it exists rather than through a single lens of a specific magnification. The combination of the scientific accuracy and absurdity of these propositions outlines environmental poetics. The two events' mathematical logic supports a poetic logic pointing to the indefiniteness of poetic interaction. Such a train of thought is consistent with the logic of critical romanticism without falling into the sounds like, looks like patter of onomatopoeia and other descriptive poetry.

Kurt Gödel and Francis Bacon contrast completeness and consistency in natural systems. Nature must build complete organisms for them to survive; it's axiomatic. But the history of poetry aims more toward perfection than consistency in line with the aspirational nature of the discipline and the religious origins of many of its exponents. But as we choose to move poetry toward a view of humanity and nature as a single complex system, we must also reduce our trust in the notion of perfection and fabricate for completeness in the sense of both Bacon and Gödel. Bacon appears to point to how we understand nature and humanity separately as any early humanist might. Gödel on the other hand simply points to the contrast rather than making a decision about which way to go.

Metaphysics develops an aesthetic practice that undercuts the tendency toward morality. But distinguished from Place & Fitterman in *Notes on Conceptualisms*, environmental poetics contrives an ethical set that overlaps both aesthetics and metaphysics and can be addressed in a way that it is susceptible to q-analysis. Neither is it limited to either/or formulations of postmodernism.

Conceptualism as instantiated in the early 21st century expresses "the desire to begin again." (Place/Fitterman). It does so by mirroring or reusing media but does not propose an alternative beyond reflexivity and is not entirely to begin again. While conceptual writing is conceptually interesting, it also proposes a pairing of the conceptual work and things one can say about it. This twin organism styles itself as a sobject (elision of subject and object) in much the same way as environmental poetics or Charles Olsen define the subject as the connections between organisms.

The chimera that Place/Fitterman proposes raises several interesting questions. First does commodifying the relationship between two organisms as a trademark reduce its value as a critique of capitalism? Second do they even intend such a critique? Third can environmental poetics align itself with such a contraption? Yes, yes, yes.

While there is some weakness in their argument in that it uses the tools of the theory they are criticizing, environmental poetics accommodates both conceptualism and its use of commodification (not a wholesale acceptance of commodification). Irony/intention is part of accepting that human creations are not unnatural. But we also have to then accept that many things that do not yet exist are natural. Such a formulation is unsettling at best.

At a deeper level so many things that we as humans leverage in an effort to improve ourselves are destructive of other parts of the environment and pollute our thoughts as well. And many of the formulations that appear as "natural" destroy human hegemony and put us as a species and as individuals at risk. How do we travel to secure sustenance? How do we differentiate and include?

To establish value in poetry modern writers have tried to revive debased content like genre fiction as in my own *In Case* or inversely the pop song "The Fifth of Beethoven". We have tried throughout this poetics text to discuss value as a type of link between things, but one can only understand postmodern writing through this devaluing process using cartoons as high art. Devaluing high art by injecting pop art exposes the weakness of cynicism in that ultimately the devalued becomes valued in art that incorporates the low into the high and I think vice versa such as cinematic thrillers based on *Mona Lisa*. One can imagine elevating a devalued nature in this way as a back door to utility. At other times as mentioned earlier I think the whole notion of nature as opposed to humanity has to be exploded.

But in the end these judgments can only be made by understanding how they are used. If the writer is too pleased with his irony or too intent on earnestness, then the reader is denied the completed thought and retrieves only the residue. Effective environmental art moves from synthesis toward completion. Components are added and the whole fails again and again until it doesn't. Then retrofitting (edits) can be applied to improve efficiencies if obsession demands it.

Such a synthetic process can be viewed as ad hoc until we understand that there are universalities in the laws of scaling. Universal does not mean total here but rather collective or in common. Neither do these scaling universalities imply that there are other more desired universal laws like love or certain moral commandments. We do not know where we're going to end up by postulating universal scaling. Unpredictability is a characteristic of complexity.

Scaling universality means that how we add and subtract from the whole can either render a whole unworkable or simply change its dimension. What are the ways to understand which arithmetic collapses an organism and which arithmetic allows the organism to continue functioning in more or less the same way but in different dimensions? Death for example is a subtraction that ends certain workings of the organism but perpetuates many of its subordinate processes. Unpacking a dozen eggs improves its usability. Marriage perpetuates both species and property. Do two magnets bonding reduce their attractiveness? Trial and error, in the scientific sense, uses hypothesis to identify potentially useful interactions. How can these scaling universalities be natively described except through understanding how the small works and then scaling up?

Atkin on the other hand points to the difficulty of communication upward scaling. Atkin's method has ramifications for communication. While you can derive trees, shrubs and plants from the notion of garden you cannot easily go the other direction, since in the first instance trees exist not only in gardens but also in forests and orchards. In the second instance we must apply extraordinary civilizing process to create the idea of garden from looking at a tree in a field or in a forest.

The limitations of the relationship between humanity and nature are also manifest in scaling. Social engineers opine how there are more murders within families than without. A view of society as nature tells us how technical and corporate competition are both associated with sexual reproduction. All related social engagements tend toward competitive participation such that those which are closest to each other fight the hardest. Our battles with ourselves provide a convincing example if you care to look into it.

In seeking to understand how to work with various resources examine food finding behavior in animals. Non-competitive, non-symbiotic relationships develop between deer and turkeys which eat the same food but at different heights. The deer sweep through the forest three to five feet above the floor eating berries and grains from the plants. The turkeys come after and eat the grain from the ground as pecking birds. There is no status game or competition and neither do they improve each other, although one might say that the deer position the food for the turkeys.

I would like environmentalism to have the completeness and complexity of the over-developed mantras of postmodernism, but it's a new idea, sort of, and as such needs to be laid like a table in parallel and in waiting. I would like environmental poetics to have the terseness of aphorism, but I am too anxious and can't let it wait; I feel urgent pressure. I don't think of the urgency as a product of the imminent disruption of civilization. Rather my metabolism constructs necessity and that is either convenient or self-defeating. Up to now it has been the latter. Let us see what develops; that's the best I can do for patience.

- Environmental poetics strives for improvement of our condition where "our" is a family, a species, an ecosystem and a planet, ours. At this level the concept of public property begins to make sense.

    Participle-like stochastic behavior: Verb forms by chance
    I'm constructing this poem
    Trafficking forward by steps
    And you're succeeding it
    Until you acquire to the end
    When you annex it

The World Trade Center Environment: Strategic Dialogue

> UHF Tower Mast A
> VHF Main Antenna Bracing, Southeast
> Left Rear Wheel Assembly, Retractor
> Radome Array
> First Class Galley Convection Oven Number One
> First Class Galley Convection Oven Number Two
> —Michael Gottlieb, "The Dust"

Dialog(ue) in a Dust Cloud

I was within two blocks of the WTC on September 11, 2001, in my cubicle in the Federal Reserve Building on Nassau Street. I was on a conference call when the first plane hit, and I thought, "Someone is trying to stop the Wall Street opening." (It has happened twice in the past few years that bombs have gone off in the neighborhood just before 9 A.M.) When the second plane hit, it was much louder and the building shook. I said to my callers, "I think something bad is happening; I have to go."

I went to the window and I could see the WTC burning. I watched in a state of denial as women fell, their dresses ineffectual parachutes. I thought, "I will just go back to my desk and get some work done." Then the first building collapsed, as time had collapsed. I could see it falling toward me and raced behind a pillar at the far corner of the office. (At the same moment my son, Ben, was racing away from his school on Greenwich Street and later described how, from his vantage point looking south, "the top of the building just slid off.")

Then we were benighted by a gray dust cloud, unable to see out the windows although the air was secure in the building. After 20 minutes the dust settled and we could see out the windows again. Security evacuated the building; the Federal Reserve employees went across the street to their bunker in the bank; the rest of us dispersed. As I passed Beekman Hospital on William Street, the second building collapsed. I could see the dust cloud billowing toward me over the rooftops. I ducked into Pace University to avoid the dust cloud that slammed the door behind me.

For 20 minutes, I sat in the basement auditorium with a professor of African history, and we discussed the state of Islam. After exchanging credentials, the professor said, "I wonder why the sub-Saharan African leaders haven't been more supportive of the jihad."

"There's a difference," I replied, "between religious devotion and self-interest."

We in New York have suffered a great deal in the past few weeks. The military, financial control, surveillance, and charitable work of our government are a complex response to a singular, traumatic, personal attack on the financial center of our global commercial empire. But it's not about us.

Islamic militants are attacking us, to be sure, but their goal is to use us, and our expected inappropriate response, to destabilize secular, Middle Eastern governments and replace them with Islamic regimes. (Note from 2012: We're seeing the effects as Islamic governments are being established across the region pushing out Western and Iranian backed dictators.) The West is to be addressed later when a stronger base in multiple Islamic powers can reasonably confront Western economic power.

Islamic militants seem to have forgotten what they have unleashed in the Christian world. If militant Islam begins to succeed, it will be confronted with a far more dangerous enemy than it can imagine. The implacable justice of Islam will have to deal with brutal Christian love. And we may yet see the fundamentalists on both sides doing battle while the rest of us watch.

(Note from 2007: And true to that prediction of 2001, George W. Bush, Dick Cheney, Donald Rumsfeld and their cronies in the conservative think tanks and military industrial complex have changed the sympathy and respect that the world felt for America that day to hatred and disrespect. They have used the support of the American people to send hundreds of thousands of Iraqi and U.S. soldiers and citizens to their deaths in order to fill the coffers of America's military machine with U.S. tax dollars. They have destroyed the complex web of relations among dozens of nations. It is unclear at this writing whether America can recover from the blow to its national prestige. And none of these strategies will suppress the rising populations of Asia's southern tier. These growing cultures will have a voice. And if we are not reasonable in responding with a platform for them, militant Islam is all they will have left.)

Putting that unhappy thought aside, Islam (and throughout this section I'm talking about evangelical Islam, which is appropriating portions of the larger Islamic religion for the purposes of its conflict with the West) is not the only religion that uses long-term planning. The West has some sophisticated ideas about time that include globalization without religion at the center, although religions play a peripheral part in controlling local behavior. The confrontation between fundamentalist Islam and transnational corporate culture will be exercised for many years. (See *Our Nuclear Heritage*, 1991). During that time fundamentalism will be trying to gain control of nation-states as protection from economic transnationalism that will try to make those national borders increasingly permeable. (At the same time national borders become increasingly leaky, the West will attempt to solidify intellectual boundaries, both intellectual property and taxonomic, for the purposes of commercial control. [Compare this to immigration policy in the U.S. in 2007.])

These permeable borders will render transnational institutions more vulnerable, so we will see transnational security disguised as nationalism, separating and isolating the local cultures and rendering them more vulnerable to transnational incursions. The conflict for the West, then, is culture versus security. (And it is this book's purpose to begin construction of a viable alternative.) The more we open and mingle our societies, the more vulnerable our institutions of power become. The more we separate our societies, the more expensive it is to distribute transnational goods and services. Mass customization, the use of computers to provide individuals with unique products, designed specifically for each, was conceived to overcome this problem, but transnationals can't yet provide it at a profit. Certainly not globally. Future readers can estimate the timeliness of this statement.

Solutions appear in our culture, not our military might or financial power. The only way we can understand what fundamentalist Islam has accomplished is to understand their culture as deeply as Islam understands ours. But it will be more difficult for America and Europe to understand Islam.

Although the West has the advantage militarily and financially as well as a more educated population, we have some weaknesses in our traditional cultures and certainly in our undernourished understanding transnational cultures. Our religious cultures tend to be more literal than Islam. The Roman Catholic Church, for example, still promotes the idea that the wine and wafer transform literally into blood and body, whereas the more sophisticated Christian Orthodox belief recognizes that trans-substantiation is a metaphor. The Islamic symbols require far greater leaps of faith, so it will be difficult to perform the usual Western analysis. By dissecting the parts, we hope that viewing the details will help us to understand the causes of terrorism. Actually the causes are in us, but more on that another time. (Noam Chomsky, *9/11*, Seven Stories Press)

Our contemporary Western arts also posit literal relations. (And this notion of environmental poetics literalizes the relation between nature and culture.) In poetry, the entire corpus of imagism (circa 1909-1917, composed of poets like Ezra Pound, Hilda Doolittle, and T. E. Hulme), generating pictures when the logic of sensory perception breaks down, aestheticizes the relationship between complex image sets. Even in its emotional and primal Vorticist underpinnings, imagism turns inward to artistry to solve problems of alienation and synaptic rerouting (see the discussion of images and Bartlett in "Limiting the Social Environment for a Good Reason Is Not Enough of a Reason").

Fundamentalist Islam's restrictions on images provide ordinary citizens with a level of imagination only found in cutting-edge arts and sciences in the West. Not coincidentally, the organizations supporting Islamic fundamentalism also support local development projects. The combination of heightened imagination and good housing garners more support than the thin soup of alienated jobs and culture of competition the West purveys. How can we combat this "weaponized" culture of the evangelical portions of Islam?

To the extent that we want our alternative culture to push through the membrane into the mainstream, we need at least three-legged stability from innovative poetics. Modernist identification of form with content appears initially to reduce support rather than increase it, spiritualizing language in response to mechanization. But modernism breaks down the dichotomy of form and content replacing it with a more complex structure that move toward biological forms.

Objectivism (circa 1930s, composed of poets such as William Carlos Williams, Louis Zukofsky, Lorrine Neidecker, Basil Bunting, George Oppen, and others) reaches for poetry with a surface that matches the complexity of a Persian carpet, using collage techniques and diverse materials. Zukofsky aestheticizes politics; new connections are established. But what is the structure underneath the complexity of objectivism? How does it compare with the mathematical, naturalistic structures beneath Persian ornament or a Moorish tile? (Note: by now the reader should be prepared to accept that human mathematics reveals natural structures.)

Williams' "contagious hospital" opens another dimension using a literal adjective, thus freeing perception and opening multiple possibilities, diverse meanings. The unexpected identity of adjective and noun creates a shimmering reflection that shakes the reader with new possibility. The issues surrounding this apparently solipsistic approach are complex, but the closeness of adjective and noun establishes a magnetic field that attracts attention. Again the formal meaning of Objectivism's strategies are closer to lexical meaning, while Islam keeps the distance and hence its readiness.

Language writing finds and explores formal and grammatical meaning; that is, meaning derived from the shape and rules of language. Its investigations move a step further, by addressing more complex and remote connections. Good examples are found in the Andrews/McCaffery collaboration in *Legend* (L=A=N=G=U=A=G=E/Segue, 1980):

Water = ground

Gathered = inequalities = $5/1.2.3 + 14/4.5.6 + \ldots \infty$

And in the work of Bob Grenier words operate contrary to our experience of how things work, but a condition exists where the following events to occur:

FALL

the leaves
falling
out of the water
water by the
table
(*Series*, This, 1978)

Understanding these chasms where real events occur that are contrary to our expectation helps recognize the distance that desperate people (Islamists and populations displaced by climate change) are able to leap, but we're just at the beginning. Future writing will accept and comprehend other cultures more easily with a model that allows for diversity. Rather than simply including everything in an unexamined pluralism or divisive analysis, environmental poetics exposes how the differences of place, time, and person co-exist. The exclusionary politics of poetic groups will give way to understanding that different approaches exist side by side regardless of the vain competitive evaluations each group makes to aggrandize itself. Western ideals of reason, Islamic faith and east Asian pragmatism will all be exposed to each other and the structure of ecosystem relations will draw us together. We are not alone in our evolutionary position, but each starting configuration is different.

For more than a thousand years, Islamic calligraphy has practiced generating emotion not from an integrated form and content but from creating distance between form and content. It does so using letter forms, energy generated from the letters' tails and loops. Islam's ability to cross both geographical and cognitive borders is based on this multi-legged strategy.

The West can derive much from it. For example, Michael Gottlieb's poem "The Dust" (*Lost and Found*, Roof, 2003) addresses the injunction against using images of people in Islamic religious art. In "The Dust" a list of the components of the Trade Center bombing that goes on for pages and pages resolves itself finally into a list of dead firemen and policemen. At one level Gottlieb shows how people in these conflicted situations are treated like things, a comment on fetishism of commodities.

But he also shows how humanity is not destroyed and can be resolved through poetry from even the pulverized remains of the bombing.

Islamic art's mesmerizing of the viewer (albeit less so than the mandalas of India) and its ideological extension upon awakening leaves Muslims vulnerable to despotism. The weakness of the projective Islam is its reliance on symbols like the WTC to galvanize popular attention. A little thinking about our own symbols may decrypt Osama's plan, if truly he was the center of the plan in a niche where there is arguably and acceptably no center. Although more practical strategies have characterized Al Qaeda's more recent activities, targets like the Statue of Liberty and large sporting events provide a prime linkage with our own symbolism.

The West's nuclear religions contrast with the many paths that T. E. Lawrence describes in *Seven Pillars of Wisdom* as leading to Mecca. The de-centered or distributed focus of Islamic culture presents a landscape with problems similar to those of combating terrorist activity. The enemy is distributed, and hence the problem is solvable only with a distributed technology. (Some people have recently been asked to describe how many Muslims can be tracked leaving a mosque for how many days before the problem becomes too big to manage.) We know how to manage distributed problems, but our military, financial, and surveillance systems (drone technology has changed this point) are not organized to function in cells and then link the data for understanding. Often doing the opposite will take us in the right direction. But that too is difficult for our literal culture to execute. Unity is an agreeable approach but should not be applied universally, as diversity actually increases stability. (See Stephen Jay Gould, *A Wonderful Life*)

Western models are not particularly attuned to dealing with these kinds of complex problems. Even the disciplines we assign to handle them, like psychology and law, are deeply immersed in the culture's limitations. Ask a psychologist how violence ought to be applied to stop terrorism. Ask lawyers how to include the opium-producing Northern Alliance in our plans to overthrow the Taliban. The disciplines are isolated from one another with no well-defined linking techniques.

The confrontation of the centralized and distributed cultures needs to be approached with a more general model, such as those that are used in environmental processes to solve resource constraints, limit the spread of disease among species or resolve conflicts of interest. Forest fires destroy property, but if they are prevented, they end up destroying more property by the degradation of the environment that fire-suppression methods cause over time.

We cannot easily protect the target of the risk; we can only distribute the risk. Including a distributed cultural model will help. Whereas before we protected our ideas and argued over our differences to the exclusion of alternatives, we can now model our differences on a common ground. In this way we would link our culture with environmental processes and approaches. Nature and city would stop looking so different from each other. We would no longer have to continually protect our "unique" identity. It also enables us to think like Islam and ultimately enables Islam to feel itself on common ground. Because in the end the conflict between cultures was not provoked for the good of the people but rather as a mechanism to divert tax revenues to private corporations that donated to the Bush and congressional campaigns.

A distributed culture is a diverse culture. Varieties of opinion and even sharing opinion can allow for diverse solutions. To calm marketers' fears, a distributed culture does not necessarily have fewer shared audiences. Common themes in Islam extend from Malaysia to Morocco. Centralized communication can present many points of view. Those views do not have to be homogenized. Journalistic objectivity can ally cultures with participating populations rather than homogenizing them.

I noticed recently on a visit to England that the tabloids there are reporting more in-depth and concrete ideas on the war on terrorism than the mainstream press in the U.S., which placates to make everything seem normal. The common elements of the body and basic resources along with centralized communications are a sufficient link. We do not need to link at all points; that is to say, we do not need to integrate.

As the bombing of the Trade Center raises questions about viability of the city and its egg basket, Rodrigo Toscano's theatrical solution points the way to a multi-nodal culture and the limitations of either/or constructions. Toscano's cutting-edge "Collapsible Theater" creates a distributed, environmental structure. The stage is set with actors reading text on stage right and actors performing blocking movement on stage left. The text readers don't move more than to turn over their index cards, and the movement actors don't speak. Further, the personnel in different cities can present similar material simultaneously in multiple geographies. A planned website links the locations to highlight the isomorphs of theatrical presentation.

Adopting a distributed approach on our part will assist Islam itself to read the lines of the Koran that address a multiplicity that includes other "peoples of the book" in their cultures. How transnationalism adopts these options is already implicit in its use of ecology to control Third World countries. To that end we need to work intently to avoid a "neo-naturalism," whereby nature is defined separately from people and used as a core value and therefore as an excuse for further central control. Environmental imperialism produces no better results than any other imperialism. On the bright side, as transnationalism adopts a sustainable commercial model, cultural conflict has a model for resolution, using the girders of our smoking mass grave on Church Street.

No One Is On

A study of connections.

Formal Invention Predicts the Invasion of Art by Content

A gardener puts no scent in the rose,
Why should a poet put poetry into his ode?
The reader takes poetry out.

Places to Sit

Let us look for a place to sit,
Where nothing is crushed by our butts
And no one is poisoned by shit.
Can't find such a place, eh what?

Practical Applications

> My only motive was the wish to see what so great an elevation had to offer.
> —Petrarch, letter to his father on the 1336 Ascent of Mont Ventoux

The reader has doubtless been asking all along exactly what do I have to do, what do I have to change to address environmental degradation? Can I dim my lights, ride my mower less, avoid fur coats, buy organic food?

All of these activities are in your future, but we must also focus on changing the way we humans relate to the rest of the planet and to each other as part of it. We approach the problem this way because it's impossible to implement the difficult changes in resource utilization without reorienting our perceptions and our culture to more appropriately position people on the planet. As Albert Einstein said, "We can't solve problems by using the same kind of thinking we used when we created them." Finding specific examples is difficult, because I'm not sure that I have sufficiently changed my own perspective to be able to see the path clearly.

But we have been at this kind of juncture before, and it would be well to look at the humanism we intend to displace. Petrarch's letter to his father describing his 1336 ascent of Mont Ventoux explores reasonable expectations for environmentalism. Petrarch's goal was merely to represent a view from a different perspective. He was fairly safe with this metaphor, and his description of the ascent did not give the Church much to fear.

Most of the letter relates a Dantean ascent of the soul, but on a human scale. His ascent was simply a walk for its own sake, paving the way for a humanist path to progress. The revolutionary point of view was that Petrarch traveled without a higher purpose, just for the hell of it. That was enough to represent a changing world view. His faux naiveté represents a complex protective strategy that we must eschew to improve our integration with the biosphere.

I do not fear that changing the way we view our position on the planet appears too modest a goal. It is, rather, the practical size for the initial step of our effort to avoid extinction. I do, however, assume that we need overt projects on the road to sustainable activity even as we clarify our position in the environment.

Problems with automobile emissions, heating and cooling require both new technology and a postural change by manufacturers and energy producers. The problem is not that we don't know what to do; we simply can't act effectively without changing the will of people at all levels of society. What can accomplish that goal?

According to *New Scientist* (January 26, 2008, p. 28), "between 5 and 8 percent of global CO_2 emissions are the result of cement production. With demand for concrete set to double in the next decade," geopolymer concretes release just "10-20 percent of the greenhouse gases associated with making the standard stuff." Fly-ash and slag waste are removed from power stations and steel production. Aluminates and silicates are extracted from waste. Alkali, gravel and sand are added to make geopolymer concrete. "Researchers…plan to capture the CO_2 released from roasted limestone during cement making, and from the fuel combustion that heats the cement kilns, and use it to feed micro algae," which will produce biodiesel to power the cement kilns in a closed-loop system, or be turned into fuel for transportation.

Industrial ecology and closed-loop processes are similar to the way nature supplies its own engines with body and power, although I want to stress that none of these descriptions or solutions fully avoids the risk of unintended consequences. Such technology must be applied over time to assess its impact. Nature's method of trial and error, with a pinch of forethought on our part, provides a reasonable expectation of a successful symbiotic relationship.

But, you will ask, why wasn't this considered before? In fact the technology wasn't available, and earlier versions of geopolymer cement hardened too fast. New ideas do from time to time appear; before, we weren't looking that way. Invention and creativity do have a value, but applying them like a deity when writing poetry misses the point of the complexity involved.

Recent discussions of "uncreative" art by Kenneth Goldsmith address this issue. In his article "A Week of Blogs for the Poetry Foundation" (*The Consequences of Innovation: 21st Century Poetics*, Roof Books, 2008), Goldsmith suggests that "conceptual writing…is a poetics of flux, one that celebrates instability and uncertainty." Oops! Sounds like an environmental essay.

Goldsmith's notion of uncreative poetry acts primarily as a critique of current art and poetry, with their premium on the essentialized act of creation. One of his concept pieces was to collect all of the weather reports for New York and Baghdad for a given period. Reading these placid paragraphs raises the specter of destruction more vividly than citing body counts on the daily news. *Oops!* utilizes conceptual strategies such as rewriting a biology text by substituting poetry nouns for biology nouns, see "How Language Poetry Got Its Period" (1995, later published in *Critiphoria 2*). Goldsmith's work is "framed through the discourse and economy of poetry" as is this essay.

The idealism inherent in Goldsmith's notion is "Freed from the market constraints of the art world or the commercial constraints of the computing & science worlds, the non-economics of poetry create a perfectly valueless space in which these valueless works can flourish." Goldsmith's "value free" poetry is an idealized, asymptotic notion, and hence essentializing itself. But it makes the point clearly.

In the environmental model we need a concept of art that accepts uncertainty but pursues the reincorporation of the poetry into the larger society. Further, Goldsmith's claim that such poetry is "uncreative" is a stretch. Conceptual writing uses creativity when it conceives of the work, and less so in the execution. Like serial composition in music, the "creative" part of composing a poem is limited and relocated; it is not eliminated. The same is true of environmentalism: we reduce human inputs to our surroundings; we don't eliminate them; we encourage each component to operate in its own terms accepting lower reader efficiency to encourage sustainability. New conceptual poets' energy output is far lower per page than poets creating their own work word by word. Such an environmentally sound practice has extended poetry outreach to the White House where no experimentalism has gone before. Clearly, unmediated natural applications cannot be followed blindly except as we view poetry as a physics where the matter and energy of the texts are neither created nor destroyed but simply reformatted.

Pursuing an environmental model of poetry, albeit unintentionally, the flarf poets apply a method similar to the chance operations of Cage and MacLow using contemporary technology. Works by Nada Gordon, K. Silem Mohammad, Drew Gardner, Gary Sullivan, and others have addressed the conceptual realm of poetry in its ability to step through its veil to other poetic methods. K. Silem Mohammad says,

> In Drew's case, for example, he has taken a source text, or bits of different source texts, and *arranged* and *changed* them with the same intentionality that someone would use in selecting and combining words that are to be constrained by iambic pentameter, or rhyme, or whatever. (http://lime-tree.blogspot.com/2006_02_01_archive.html)

But the flarf poets have been careful in defending their work against charges of automation and uncreativity, rather than vigorously proposing their methods and poetry as an alternative in the way Goldsmith addresses the topic. And in fact flarf poems are usually heavily edited from the initial Google searches.

Flarf poems conceptualize the initial process and then rework results, using a variety of tactics to produce an ecology of language that can adapt to various niches and changes of cultural climate. Although there are as many strategies to flarf as there are practitioners, it works something like this: a poet conceives or finds a string of words and puts them in a computer search engine. The search engine generates a limited vocabulary that then acts as a resource for writing the poem. Usually a group of themes propose themselves in a series of paragraphs/stanzas generated by the search engine. The poet can manipulate those paragraphs generated by the search engine in a variety of ways, depending on a set of goals or merely by look and feel. The net result is not constrained by a specific politics, although a politics of resistance is implied. The economy is described by the method. The psychology is adaptive. The industry is both labor intensive and technology dependent. Yes, I'm building a case for flarf and conceptual poetry as an environmental writing.

Most innovative poetry has an environmental slant to it because the most thorough critique of contemporary society addresses human over determination of the objects of its attention. This does not mean everything in nature is good. The danger of natural pietism looms among many ecological theories including new nature poetry. If we separate ourselves from nature we become prone to a quick if flashy finish. New conceptual poetry and flarf show early examples of how awareness of environment can improve poet's impact on the larger culture.

Recently I took one of the chapter titles of this book "Passive Voice: Forcing Amaryllis" and put the four words into Google. The search engine returned 687 paragraphs of information from various sites and blogs. Using these resources, I built the following poem. Not all my methods were environmentally informed; I'm not sure how to do that yet. But here is a result.

Passive Voice: Forcing Amaryllis

A single explanatory framework may account for the many levels of literary production.—Franco Moretti

For the diarist in search of a life
The passive voice tastes good during breakfast.
It somehow lends my work authority,
Freedom's foundation, hope-flack,
That jumping spider, that achy-breaky organ
Crawling to middle ground
That implies,
As here,
She had forgotten how the passive voice
Multiplies your syllables.

II. An EKG Addressed to Monody's Cloven Hoof
Forced change is climate's government.
Poverty has paid our citizens passive,
Strangely, yet some of the men join
As founding member and second violinist.
In further financial suppression
It's all they can do wop.

The women vivify
A figure of endurance, ululating
Where the living operate as segmented thought,
And all the Dead know is storytelling.

Humans are active in space but passive with regard to time,
And now dates pile upon us as has been.
Sweeter far than earthly strain,
Ourselves be bling:
If you refuse to follow the spoor, it's quite useless to force you.

III. Shall Pull Us To Glory Like Bricks
This project gives public voice to submerged questions.
Thus the voice of reason cries with winning force,
"But, but,"…
The power of one organism fails.

Couching ontology as mathematical bundles and cross-sections,
You can't get less vague from here.
I leap to March beneath shriveling swords
And capture intuitions
Such as Bruce has been existing for a long time,
And Harryette is exactly what one would call a role model.

Science, that vast left wing conspiracy,
Shifts l'obéissance passive, le lot quotidian,
To moral force only occurs as part of a word—am, amar, rill.
Being misconstrued as the whole highlights the limit
Of the analysis, e.g.
Adding moving word fields that interact
With all the news
My schooled and slangy boy speaks.

IV. To Act On With (Apparent) Centrifugal Force
Sparkling centrifuge
(meek. o'pasiv.o, voice calling;
debt (owed to another), liability (communication
As non-violent aggression,
As re-domesticating women after the revolution).

My voice spins out. For what can force or guile,
Their march loose from the rapid cars,
Do to make the world safe?

Long before Origin of Species appeared
Evolution had been reconciling the tangled bank with disciplined thought.
A person : an organism = an idea : a discipline = a poem, an ecosystem.
Gone from a passive pursuit to no longer a voice in the wilderness,
We were the agency and audience to reversing evolution.

V. Font Dog Handbrake Virus!
Dedicated to the one whose
Spelling hours transformed eyes measure,
Whether as vital force or communicated wave,
Cells make markets.
But I-tunes does not play unemployment.
Western tears fall in lyric bullets
For my valentine's ringtones

While delusions of reference stream in retribution:
Welcome to the Subscription Center and enhancement plan.
Tamales in Sparta built worldwide:
SIM-kortin PIN-koodin antaminen
Tuottaa ongelmia, joten koodin kysely on poistettava
And a free ebony sex judge advocate group
Of Derbyshire girls hugging cranky seniors,
Living in fencing, are some of the causes of sequined incontinence.

VI. Vodka Gift Baskets for Pre-Med Nic Patches
Faceless Female Persona as Their "Other". A title

Everywhere you look these days
Electronic orgasm kick ass illustrated lovemaking techniques're
Bustin' out cheat codes for Xbox realty.
Are all the risky nodes in art networks included?
Does novel poetry cheat happy sport street?
Where can I report a bad decision?

Funny pregnancy wrestling cake decorations
Disappoint the gun lobby and drain the effects of sound on plants.
Giving-no-quarter ignores we're all in this together.
Art as if I'd filter failing members' efforts.
In the culture of personal taste, the rough parts are phased out,
Civil cases files against conceptual low-protein diets.

Old kosher firmware loudly leans on over-digested results,
Animated girl wallpapers flock the museum, personal data assistant
With permanent digital self-effacement published each week inside.
I don't know about you but I really gotta have one.

VII. Loose Coupling of Theory and Practice
Looking for poetry in all the wrong places,
Fixed connections come with a good time
And extended warranty,
So it's not easy to break those links
And take a risk. Word up, you all:
Frequent glass for welding grands prix verbs.

Penile implants, the women's perspective!

John the Baptist training teaches you not to lose your head.
Some are images, some are not; can you control it? Does it matter?

Well, what happens when you release control
Of yourself, of your relations, of your views?
L-bloom node 1 maker, node 2 presenter, node 3 user node 5 funeral home,
Loose coupling of theory and practice reuses connectors,
Fit for purpose rather than pinning the pining forever to the page.

Subwoofer pet tags for example.
Forced lactation, inadvertent ejaculation, casual poetry gesture,
How does the human brain infer from little information?
The angel's bended knee humanizes assembly.

VIII. What Did Lewis Carroll Do in Mathematics?
Our prophetic mariner walking shoe
Maximizes the likelihood of ideological validity
With the method trees use to estimate
And because it's already been done.
The first time's often, of course, sketchy.

Conscience free creations rule
In Kevin Killian coloring book.
Just how much thought is required?

Dancing deer coupons pose with vintage prose connectors
And paralyze lawyers in Orlando labor flickr pose.

The former head of the NEA still having sex alone,
Used Costa Rica facts improve the end rhyme;
You think arbitrary is a problem? Arbitrary is a solution!
Look around you!

The Four horsemen juicer amaryllis toxicity,
The art object disappears.
I've got spurs at the Depleted Uranium High School
D.U.H., the wireless popover belch.

IX. Command-Operated Sheep Cruise (Cardamom spoofing)
Large blooming amaryllis will have been forced.
The Missouri compromise would have been mapped
By the Knicks Albanian hair removal art faction, if not
By the Hindu clownpenis, safe and alert for orders.
The kingdom of god suffers Epsom salts.
Then we're all set for a ride on the Martian passive voice.
Teaching liar mechanics to undergrads

Grievous coloring books
Dream of Jeannie anti-glare coating
And so learn to write like Alan Davies?

Amaryllis nutrition.
How to accept multiple solutions!
To government health care
To diarrhea tractors
To feeding 9 billion amaryllis
Guantanamo amaryllis
Cheap, free, dual-channel, diesel-driven, nutrition-labeled, hackneyed, anti-theft, Ciceronian, amplified, framed, double, mobile, absolute, inevitable, ideal, long-stemmed amaryllis

Spiritualizing Comprehension

> I have read that in the old days the truest and surest oracles were not those delivered in writing or offered by word of mouth. Very often even those who were reckoned subtle and ingenious have been mistaken in them, both because of the ambiguities, equivocations, and obscurities in the words, and because of the brevity of the sentences. For which reason Apollo, the god of prophecy, was surnamed Loxias—the Indirect.
> —François Rabelais, *Gargantua and Pantagruel*, Chapter 19.

The value of poetry in both its performative and communicative modes resides in its ability to link concepts in multiple dimensions. Poetry's polysemic, metaphoric, and other linguistic methods maneuver meaning rapidly through multiple dimensions in a way that requires endless explanation in other modes of discourse. Poetry facilitates meaning, but using poetry as a cultural leader incurs significant risks not the least of which is the unintended results of even carefully wrought poems.

Formalizing poetry's communication and presentation to support environmentalism may destroy the immediacy of its language. On the other hand shaping poetry to support spiritual practices pressures us to ignore our material environment while striving for epiphany. Such efforts lead us to walk away from the problems with climate change. Can environmental poetics support both material and eschatological poetic strategies?

The systematic analysis and representation of poetry as a method of increasing environmental awareness raises resistance at many levels. Professional and academic protests range from the way systematization transgresses on accepted beliefs about the ultimate inexplicability of the creative process to objections to using poetry for activism. I recently submitted some work from this book to an editor who assailed its activism, "James, can't you leave us poets alone in our corners?"

These contrary positions may be tied to characteristics of the academic discipline, to personality or both. In any case such objections are largely coupled to the use of poetry to address the spiritual inclinations that all people to some extent experience. These feelings are revealed in the Geist of identity poetry, be it personal revelation or group affirmation, and in nature poetry that indissolubly links the spirit of humanity to beauty in nature.

Lest the reader think exposing the spirit through poetry operates only as the product of weak-minded romanticism or neurotic individualism, let me point to an example, in the Epilogue spoken by Prospero in *The Tempest*:

> Now I want
> Spirits to enforce, art to enchant,
> And my ending is despair,
> Unless I be relieved by prayer,
> Which pierces so that it assaults
> Mercy itself and frees all faults.

Culture is familiar with evoking the spirit through poetry and its affinity with prayer. Such poetic strategy acts as a link between the world and the mind in their divergence. While reassurance weakens the will and distracts from the job at hand, I suspect no one is free of some desire to recapture our oceanic infancy of consciousness. (As discussed in the sections on Ron Atkin's q-analysis, the value of poetry to easily move dimensionally upward possesses the imagination of many readers. But keep in mind that Shakespeare's breadth of vision and vocabulary render an entire world rather than only extracting the epiphanies of human emotion. Environmental poetics would repurpose poetry's dimensional machine for environmentalism and demonstrate the way each poetics fits into the culture and the larger world.)

Reliance on poetry to reveal one's inner workings is intentionally not well understood. Many readers would rather appreciate poetry's value as a canon of faith even as its methods become increasingly mechanical and linguistic. Their response to questioning that faith releases all the fear that drives them to seek solace in the first place. And they defend it vehemently. Although I do not support this faith in poetry, I, nevertheless, do support the process of its creation, some of the people who make it, and some of their results.

Clinging to the mystique of poetry, however, plays into the hands of those who would control poetry, its ideas, organizations, markets, and reader acceptance for purposes such as support of market ideology, religion or the cult of the individual. As I have noted before, such manipulation of people's inclinations by highly productive individuals appears at all levels of the taxonomy of knowledge.

This belief in intuitive understanding extends to our entire cultural apparatus. In my effort to draw poetry out of its lair, I cite a recent article in *New Scientist* as an example of the cultural bias against thinking that appears in the story of Ralph Guldahl, a golf star of the 1930s. Guldahl won three major championships in three years including the Masters. Bobby Jones described Guldahl's playing as the finest he had ever seen. Then Guldahl wrote a book about how to golf in which he claimed that nobody "'is so good he never has to consciously be aware of a number of things to keep his swing in the groove.'" After finishing the book, the legend goes, Guldahl never won another championship. Many said it was the book that did it.

In 2007 Sian Beilock of the University of Chicago

> put a group of golfers to the test. Beilock found that distractions, such as recalling a list of random words, affected the performance of novices, but expert golfers were not so easily thrown off—with one critical exception. The way to make an expert golfer miss a shot, Beilock found, was to ask them to explain what they were doing. 'Golf is a great game to study choking because it is a complex motor skill that people spend a lot of time practicing to perfection,' says Beilock. 'Even the simplest well-practiced shots can go awry.'
> ("How Ralph lost his groove," *New Scientist*, June 13, 2009, p 44,5)

Other studies showed that explaining a successful putt resulted in skilled golfers taking "twice as many putts to sink their next ball." The need to describe movements that have become automatic shifts the brain from motor skills to language, "and the need to find words to explain something normally done without thinking." American culture takes this reliance on gut instinct to new levels of absurdity and the instinctive actor dominates the popular culture. In reality Guldahl's short term slump did not continue. He won the Milwaukee Open in 1940. And the effect of describing one's shot on subsequent shots quickly evaporates. But it does retain an immediate effect.

Losing a major tournament also depends on the strength of other players. And a more objective indicator, the number of strokes per game, shows that Guldahl in his victories tended to hit more strokes than most tournament champions. His relational play was superior in those three years, but his measurable skill was not as great as his temporary success would indicate. The power of the ideal of instinctive greatness leads us down the primrose path to assuming that thinking diminishes our natural power when what is more important is that humans are generally not strong at multi-tasking.

There are critics who will try to use this material to categorize me as a writer trying to scientize poetry, an activist and (to my humiliation) not a pure poet. The critic will even go so far as to say that I am using this paragraph to deflect attention away from that fact by directly denying it. The critic will use the argument as an appeal to a higher, purer poetic mystique. But the critic misses the point that Wittgenstein presents so clearly: "Essence is expressed by grammar."

The scientific material herein is a way to show how all disciplines are parts of the integrated human condition, not an attempt to subvert art with science. All our activities are capable of being linked for both near and long term progress as a bulwark against the degradation of our planetary and mental environment. And I am provisionally exploring which ones appear suitable to link, although it is clear such suitability is not universal.

If I were to be my own devil's advocate I would cite this work as a misuse of poetry as it exists today. But leaping these chiastic discrepancies (I might even say chiasmic) of reasoning seems to me less a misuse of poetry than the notion that the cosmos or still less god herself has bestowed this idea on the poet. Of course, if you like I will say that god told me to take this step. Yet my appeal to humanity and nature as a chimera does raise a question of identity, onus and origin. Differences in how we view ontological concerns cannot be addressed unless we agree about the scope of the substances (poems, essays about them) we seek to comprehend and by knowing their origins. In the case of poetry, I would like to say that ontology means intention or purpose in writing the poem. Intention is unlikely to be communicated except in error and, if adhered to, is likely to have unpredictable and horrifying results. Finally, my view of decision-making in poetry as a poet's analysis of risk points to the difficulties of accurately achieving one's intention or of avoiding connections with natural processes.

Poetry of the modern kind has been mostly about meaning or understanding, depending on whether you're the writer or the reader. From Baudelaire and Mallarmé to Andrews and McCaffery modern poets have proclaimed new ways of making meaning and readers have said they didn't understand them even when they understood the method. (A small group of cognoscenti including me prattle on about meta poetry, but poetry of this type has lost its power over the reader.)

Wherever writer and reader pass each other without recognition, but there is a further problem that causes a lack of comprehension. Readers often come to new writing with preconceptions about what they are reading, and the poets often don't explain and even resist explaining their assumptions. Yet readers persist in attempting to understand the writer's intention: "What did you intend by that?" And although intention is often concatenated with meaning, it is different than meaning in obvious ways.

Writers seek acceptance by the reader of the finished work, not the original intention except in poetry where method extracts content as in MacLow or Conceptualism. There may be a continual renewal of intention, and the finished poem may have a different intention than the source intention, which might be called inspiration. Writers want to know whether their intention was communicated through the writing, but their primary focus is on approval of the finished product.

As an editor, often the first reader of a poem, I am asked, "Will you read what I wrote?" not "Do you know what I intended?" The latter is actually an embarrassing question, because it immediately sets up a barrier and presents several obvious risks.

Nevertheless the expectation of giving a work to an experienced reader is that she will read it, understand the intention and appreciate the execution. These three and other expectations of writers make it difficult to talk to writers about their work. Recently I have been writing reviews of a collective literary memoir by a group of the Bay Area language writers. Focused on the Grand Piano reading series from 1976 to 1980, the set of 10 books begins with a volume whose topic is defined by Bob Perelman as "Love." In reading subsequent volumes, I continued to look for "assigned" topics but was disappointed in my search. In fact I received an email from a reader of *Jacket* (an online magazine at jacketmagazine.com), in which I have been publishing these reviews, asking what the topics of the subsequent books were.

I responded in an email,

> There's some inconsistency on that question. Clearly the first one is about Love and it says so in Perelman's introductory piece, but subsequent volumes may or may not have had subjects, depending on who you talk to. The most recent one [as of this writing], *Grand Piano* 4, for example, appears to be about everyday life, but in corresponding with one of the writers, my assumption about an overarching theme did not meet with his agreement. I'd suggest that *Grand Piano 3* provides a forum for the contributors to write about their own work, but not everyone agrees with that either.
>
> I think they talk vaguely about theme and then go their own way if they feel like it. In that sense it's more about writing the work at the moment when it is being written than an a priori, must-write-about-this, kind of theme. L=A=N=G=U=A=G=E magazine frequently assigned themes to its issues or parts of the issue and I think the Bay Area crowd is responding to that with a more free-form approach to thematics.

From the writer's point of view the problem arises when she expects her privileged ideas to be absorbed from the page in a consistent way by readers of many classes, ages, and circumstances, in different hours, seasons, and states. Any writing that seeks to sustain the author's intention through various readings suffers from a fixed idea of meaning and as such is suspect if it purports to change the field or represent the world. (If the writing is intended as an exposition of the writer's internal state for her own needs, then she retains the freedom of Dada and remains in the role of specialized poet. But of course I am representing that kind of freedom as dependent on the writing. Its effect on the world would be toxic. A bit of poison is often a useful remedy, but to generalize it pollutes the environment. So we need to distinguish between writing for its own sake, presentation, and writing for communication. Environmental poetics is inclusive and both approaches fit into the same dimension.

Notions like ontological intention cannot be sustained without being fostered by the mainstream or reified through several readings by many people over time. The history of a thought is even less reliable than our collective memory of historical events, as it has fewer perspectives to rely on. A more flexible idea of meaning needs to be proposed, propounded, explicated, promulgated for the world, in a way that sustains our presence in it.

For their part, readers stand little chance of returning to the original intention of the work except by the roundabout and problematic exercise of reinventing the writer and her history in order to decipher the moment of creation. And in a long work there are many moments of creation that are linked by sustained intention but separated by conditional intentions at each writing or editing session. Writers style them together, but then both local and initial intentions are obscured. Both the reader and the writer tend to forget the process of writing, the method of writing and what happens while the writing is being turned from a general idea or specific event into a readable text. As Ron Atkin points out, moving from lower to higher levels of abstraction requires a longer, slower traffic and even so produces a range of meanings rather than a single definable result. Such complex traffic represents part of the reason why poetry is exciting as a cypher for ecosystem change.

Poems provide the transportation that allows the reader to move rapidly and comprehensibly through sets of increasing abstraction. Sometimes the movement in the text takes place from description to metaphor and then returns to the original description. Sometimes the description continues to carry on and use the context of the metaphor or layers of metaphor throughout the poem. The latter is the method by which the spirit has been said to play, consolidating multiple conditions and conclusions into a single instance of language, a metaphor, making the whole comprehensible together instead of in parts. Used in this way spirit is no more than a one word designation of a more complex natural process whereby the mind creates images when the logic of the situation breaks down. Using the word spirit in this way allows poetry to be linked to faith. The logic of the metaphor is followed rather than returning to the original context.

While readers and writers usually ignore the intervening mental activities, they tend to emphasize a process of comprehension and the product of the writer. But the steps of the writing process can be traced. They are neither given from on high nor are they only part of an ineluctable subconscious procedure. When writing a poem, comprehension is not looked at directly but peripherally, and as such it is only approximated. This formulation of meaning explains the impact of John Ashbery, Jack Spicer, or Ron Silliman.

Such imprecision might be said to be closer to the way human understanding actually works, as I have pointed out in the discussion of Frederic Bartlett's work on images, but I cannot say that I perceive the data I get from reading imprecisely or process it imprecisely. I process at a human level, and that means in a discontinuous rather than precise or imprecise way. I do not see with the eyes of a hawk or think like a computer. But I do process in a complex manner that is similar to the process of writing. There is not that much distance between the reader and the writer. Why not understand the space between? What would be lost by such understanding, a vague feeling of contentment backed by the inevitable unease that stems from the fact that we know we cannot remain in that state of grace for long?

I am not condemning the reader's trance-like absorption as does Charles Bernstein in *Artifice of Absorption*. I am sure that kind of absorbed reading will always have an important place in art, since it provides a useful respite. I am concerned about the self-interested defense of understanding by faith against all reasonable and unreasonable alternatives. Sam Harris, in *The End of Faith* (WW Norton, 2005), provides an interesting if polemical attack on reasoning from faith. Our discussion of q-analysis, on the other hand, predicts that if one doesn't accept probabilistic results, reliance on faith, or as Shakespeare says "despair," is the likely outcome of attempting to understand increasingly abstract concepts.

By mapping the different mechanisms of comprehension that the reader and the writer use, I am suggesting that we can know something about them without sacrificing poetry, creativity and poetic imagination. We ignore several well-explored parts of writing in favor of the unknown as an act of faith and as a mechanism for leaping into higher dimensions. Environmental poetics creates a composite poetry based not on the unknown but on multiple sets of action (some of which are kinds of understanding) operating simultaneously. To recognize, for example, that we are often reading the final version of a well-wrought poem rather than the poet's original intention might help avoid the confusion that results from looking for some rough, heroic impulse as opposed to a refined language and digested thoughts of that impulse. (Some poems are written in one breath but most are not unitary and entail much retracing of steps.)

The creative process and meaning are not easy to nail down because they are complex, shifting and sometimes threatening. But to remain silent about the mystery of writing or that the process is not comprehensible surrenders understanding, which participates at many levels in this same kind of complexity. The process is not incomprehensible.

Spiritualizing uncertainty is an adaptive solution. Seeing an unidentifiable lump in the dark as a threat may occasionally make you run away from a stump, but if you assume the lump in the dark is a stump you may turn your back on lions and tigers and bears. Doing so may not always prove the right perception for survival. Materializing the spirit is a similar adaptive tendency and does not prove anything other than that an adaptive process is active.

Faith-based worldviews on the other hand draw nature into another kind of universe that exists in the collective imagination. As such they provide reassurance and community, but they tend to be exclusionary. As such faith-based notions must remain in specific niches however much they proselytize. Environmental studies that purport to be a general structure of nature risk disregard and disinterest when allied too closely with religions. They invite consideration of the supernatural and are subject, as in most specialized disciplines, to a separate consideration of nature rather than a more realistic approach in which difference and similarity are part of a larger matrix of relationships. On the other hand, if nature is god's work then we must revere it and protect it. But most religions put humanity on top of a hierarchy of beings and give permission for people to dispose of god's works as they see fit— that's been the interpretation in most cultures for the past 1500 years.

This tendency to spiritualize comprehension by faith is linked to all sorts of religious writing that achieves the status of poetry. From the Psalms and Milarepa to John Donne, Gerard Manley Hopkins and Allen Ginsberg, poetry has had a spiritual flavor derived from religion, and some people have even referred to poetry as a kind of prayer. And for some people it is. ("Please, God, let someone read this poem.") Some schools of Buddhism have taken on the important role of providing succor to people who want to believe in a benign view of nature.

Zen and other esoteric groups have a stated goal that is, according to poet Alan Davies, "entirely about living in the world as it actually is." This identification with existence is achieved by the individual through a practice of meditation. Rather than live in the world as it actually is, environmentalism presents the world as it actually is in order to change humanity's relationship to it. I am not satisfied with the status quo. I have proposed here a mechanism for society to move toward an environmentally supportive process.

Certain schools of Buddhism and Daoism have strong ecological ideals and methods "especially concerning the powers that create and animate." (*Daoism and Ecology*, "'Nature' as part of human culture in Daoism," Michael LaFargue, Harvard University Press, 2005) Pinning down a Buddhist point of view that supports anything beyond its practice, beyond adherence, is difficult because while the ideas we have been developing here point to a probabilistic result, Buddhism insists on an ultimate unitary notion of existence rather than the combinative methods proposed by environmentalism. To address Wittgenstein's point from a different perspective, the world may be "all that is the case", but its methods and solutions are dynamic, unpredictable and various.

Nevertheless the Heart Sutra's phrase "not this, not that" points to a relational model that is consistent with the point of view of the present volume. The complexity established by Buddhist practices, koans and dicta is used as a means of control that puts the religion's leaders in charge of knowledge that is not easily shared except by the practice of Buddhism. Therefore I am always wrong about Buddhism except when I am a practitioner. No external critique is possible with such a hermetic view. In this way Buddhism is treated as a cult in Thompson's terms. The hermit is one component of culture and has a place in Thompson's social structure.

It is basic to reading poetry to know what we are reading. The modern poets, who want to throw us off guard with the unexpected in a koan-like thrust of verbiage, be they Buddhist or Dadaist, are not easily integrated with the rest of society. Nevertheless their work has a place and can be a powerful force by providing an image in contrast, a point juxtaposed to the plane of the larger social structure.

Buddhism also creates a political hierarchy that is difficult to unwind in the context of my attempts to flatten the taxonomy of human thought and our views of the biosphere. Even as Buddhism seeks to break down hierarchies, it has built up a system of oligarchic governance at the institutional and national levels by which people work to feed the priests. The resultant theocracies have been toppled throughout the world, mostly by autocratic regimes, going from bad to worse. The mechanisms by which an environmentally supportive society can avoid these more rigid social structures may be worked out through the democratic liberalism of Western culture, but it's not clear to me how that will take place from here.

Daoism, an indigenous Chinese religion based on reverence for our surroundings, is in some ways another historical precedent to environmental poetics' integration with nature.

> Deliberative human consciousness is seen in the *Laozi* as the primary threat to organic harmony. But this does not apply to deliberative human consciousness of any kind, in and of itself. The danger lies in the ability of human consciousness to separate itself off from a system on which it depends or is trying to manage and to vigorously pursue ends thus so separately conceived, working against given forces in the system.
> ("Nature as Part of Human Culture in Daoism, Michael Lafargue, *Daoism and Ecology*, ed. N.J. Giradot, et al, Harvard University Press, 2001, p52, 3)

I read Lafargue as a statement about risk homeostasis. An effort often misfires and the law of unintended consequences takes over. The Daoist concept of *wuwei* (not doing, or more accurately, doing in context of the surroundings) aligns itself with the concepts of environmental poetics. Daoist artists sought to find the useful object in an ecosystem resource and to extract it much like the well-known story told by Vasari of Michelangelo finding the statue of David in a marble block. Connecting human and natural activity in this way supports one of the important points of this book.

A deeper look at the way these ideas are implemented in Daoism exposes its "idea that 'nature' is part of the human cultural ideal." (LaFargue, p. 54) Clearly human understanding of the biosphere comes through culture as much as direct experience of ecosystems. Daoism's way of subordinating nature to a cultural construction sounds more like pragmatism than environmentalism. Although we have pointed out that a cultural construction of nature is needed, it is a tool of society, useful in environmental and political practice, a characterization rather than a complete description of nature. For human activity to continue it needs to find the ways it can imitate ecosystem processes sometimes by subordination, in method and details, while retaining those practices and privileges that allow us to participate as a species in adaptive mechanisms, those practices that enable us to thrive when the ecosystem turns unfriendly.

Daoism does have an innate fascination in its complex relationship to the planet, but relying on the past drags with it a lot of other cultural affiliations with the Chinese aristocracy that I would not want to associate with contemporary environmentalism. Limiting such appreciation of the biosphere to a few highly functional individuals, however, is a very real risk for such an endeavor dependent on subtle distinctions. Nevertheless Chinese notions of integrating nature and humanity provide some reassurance that culture does not always conflict with its environment. Yet downstream, contemporary China doesn't have a good track record on environment.

Cultural tendencies based on reverence for nature as distinct from humanity, on religion and on spiritualizing comprehension in Buddhism, Daoism or poetry represents a useful strategy for survival when nature is the dominant player and humanity fights for survival. These attitudes and practices are insufficient for the purposes of sustainable human culture in our current context where people can often dominate and disrupt ecosystem processes. Environmental poetics ultimately has to modify humanity's position to one that does not pluck all the fruit from the tree of life while revering the bare branches we leave behind. Environmental poetics requires labor in support of these ideas in addition to the appreciation of what we are trying to achieve on our own behalf. Environmental culture needs a contemporary cast.

Resistance has grown in response to humanist disregard for traditional cultures and even well-understood planetary forces have an important place in changing our perception of the biosphere. Resistance is wide spread and has surprising allies. Resistance is the genesis of any major cultural change. Resistance will be part of any framework that accommodates the tremendous diversity of human and non-human relations. Resistance takes this role in environmental culture, by political power or as a response to climate change, and continues as part of the focus of global as well as local culture. Resistance raises other issues. Poetry may be innovative and resistant.

Appendix B: Scenes from Fallen Arches: A Mystery Play in Eden

This compost.
—Jed Rasula

Characters:

Giraffe Good-natured optimistic beast
Sheep   Sheep
Skunk   Self-destructive critic
Dodo   Purist
Adam   The First Man
Eve   The First Woman
Devil   Fallen Angel
Snake   Scapegoat with no legs
Gabriel Messenger of God

Act I

Scene 1: The Garden (music: "The Hucklebuck")

Giraffe: I don't know.
Sheep: Beats me.
Skunk: What to do; what to do.
Giraffe: I don't know.
Sheep: I don't know.
Skunk: I don't know.
Giraffe: Beats me.
Sheep: Beats me.
Skunk: Beats me.
Giraffe: What to do; what to do.
Sheep: What to do; what to do.
Skunk: What to do; what to do.

Scene 2: The Audience

Giraffe: Get your hot programs here. I've got hot pabulum here. I am a hot pogrom here.
Skunk: Get lost lady. Let an experienced hand do the job.
Giraffe: Ok, big boy, but don't bend it all out of shape.
Skunk: These are your hot programs. All the programming you want

	in one program.
Sheep:	Honey, you stink at this. Let me try.
Skunk:	Don't tell me what to do.
Sheep:	I'm a wooly prognosticator, I tell and don't tell.
Skunk:	Here! I didn't want to preach the rates anyway.
Sheep:	Whatever you want here. You name it and this is it. Your whole desire cranked into this flyer. Here's the info on what you need, where you need it, and when. A whatever you think it is infobot selected to be yours by me from among all I could think of without being anything at all except this.
Devil:	Isn't that a little far-fetched?
Sheep:	It's really the way it is.
Devil:	I beg your pardon.
Sheep:	Reminds me of my first trick, I mean caper, I mean gambol when I was told what to do.
Devil:	I bet you didn't want to.
Sheep:	I'll take that wager and the money that goes with it. I wanted to, you bet honey bunch, but I wanted to on my own terms.
Devil:	What terms are those?
Sheep:	I let you watch and you pay me to do it.
Devil:	You'd better be good.
Sheep:	I give you what you need.
Devil:	If I'm paying I get what I want.
Sheep:	You don't anywhere else. You buy the dishwasher as is. Why should an artiste, such as myself, be forced into servitude to your vulgar tastes?
Devil:	Because they made the dishwasher for me.
Sheep:	That's what they say.
Devil:	Now that you mention it....
Sheep:	At least an artiste, such as myself, I might add, expresses her inner life and satisfies herself about quality. At best she changes the way we think. And we know quality assurance in the arts is a big thing these days.
Devil:	I got what you need, babe.
Sheep:	Save the macho crap for someone else, bozo. (Exit Devil in a huff.) I told you I had the goods.
Skunk:	Some goods are not as good as others.
Sheep:	Stop evaluating.
Skunk:	I can't.
Sheep:	(Aside) He doesn't know what's good for him.

Scene 3: The Garden (music: "Amazing Grace")

Giraffe: He is one of us. He is one of us.
Skunk: Not that I can see. He is a two-legs.
Dodo: And what do you see here? I mean what's below this toupee? Can you count?
Skunk: 1,2,3,4,
Dodo: I mean count my legs and divide by two.
Skunk: No offense, but you don't count.
Dodo: Sure I do. One, two, three, ha!
Skunk: And that's the proof about two legs. They are not born inferior, but being born with two legs they develop unstable behavior.
Giraffe: Certainly it must be open to question.
Skunk: It is a question why we don't just get rid of them.
Giraffe: They are born animals like us. They drink milk from their mother's breast. They beat their chest when they are threatened. There is no proof that they shouldn't get equal rights with all the other animals, assuming they survive the test.
Skunk: Gravity is just too much for them and their nerves fray as they learn to walk. What other animal has to be taught to walk? Human culture is shaped by the genes. And their belief in god is a survival instinct.
Giraffe: And are their genes shaped by their culture? Darwin said there's no feedback. The mechanism either works or gets whacked out. I mean look at who's talking.
Sheep: Boys, boys. Calm down. God is infinite and dismal. We must allow his plan to work. Even though it bores us, we cannot interfere.
Skunk: Just follow along, right to the slaughter. How'd you like to follow this. (Exit smelling)
Sheep: What a gas.
Giraffe: I'll keep above this one. (Exit)

Scene 4: Naming the Animals: A Rehearsal

Adam: Lemme see. You look like a sheep. I call you sheep.
Sheep: Lots of luck, big boy.
Adam: Wow, what can we call this one?
Eve: I'm not the taxonomist around here.
Adam: I'll call you nectarine.
Giraffe: You want to saddle me with a name like that. Everyone'll

	say, "Look at the neck on that nectarine."
Adam:	I didn't saddle you with anything; you're not a horse; a horse is a horse of course; and you're not one. You are what you are and you're a nectarine.
Eve:	Adam, darling, maybe she's right about the neck thing.
Giraffe:	Well, I suppose it's ok to be a nectarine, but I wasn't one when we started this conversation, you know; you made me one. You keep saying I am one, but...
Adam:	What's the big deal? Either you are one or you aren't one. And since I say you're one, you're one.
Eve:	Just a second. It says here under nectarine, a smooth-skinned variety of peach.
Sheep:	That's what you said to me last night, Adam.
Adam:	Shut up. Drat. Well, if it can't be a nectarine, what can it be. Nobody appreciates my work here.
Eve:	Don't get all testy, darling. What we're doing here is naming the animals. You don't have to name them all yourself. Why don't you let this one choose its own name.
Adam:	Can't do that, sweetie dumpling. If I let this one choose its own name, they'll all want the privilege. And then if we get two animals wanting to be called Lion, then I'll get a discrimination lawsuit from the one who chose second.
Eve:	Ok, if you have to make all the decisions then you can't object when you contradict yourself. It's your own fault.
Adam:	OK OK OK OK OK OK OK. What do you want to be?
Giraffe:	Oh, I don't know, let me see. I see, I see a beautiful long-necked creature enamored of leaves high up in the beautiful trees.
Adam:	Be not see. We all see you, and quite a sight it is. What do you want to be. Be, be, be.
Eve:	Bee, a winged insect...
Adam:	Pulease, do you have to.... Beauty is not your forte, It's secondary to your neck, Nectarine!
Giraffe:	That's it: Do you have to?
Adam:	You can't be called Do You Have To.
Eve:	Dewey Half-twos. Half-Jew. Giraffe. How about giraffe?
Adam:	Well, how about it? We haven't got all day, you know. I mean a day is now about 4% of all time on God's earth.
Eve:	Whose, honey?
Adam:	God's, silly. Don't tell me you haven't heard.
Giraffe:	Ok. Giraffe is ok with me. I wanted to be Marilyn, but I'll accept giraffe. And by the way, we've been here a

	lot longer than a couple of weeks. Why I know my great grandmother. So you don't have to buy that God made the earth in seven days. It's what you want that you think is.
Eve:	I know I should think something, but I'm just not sure what, so I don't.
Adam:	Next.
Skunk:	I'm nothing, you're nothing, and nothing makes sense except supping, sleeping, and shagging, with an occasional foray into the higher arts, of course.
Adam:	Of course.
Skunk:	And besides, no one gets near enough to me to call me by name anyway.
Adam:	I think then you're a Faraway.
Skunk:	Why don't you call me a Stink? You are so literal. What's in a name but my image? And besides, whatever you call me, I'll try to call myself something else.
Adam:	As a citizen of the Garden, I'll let you call yourself whatever you want at home. But in the body politic you have to have a name to distinguish you from the others.
Skunk:	Private Smelly Skunk, serial number 1234567, sir.
Adam:	A citizen has responsibilities. But this ain't the army, brother.
Dodo:	I won't even participate in this charade. I will not have my identity condensed into a name. I shall go forever nameless.
Adam:	Then thou shalt not go much longer. No name, no consideration.
Dodo:	This is just another way to control me. You want to have my name so you can tell me to do things. Once you name me I have lost half my self-determination. The whole idea of freedom is based on being able to change oneself as one changes a coat, a new one for each season.
Adam:	And then you'll be harvested once and for all.
Dodo:	So if I don't consent to have a name, you threaten me with death. Are you the executioner we've been hearing so much about?
Adam:	I'm not threatening anything. I'm just telling you like it is. If you don't have and use your name, I can't call you to receive the blessings of the Garden.
Dodo:	I did just fine until you came along.
Adam:	I think I'll call you Thank You.
Dodo:	You're welcome.

Adam: No, your name is Thank You.
Dodo: Reminds me of my cousin, Last First. Just couldn't fit the form.
Adam: I'm trying to say what I mean and you keep twisting it around.
Dodo: And your coercive naming principle is not twisted? Please.
Adam: You're just a don't do.
Snake: Not bad, Don't-do.
Dodo: I do so.
Adam: Then you're a doo-doo.
Dodo: Don't say doo-doo, say Do-Do.
Adam: And you're a snake.
Snake: Whatever you say, sir.
Adam: Now that's more like it. See, why can't you be more like him?
Dodo: Because I'm more like you.
Adam: What do you mean?
Dodo: You believe in progress, don't you?
Adam: Of course, it's getting better all the time.
Dodo: And you let that snake in the grass coddle up to you while you argue with other warm bloods.
Adam: I thought we were all one here in God's neighborhood.
Dodo: We are not. There is a definite hierarchy, and some claim a reason for the hierarchy. That's why we'e all afraid of you.
Adam: What do you mean?
Dodo: To be and not to be. That is reality. Whether it is nobler in the mind is not the question. Can you admit it varies?
Adam: I'm lost.
Dodo: We are all lost. The question is whether we should make up arrows pointing nowhere to reassure ourselves or can we admit uncertainty is our condition. No guarantees of being good enough to survive. Just survive as well as you try. No threatening life insurance, no organized reassurance. I am pure and I remain pure and nameless.
Adam: You too. You're a Dodo...or a Sergio Leone fan.
Dodo: Watch it, bud. I happen to have a perfect attitude.
Adam: Time's up. Now, sweeties, what I'd like to do here is run that through one more time for real, for the big boys.
Skunk: Just what I always wanted, an audience. (Enter angels)
Gabriel: Our lord your God has ordained that we be treated to the

Adam: naming of the animals.
Adam: I live to serve your lordships and my words shall be my name.
Gabriel: Let the procession begin.
Adam: A wooly lamb precedes this Sheep into the world.
Sheep: I'm here for the sheer pleasure of it.
Gabriel: We see the beauty of your name and your person. You are a hallowed presence in our Garden and presage the coming of our lord and his followers to earth.
Adam: To prune the highest trees our Giraffe will ecologize.
Giraffe: I rise to the theme of the impending crisis of faith that our Adam staunches.
Gabriel: Faith is renewed by his great works and by the sense of relief we feel. We understand that it needs renewal like the trees who lose their leaves.
Adam: And beyond the pale our Skunk wanders like a flower who lost his roots.
Skunk: It's not me that smells so bad, it's you who are smelling it. To me protection is divine.
Gabriel: You have such a wonderful smell. Would evolution have made such a hell?
Adam: The Dodo will not do that which he is supposed to do and so he will be outdone in time of which we know the outcome.
Dodo: I have said it once, and I've said it twice. This guy Adam is not treating me nice. I want to put in a formal complaint against this guy who says what he ain't. You are all making a pitch for God. To me it seems a trifle odd that I should believe what such as you say, who are all in the Big Guy's pay.
Gabriel: Oh, ye of little faith or brain. To speak so in his Garden is a little vain. But only time can heal the wound. I fear you don't know just how soon your time is going to be unturned.
Dodo: I will fight with my dying breath to end the injustice of being named.
Adam: And finally, your loving Snake who does what should be done when told.
Snake: I beseech thee to tread on your humble snake.
Gabriel: Quite a performance, Snake, but we remember you.
Snake: If you doubt my sincerity, put me to the test.
Gabriel: Since we are concerned to preserve the Garden, I would make you supporter of Adam in his role as resource manager, since this is why we have started the naming

Skunk: convention.
Skunk: I don't see too many Shriners around here.
Adam: Ask not what your Garden can do for you but what the God did for me when I was in Egypt.
Gabriel: Please, no hucksterism in the sight of God.
Dodo: Isn't that an oxymoron?
Adam: You've had your say.
Gabriel: I don't like the way this is progressing.
Adam: Depends on your model. If your goal is Armageddon, you can get it by positing a single point of origin. If your goal is advancing the cause of life on earth, you can get it too. The problem is stating the policy of multiplicity.
Gabriel: We must get back to our silver-lined cloud. These issues are too earthly.
Adam: We will remember you as you are here with us. (Exit Gabriel and angels)
Skunk: Now that you have categorized us, what shall we do? Fall to fighting among ourselves, no doubt.
Giraffe: I like knowing who I am.
Skunk: It's not who you are; it's what Adam says you are.
Sheep: Don't be so negative all the time. It makes my fleece shrink.
Skunk: I'm telling you what I think, not what you think. That's the difference between Adam and the rest of us. He's trying to set an agenda by his name game.
Dodo: I still refuse to be considered to have been named.
Skunk: That's quite a tense situation you've got there, sir. Or is it ma'am?
Giraffe: We giraffes don't have to talk to such riffraff.
Adam: And so you will not talk. (Exit Adam)
Snake: Well, I haven't offended anyone. You can talk to me.
Giraffe: (Points and gestures)
Dodo: See, it's started. She can't get a word in edgewise or any otherwise wise. I told you this would end badly.
Sheep: You are the bad end, Don't Do. If everyone had gone along with Adam, we wouldn't be in this fix.
Snake: I am getting an idea.
Skunk: Don't have a cow.
Snake: A snake can't have a cow any more than a chicken can have an egg.

Scene 5: Adam Downsizes Eden

Adam: I think the animals have too much freedom and are beginning to not appreciate all that we've done for them.
Eve: You mean productivity is down and waste is up; borrowing is rife and savings are drained; they are using too many resources and not replenishing the environment; they harbor ill-feelings and act in an anti-social manner while accepting the largess of the public weal; they are screwing around with the divine order you have established and not mentioning your name often enough in their scripts; they are heightening the blubber while not accommodating the gizmos on which we depend for evaluation; they mean nature in one scene and the masses in another and you're not in control of which; they market their homegrown and ask for foreign aid; they want more pay for less work; they want the profit while you take all the risks? You mean to say they take take take? Can you believe it?
Adam: I couldn't have said it myself.
Eve: Of course you can say it.
Adam: All right, it.

Adam decides that he should move the animals to the other side of the Eden border so that they can be made to work harder to get their food. Eve suggests they use the snake to woo the other animals to the border, while offering them not just the safe little world of Eden but a big world of opportunity and freedom.

Scene 6: Shift of Fools

Snake: I couldn't agree more.
Of course.
I concur
I absolutely think you're right about that
Certainly
You have hit the nail on the head
Right
That's right
While everybody else was going the wrong way, you were already staking your claim to reality.
There aren't many people who knew what to do in those days
Uh, huh.
Sure is.
Right

      Correctamiento
      Exactamiento
      Precisely what I would have done
      That shoe is on the right foot
      Fits like a glove, I'd say
      I sure would
      Yes, yes, yes.
      I couldn't disagree with that one.

Scene 7: The Garden

Sheep talking about her vulnerability as a sex object in a different character than she portrays as a sheep, perhaps a hardened Lower East Side actress.

Scene 8: Crossover

Adam: How did we get over?
Eve: I didn't know we were sick.
Adam: Feels like some kind of sick. Struggle and longing. I've had enough.
Eve: It's only been five minutes since we crossed.
Adam: More like eternity.
Eve: No, that's where we're going to burn for that fruit.
Adam: What a ghastly thought. Fried for a fruit.
Eve: Maybe it means something else.
Adam: Like what?
Eve: He's testing our resolve. He wants to see if we are still faithful to him after our punishment. Maybe if we stay faithful to him we'll be reinstated.
Adam: How do you know we've been exiled?
Eve: Gabriel left little room for doubt.
Adam: And the snake. I feel guilty about the snake.
Eve: Worry about yourself, Adam. You've got a lot to do.
Adam: Can we go back?
Eve: Back into the space where it was, but it's not there now. Not for us.

Scene : In Eden After the Apple

(Sounds somehow different)

Giraffe: Futsky, butsky, futsky.
Skunk: Bitsky, shitsky, whiskey.
Dodo: Sucksky, wucksky, sucksy.
Snake: Sssssssssssssss.
Adam: What are they talking about?
Eve: Sounds pornographic to me. Shall we try it?
Adam: Fuck ing shit suck.
Giraffe: Who let them back in?
Snake: I posted the memo the other day. Hereinafter the aforementioned Adam and Eve shall without restriction be allowed to move freely across the boundaries of Eden. Any denizen of Eden who notices a change in the behavior pattern of Adam and Eve shall keep their noticing of such a change to themselves.
Sheep: Then you're in violation again, snakey-pooh.

Continues.

James Sherry is the author of 11 books of poetry and prose. His work has been translated and published in 9 languages. Several of his other books are available on the Electronic Poetry Center (http://epc.buffalo.edu/). He is the publisher of Roof Books (http://roofbooks.com) and founder of The Segue Foundation, Inc., a multi-arts publisher and arts producer. Mr. Sherry is currently working to create a sustainable pension project in conjunction with 350.org and the fossil fuel divestment movement. He lives in New York City.

Made in the USA
Charleston, SC
14 June 2013